THE SIEGE

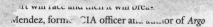

[...] will race and then it will break[...]
Mendez, form[...] CIA officer an[...]or of *Argo*

'M[...]culously researched, beautifully written: an unstoppable read. This is not your ordinary thriller' Ahmed Rashid, author of *Descent into Chaos*

'Totally unputdownable, utterly absorbing – a minute-by-minute account of a city under onslaught. Here we have victims, hostages, police and terrorists; their every fateful action and decision; the moments of sheer chaos and the crucial seconds of clarity' Paul French, author of the Dagger and Edgar Award-winning *Midnight in Peking*

'A heart-pounding read and an investigative tour de force, *The Siege* is an essential primer on terror in the twenty-first century. It shows where mass-murderers come from, how they think, and what it is like to be caught in the cross-hairs of their madness' Blaine Harden, author of the *New York Times* bestselling *Escape from Camp 14*

'Scott-Clark and Levy recreate this cataclysmic disaster with all the pulse-pumping intensity of a cinematic action thriller . . . [They] recount astonishing episodes of personal heroism while issuing a sobering indictment of the ineptitude of the agencies that failed to prevent the attack' *Booklist*

'Revelatory . . . a riveting human drama. An insightful and dramatic account of an extraordinary episode in modern warfare' *Publishers Weekly*

'A beautifully written account that at once terrifies you with the story of how terror is masterminded and inspires you with the heroism of average people who fight back in extraordinary circumstances. [*The Siege*] is a major contribution to our understanding of terror' Bruce Riedel, former CIA analyst and counter-terrorism expert, and advisor to four US Presidents

'*The Siege* reads like a thriller, but it also raises important questions' *Wall Street Journal*

'A spectacular narrative . . . Scott-Clark and Levy's retelling of the disaster from the vantage points of trapped and imperilled guests and staff, as well as from the perspective of the terrorists themselves, reads like an expertly constructed thriller that's all the more heart-stopping because it actually happened . . . A painstaking and gripping recreation' *Daily Beast*

'I devoured [the book] in just two sittings. It is a desperate story
of the depravity to which perverted religious belief and economic and
social deprivation can lead. It is also an uplifting story of the courage which
ordinary men and women can find in themselves, when faced with
challenges . . . A remarkably well-told story . . . riveting due to the
personal detail that it reveals' *Asian Review of Books*

ABOUT THE AUTHORS

Cathy Scott-Clark and Adrian Levy are the authors of four books, most recently
the acclaimed *The Meadow: Kashmir 1995 – Where the Terror Began*. For sixteen
years they worked as foreign correspondents and investigative reporters for the
Sunday Times and the *Guardian*. In 2009 the One World Trust named them British
Journalists of the Year, having won Foreign Correspondents of the Year in 2004.
They co-produce documentaries, including *Kashmir's Torture Trail*, winner of a
2013 Amnesty International Media Award. Currently they are filming several
new projects in South Asia.

The Siege

CATHY SCOTT-CLARK AND ADRIAN LEVY

PENGUIN BOOKS

PENGUIN BOOKS

Published by the Penguin Group
Penguin Books Ltd, 80 Strand, London WC2R ORL, England
Penguin Group (USA) Inc., 375 Hudson Street, New York, New York 10014, USA
Penguin Group (Canada), 90 Eglinton Avenue East, Suite 700, Toronto, Ontario, Canada M4P 2Y3
(a division of Pearson Penguin Canada Inc.)
Penguin Ireland, 25 St Stephen's Green, Dublin 2, Ireland (a division of Penguin Books Ltd)
Penguin Group (Australia), 707 Collins Street, Melbourne, Victoria 3008, Australia
(a division of Pearson Australia Group Pty Ltd)
Penguin Books India Pvt Ltd, 11 Community Centre, Panchsheel Park, New Delhi – 110 017, India
Penguin Group (NZ), 67 Apollo Drive, Rosedale, Auckland 0632, New Zealand
(a division of Pearson New Zealand Ltd)
Penguin Books (South Africa) (Pty) Ltd, Block D, Rosebank Office Park,
181 Jan Smuts Avenue, Parktown North, Gauteng 2193, South Africa

Penguin Books Ltd, Registered Offices: 80 Strand, London WC2R ORL, England

www.penguin.com

First published by Viking 2013
Published in Penguin Books 2014
001

Copyright © Cathy Scott-Clark and Adrian Levy, 2013
All rights reserved

The moral right of the authors has been asserted

Typeset by Jouve (UK), Milton Keynes
Printed in Great Britain by Clays Ltd, St Ives plc

ISBN: 978-0-670-92259-8

www.greenpenguin.co.uk

MIX
Paper from
responsible sources
FSC® C018179

Penguin Books is committed to a sustainable
future for our business, our readers and our planet.
This book is made from Forest Stewardship
Council™ certified paper.

For Zed and Ava

Contents

Dramatis personae

Guests/diners

Will Pike and **Kelly Doyle** – Will, twenty-eight, and Kelly, thirty, from London, were at the end of a two-week holiday in Goa when they decided to stay one night at the Taj, checking in on the afternoon of 26 November 2008. They were due to return home the following morning. It was Will's first visit to India.

Andreas Liveras – the multi-millionaire Andreas, seventy-three, made his fortune in the bakery business in London after emigrating from his native Cyprus as a young man. Ranked 265th on the *Sunday Times* Rich List with an estimated fortune of £315m, he also owned luxury yachts. In November 2008 he was in India with his friend Nick Edmiston and his Indian cruise director, Remesh Cheruvoth, to launch a new yacht charter business in the subcontinent.

Sabina Sehgal Saikia – forty-five, was a formidable foodie and restaurant critic, a TV celebrity and journalist. She lived in New Delhi with her husband, Shantanu, and children, Arundhati, fourteen, and Aniruddha, eleven. She had come to Mumbai to review a new outlet at the Taj and attend a society wedding.

Bob Nicholls – the British-born security expert, forty-four, ran a VIP protection company based in South Africa. He came to Mumbai in November 2008 with six colleagues, Faisul Nagel, Reuben

Niekerk, Reagan Walters, Zunaid Waddee, Charles Schiffer and Zane Wilmans, after winning a contract to provide security for the forthcoming Champions League Twenty20.

Ravi Dharnidharka – a captain in the US Marines, the 31-year-old Ravi had spent the past four years flying combat missions in Iraq, including during the bloody battle for Fallujah in November and December 2004. He was visiting Mumbai for the first time in more than a decade to reconnect with the Indian side of his family.

Mike and **Anjali Pollack** – the New York-based Mike Pollack, thirty-two, a managing partner at Glenhill Capital, a public equities investment firm, had come to Mumbai with his Indian wife, Anjali, thirty-three, to visit her parents. On the night of the attacks they were due to have dinner at the hotel with friends, leaving their two young sons with Anjali's parents.

Amit and **Varsha Thadani** – the heir to a Mumbai textile and restaurant empire, Amit, thirty-two, had booked his wedding reception in the Crystal Room on the night of the attacks. He and his new wife, Varsha, thirty, who had taken their religious vows the previous day, invited 500 guests.

Bhisham Mansukhani – was an assistant editor at Paprika Media, publisher of *Time Out India*, specializing in food and drink. Aged thirty, Bhisham was at the Taj to attend the wedding reception of a school friend, Amit Thadani.

Kuttalam Rajagopalan Ramamoorthy – was a 69-year-old banking executive from Tamil Nadu, known to his friends as Ram. He was on a business trip to Mumbai on 26 November and had checked into the hotel after lunch, having turned down an offer to stay with his nephew in the city outskirts.

Line Kristin Woldbeck – a marketing executive from Norway, Line was on a month-long holiday in India with her boyfriend, Arne Strømme, a landscape architect. Both Line and Arne were keen photographers and avid travellers and this was their fourth trip to India. They arrived in Mumbai on the morning of 26 November from Gujarat and were due to fly on to Delhi the following day.

Staff

Karambir Kang – the 39-year-old General Manager and Vice-President of the Taj, Karambir had worked for the hotel chain since graduation, starting in sales. The son of a Sikh general in the Indian army, he had taken over the reins at the Taj a year before, moving  his wife, Neeti, and sons, Uday, twelve, and Samar, five, into a suite on the sixth floor.

Amit Peshave – the son of two GPs from Pune, 27-year-old Amit had worked at the hotel for seven years, starting off as a trainee waiter. A few weeks prior to the attacks he was appointed General Manager of Shamiana, the hotel's ground floor twenty-four-hour coffee shop.

Hemant Oberoi – the Taj's 53-year-old Grand Executive Chef had worked for the Tata group his entire career. Widely known across India, Oberoi had a blossoming book and TV career and had inspired several restaurant chains, as well as personally designing most of the Taj's restaurants.

Florence and **Faustine Martis** – Faustine Martis, forty-seven, the head waiter of Sea Lounge, the hotel's first-floor tea-room, had worked at the Taj for more than two decades. Originally from Kerala, he lived in Thane, north-east Mumbai, with his wife, Precilla,  and children, Florence, twenty-one, and Floyd, sixteen. Two months before the attacks he managed to secure a job at the hotel for his daughter, as a trainee computer operator in the Data Centre.

Security services

Vishwas Nangre Patil – appointed Deputy Commissioner of Police for Zone 1 in June 2008, a job that gave him jurisdiction over most of Mumbai's five-star hotels and the heart of the tourist sites. Brought up in a village in southern Maharashtra, Patil, thirty-two, joined the police in 1997 and rose quickly, making his mark by clamping down on illicit parties in the state's second-largest city of Pune.

Rajvardhan Sinha – Deputy Commissioner of Police, Special Branch 2, Rajvardhan had responsibility for monitoring foreigners in the city. Born in Bihar, he was a veteran of jungle warfare against Naxalite militias operating in eastern Maharashtra, and a batch-mate of Vishwas Patil, meaning they had trained together.

Rakesh Maria – the legendary Crime Branch boss of Mumbai, Joint Commissioner of Police Maria, fifty-one, made his name by hunting down the perpetrators of a series of bomb blasts that rocked the city in 1993. The story of how he solved the case was later turned into a Bollywood film, *Black Friday*. Maria, whose father was a Bollywood producer, was a major character in Suketu Mehta's memorable non-fiction work *Bombay Maximum City*, appearing under the pseudonym of police chief Ajay Lal.

Hasan Gafoor – Mumbai's Commissioner of Police, Gafoor, fifty-eight, was only the second Muslim to hold this rank in Mumbai. The son of a *nawab* from Hyderabad, Gafoor was among the many privileged officers who dominated the upper ranks of the Mumbai force.

Deven Bharti – Additional Commissioner of Police Bharti was second in command to Rakesh Maria at the Crime Branch. He was also a veteran of the Naxalite insurgency of eastern Maharashtra.

Govind Singh Sisodia – Brigadier, the Deputy Inspector General of the National Security Guard, India's specialist counter-terrorism force. Joining the Indian Military Academy, the subcontinent's elite officer-training college, in Dehradun, Sisodia graduated in 1975, and was commissioned into the 16 Sikh Regiment.

Terrorists

David Headley – born Daood Saleem Gilani in
Washington DC in 1960; his father was a renowned
Pakistani broadcaster and his mother an American
heiress. He was brought up in Pakistan but moved
back to the USA at the age of sixteen. During the
eighties he was arrested for drug smuggling, and
became an undercover agent for the Drug Enforcement Adminis-
tration. Anglicizing his name to David Headley, he joined the
Pakistani militia Lashkar-e-Toiba and helped plan and craft the
Mumbai attacks. He also worked for the US intelligence community
throughout this period, passing back information about Lashkar's
intentions for Mumbai.

Ajmal Kasab – born in 1987 to a poor family in the
village of Faridkot in the eastern Punjab, Pakistan,
Ajmal was one of ten young men recruited and
trained by Lashkar-e-Toiba for the Mumbai attacks.
He underwent religious instruction and nearly a year
of physical training before being dispatched to India
in November 2008.

Lashkar-e-Toiba – a Pakistani militia formed
in 1990 to fight in Indian-administered
Kashmir. The activities of Lashkar, which
was funded and armed by Pakistan's Inter-
Services Intelligence Directorate, were
focused on sending highly trained *fidayeen*
(guerrilla) units to fight Indian troops until
the death.

Hafiz Saeed – the *amir* (spiritual leader) of Jamaat-ud-Dawa, the parent organization of Lashkar-e-Toiba. Born in the Punjab, Saeed, aged fifty-eight at the time of the Mumbai attacks, was an Islamic studies lecturer in Lahore until he travelled to Saudi  Arabia during the eighties and began actively supporting the *mujahideen* fighting the Soviets in Afghanistan. Soon after he returned to Pakistan he formed an Islamic movement underpinned by the Ahl-e-Hadith sect. It would lead to the establishment in 1990 of Lashkar-e-Toiba.

Zaki-ur-Rehman Lakhvi – the *amir* and co-founder of Lashkar-e-Toiba, *chacha* (uncle) Zaki, as he was known to all Lashkar recruits, was born in Okara, the same district of the eastern Punjab as Ajmal Kasab. During the eighties he abandoned his studies to fight the Soviets in Afghanistan. He was Lashkar's chief military commander and was described by Indian investigators as the mastermind behind the Mumbai operation.

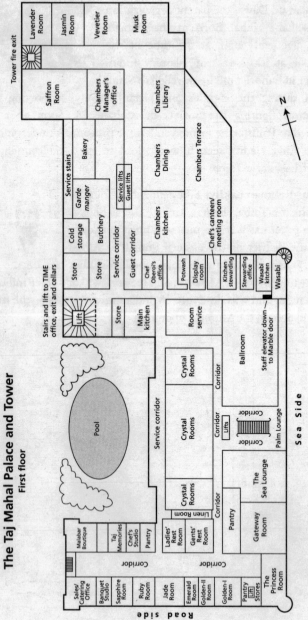

The Taj Mahal Palace and Tower
First floor

N

Tower fire exit

Lavender Room
Jasmin Room
Vevetier Room
Musk Room

Saffron Room
Chambers Manager's office
Chambers Library

Service stairs
Bakery
Garde manger
Chambers Dining
Chambers Terrace

Cold storage
Butchery
Service lifts
Guest lifts
Chambers kitchen
Chef's canteen/ meeting room

Store
Store
Service corridor
Guest corridor
Chef Oberoi's office
Potwash
Display room
Kitchen stewarding
Stewarding office
Wasabi kitchen
Wasabi

Stairs and lift to TIME office, exit and cellars

Lift

Store
Main kitchen
Room service
Ballroom

Staff elevator down to Marble door

Pool

Service corridor

Crystal Rooms
Crystal Rooms
Corridor
Corridor
Lifts
Corridor
Corridor
Palm Lounge

Sea Side

Malabar Boutique
Taj Memories
Chef's Studio
Pantry

Ladies' Rest Room
Gents' Rest Room
Crystal Rooms
Linen Room
Corridor
Pantry
The Sea Lounge

Corridor
Corridor
Corridor

Sales/ Catering Office
Banquet Studio
Sapphire Room
Ruby Room
Jade Room
Emerald Room
Golden-II Room
Golden-I Room
Pantry Stores

Gateway Room
The Princess Room

Road side

The Taj Mahal Palace and Tower
Ground floor

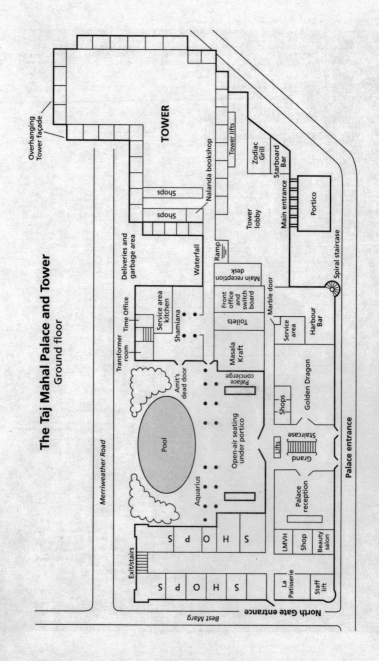

TOWER

Overhanging Tower façade

Merriweather Road

Transformer room

Time Office

Deliveries and garbage area

Service area kitchen

Shamiana

Amit's dead door

Pool

Aquarius

Open-air seating under portico

Palace concierge

Masala Kraft

Waterfall

Shops

Shops

Nalanda bookshop

Ramp

Main reception desk

Front office and switch board

Toilets

Marble door

Service area

Tower lifts

Tower lobby

Main entrance

Zodiac Grill

Starboard Bar

Portico

Spiral staircase

Harbour Bar

Golden Dragon

Shops

Grand Staircase

Lifts

Palace reception

LMVH

Shop

Beauty salon

La Patisserie

Staff lift

Exit/stairs

S P O H S

S P O H S

North Gate entrance

Best Marg

Palace entrance

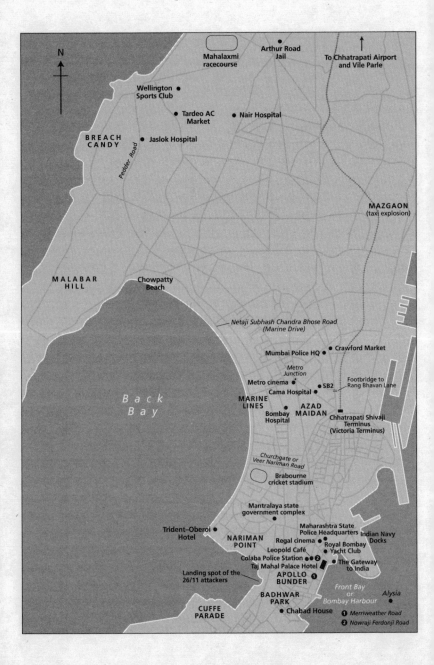

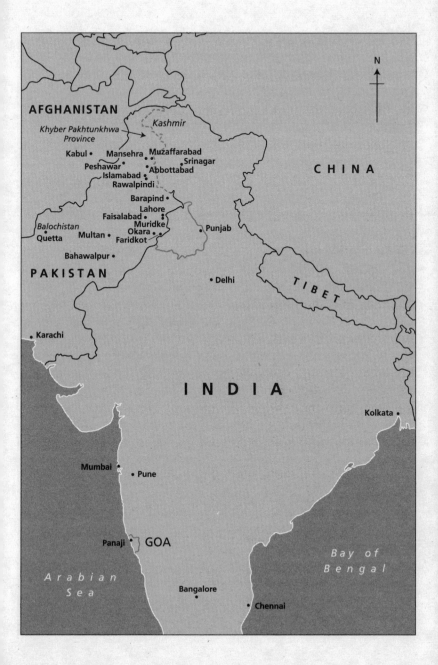

'Mughal ceilings, let your mirrored convexities
multiply me at once under your spell tonight.

He's freed some fire from ice in pity for Heaven.
He's left open – for God – the doors of Hell tonight.

In the heart's veined temple, all statues have been smashed.
No priest in saffron's left to toll its knell tonight.

God, limit these punishments, there's still Judgment Day –
I'm a mere sinner, I'm no infidel tonight.'

Agha Shahid Ali, 'Tonight', in *Call Me Ishmael Tonight: A Book of Ghazals*
(W. W. Norton and Company Inc., 2003)

Prologue

Wednesday, 26 November 2008, 8 p.m.

A sliver of moon hung over the Arabian Sea as the dinghy powered towards the 'Queen's Necklace', the chain of lights strung across Mumbai's Back Bay. The ten-man crew of Pakistani fighters rode the black waves in silence, listening to the thrum of the outboard motor and hunched over Chinese rucksacks, printed with English logos that read: 'Changing the Tide'. Ten AK-47s, ten pistols, ammunition, grenades, explosives and timers, maps, water, almonds and raisins – they laid out the contents in their minds. It barely seemed enough to take on the world's fourth-largest city. 'Surprise will get you in and fear will scatter the police,' their instructors had assured them. They had practised night landings, and planting timed bombs in taxis set to explode all over the city, hoping to create the illusion that an army had invaded Mumbai. Brother Ismail, the team leader, held high a GPS unit, programmed with landing co-ordinates, as the sea sprayed over them, stinging their sunburned faces.

They had volunteered for jihad a year before, and been put through religious indoctrination and military training that had taken them from secret mountain-top camps in Pakistan-administered Kashmir down to safe houses in the swarming port city of Karachi. Four days ago, at dawn on 22 November, they had finally weighed anchor.

One day out in open water, they had hijacked an Indian trawler, the first test of everyone's mettle. The second had been saying farewell to their handlers, from whom they had become inseparable, and who melted away into the sea mist, heading back to Pakistan. The third was forcing a captured Indian captain to navigate the seized trawler on towards invincible Mumbai, 309 nautical miles away, in the knowledge that this was the first time they had been alone.

In reality they were not by themselves. A satellite phone linked them back to a control room in Karachi that called regularly with updates. But these were landlocked boys, from impoverished rural communities, who knew only about chickens and goats, and they were stupefied by shooting stars arcing above them. On the second night, 24 November, they had all lain up on deck and imagined being sucked up into the heavens, while one of the ten had told the story of Sinbad, who had explored the Arabian Sea, where 'the rocky shore was strewn with the wreckage of a thousand gallant ships, while the bones of luckless mariners shone white in the sunshine, and we shuddered to think how soon our own would be added to the heap'.

Finally, on 26 November, the GPS had sounded their arrival off the coast of Mumbai, and they had called Karachi to find out what to do with the captured captain. It fell to Ajmal Kasab to act. He had just turned twenty-one and felt compelled to prove his worth. Two others held the Indian sailor down, while Ajmal slit his throat. Blooded, they jumped into a yellow dinghy that pulled them onwards towards the glistening Indian city.

Each of them, Ajmal recalled, seemed lost in thought. This was a one-way journey that was supposed to culminate with their deaths. There would be no hero's return, no village *tamasha* (celebration) to fete their victory, and no martyr's poster in the local mosque to immortalize their bravery. There would be no ringing eulogy printed in a jihad magazine. As they approached the city, Ajmal's mother, Noor Elahi, was crouched at home by the fire in Faridkot, frying stuffed *parathas* for his younger brother and sister, a pot of thick curd sitting up on the kitchen shelf. She had no idea her favourite son was staring at a rapidly nearing foreign shore, his head filled with instructions to 'kill relentlessly'.

Ajmal had started on this road in November 2007, with another boy of his age, both of them pledging, *mujahid*-style, to fight for each other until the end. But this boy had had a family who had talked him back home, while other cadres got homesick and were also fetched by concerned fathers, brothers or uncles. By May 2008, half of the would-be warriors had changed their minds. Ajmal had waited at the camp gates, but no one had come for him. In the end, and alone, he had given himself over to the outfit, signing a testament in which he pledged to 'cut open the kafir's jugular to quench my anger'.

Then, the handlers had packed his rucksack and put him to sea with nine others, all of them wearing new Western clothes, sporting cropped hair and carrying fake Indian IDs.

At 8.20 p.m., dry land reared up. As he slipped on the pack, Ajmal remembered a promise made by their *amir*, the cleric who had sent them on their way, conjuring up their deaths: 'Your faces will glow like the moon. Your bodies will emanate scent, and you will go to paradise.'

The higgledy-piggledy fishermen's *chawl* (tenement), close to the tourist mecca of Colaba, was deserted when they leapt ashore. Residents were distracted, watching an India–England cricket match on TV. Only local resident Bharat Tandel challenged them, as they ran up to the road: 'Who are you and where are you going?' A shouted answer came back: '*Hum pehle se hi tang hain. Hume pareshaan mat karo* [We are already stressed, so don't pester us].'

An hour later, the growl of gunfire and the bark of explosions reverberated across the city.

I.

Jadu ghar (House of Magic)

Faustine Martis wanted a memorable death. But the senior waiter, who had worked at the Taj for more than two decades, could not find the right time to broach the subject with Florence, his dizzy, 21-year-old chatterbox of a daughter. On their way into the city, Florence loved to talk and normally Faustine was happy to listen. Recently he had got her a job at the hotel, but often their shifts were incompatible. Even when they were on the same roster, they had to contend with the geometry of their commute.

Most mornings, Florence, her black hair streaming, clung on to her father as he weaved on his Honda motorbike through Mumbai's deafening north-eastern suburbs. Parking up, they then plunged into Thane train station and the crush of the central line. She sat for an hour, humming a *filmi* love song, while he stood jaw to jaw with the other commuters, stacked up like *paratha*s in a tiffin.

At Chhatrapati Shivaji Terminus, one of the busiest stations in India, they took a moment to check their watches beneath the old Victorian railway clock, before picking their way across the heaving concourse to catch a bus to Colaba. Getting off at the Regal cinema, Faustine, decked in his broad-brimmed hat like a cricket umpire, and Florence, fine-boned, tall and picky like a wading bird, strode past the invitation-only Bombay Yacht Club that smelled of stale bread and lemon cake, before entering the heart of tourist Mumbai. Ahead, the Taj rose up, like a grand sandcastle tipped from its mould.

At the hotel's staff entrance, the Time Office on Merriweather Road, Faustine, forty-seven, placed a thumbprint on his staff card, while his daughter, just three weeks into a probationary contract, clocked in, using the antiquated machine on the wall. Kissing her father goodbye, she set off for work in the second-floor Data Centre, from where the Taj Group's global systems were monitored, while he descended to the basement to change into his white jacket and black trousers, before heading to the first-floor Sea Lounge, where guests took breakfast and high tea.

The next opportunity for talking would not come until evening, around 9 p.m., in the Palm Lounge, an airy conservatory adjacent to the Sea Lounge. Florence liked to sit there on her break, admiring the crowds of honeymooners and tourists swirling around the brightly illuminated Gateway of India, while the chefs spoiled her with a scoop of coffee ice cream.

Faustine had been dwelling on his death for many days now, while Florence had avoided listening to 'his mawkish thoughts'. The idea had come to a head in the lead-up to his copper anniversary, twenty-two years wed to Precilla. Now, on 26 November, the date was upon him and he had renewed his wedding vows by presenting his wife with a new *mangalsutra*, a gold pendant strung on a yellow thread, and a shimmering gold and green silk sari. To celebrate, he had given Florence a pair of white plimsolls, which she had put on straight away. Faustine had promised to bring something special back for Floyd, his sixteen-year-old son, later that night.

The Taj had been in Faustine's life longer than he could remember. A Christian, originally from Kerala, he had started working there when the city was still Bombay – a name coined by sixteenth-century Portuguese settlers who had marvelled at its *bom bahi* (good harbour). This view lit up many of the hotel's restaurants and bars – and could be seen from the best suites, which nowadays commanded up to £5,000 a night.

Faustine had begun, his head crowned with a luxuriant mane of chestnut hair, in room service, where he had remained until the city was renamed Mumbai in 1995 by the Shiv Sena, a Maharashtrian grass roots party, who, railing against migrants and Muslims, turned base chauvinism into political gold. Soon after, he had become a waiter, and finally the balding Service Captain of the baby blue Sea Lounge, a place for a tryst, with its lucky lovers' seat, a ying-yang coiling chair. There he was paid to be whatever the customer wanted. It was for this reason that when the time came he wanted to be served by others, his invisible life celebrated by a great and uproarious crowd of mourners. Now all he had to do was pin Florence down, and make her understand.

Tuesday, 25 November 2008, 7 p.m. – the purchase department

A grand hotel such as the Taj was like a galleon inserted in a bottle, a private world that, once entered, the well-heeled need never leave. It consisted of the Palace, the original U-shaped grand hotel, built in 1903 facing the harbour, originally five and later six storeys, plus a modern Tower added in 1973. On the lam from south-west France and fancying a *croustade*, why not try La Patisserie, in the southern corner of the Palace? Back from Af–Pak and needing a book on Gandharan sculpture? The bellboy would show you across the Tower lobby to the Nalanda bookshop. A chiropractor was on call, while Pilates classes were by the pool and depilation and detoxification could be done in the privacy of your room. On the top floor of the Palace, where the most exclusive suites were located, teams of liveried butlers catered to every whim.

The Taj was a beacon, conceived of in the Belle Époque, when its unique grey-and-white basalt façade had become the first landmark visible from the deck of approaching Peninsular & Oriental liners. A confection of ornate balconies and bay windows, topped off by triumphant pink cupolas and a central dome, it had shimmered in the early-morning haze for more than a hundred years, and was described as Mumbai's *jadu ghar*, the House of Magic.

In the old days, as the passenger ships came into view, a bell rang in the bowels of the hotel, alerting the staff to the imminent off-loading of wealthy travellers, who would be welcomed with the ethos *atithi devo bhava* (the guest is god). This idea was conceived by the hotel's founder, Jamsetji Tata, a Parsi industrialist and philanthropist, who had wanted to build a hotel that pointed to the future, making everyone forget the dying years of the nineteenth century, when Bombay had been ravaged by plague. Today, new recruits like Florence Martis were issued with crib cards that they carried in their shirt pockets and that set out Tata's historic values.

This entire spectacle took martial organization, overseen by the man described by his staff as the god of the backstage, Grand Executive Chef Hemant Oberoi. Small, portly and poised, with a salt-and-pepper moustache and a high forehead that glistened when the kitchens galloped at full tilt, Oberoi ruled his realm from a tiny cabin he called his *adda* (sanctuary), which was crammed with more than two dozen Ganeshas, flags and citations from leading chefs around the world. It was situated at the heart of the first-floor service area that straddled the Palace and the Tower, and a ceramic tile hung on the wall: 'So bless my little kitchen, Lord,/And those who enter in,/And may they find naught but joy and peace,/And happiness therein.'

Planning for the day ahead started the evening before, after Faustine Martis and the Sea Lounge day shift had gone home. Oberoi had to make sure there was just enough of anything perishable (kept in walk-in cold stores) to get them through the lunchtime and evening sittings: sole for the French-themed Zodiac Grill, shellfish for Masala Kraft's signature prawn skewers, and fatty tuna flown in daily from the Maldives for Wasabi's sushi chefs. For meat and poultry alone there were more than twenty suppliers kept on call to ensure that nothing ever ran out.

Serving fresh dishes from around the world – in a city where temperatures sometimes reached 38 degrees Celsius and the air could be laden with 80 per cent humidity – required special measures. Super-cooled containers from the city's docks fought for space outside the delivery entrance with lorries filled with sticky Alphonso mangos from down the coast in Ratnagiri, and musty truckles of Kalimpong cheese from the hill stations of the north-east. Cycle rickshaws and handcarts darted in and out, delivering fruit, nuts and herbs from local markets, with spice mixes like masala powder ground to each chef's taste. In the delivery hall, boxes were sorted and dispatched by hand: chickens and lamb to the butchery on the first floor of the Palace, *charcuterie* to the cold store behind. Too much, and it would all turn to mush. Too little, and Oberoi's chefs would grind to a halt.

By midnight, on the cusp of 26 November, when the sleeping crows were propped up like dominoes in the trees around Apollo Bunder, Chef Oberoi was still working. The hotel was in the jaws of the wedding season and he knew that tomorrow every one of the Taj's dozen restaurants and bars was fully booked for breakfast, lunch and dinner. His kitchens would be expected to turn out thousands of meals that broke down into 100 kilos of rice, 20,000 eggs, 200 kilos of prawns to peel, hundreds of fresh coconuts to chop, 200 kilos of flour and six trucks of vegetables and fruit. Later, there would be 30,000 pieces of linen to wash down in the laundry, soaking up 100 gallons of cleaning products. He wearily ticked the boxes, signing off on everything.

Wednesday, 26 November 2008, 4 a.m. – the kitchens

Chef Oberoi went to bed late and the cooking began early. While wealthy guests lay between Egyptian cotton sheets, the Taj bakery fired up. In the bakery, a predominantly female corps was up to its elbows in flour, salt and yeast, filling the air with the sweet smell of fermentation. Soon, the chrome trays by the door were stacked with sticky delicacies.

By 5 a.m., the stainless steel kitchens were clattering as the executive chefs, sous-chefs, *sauciers*, commis and pot washers arrived. By 6 a.m., the *garde manger* was boisterous, with salads washed and pared while across the corridor in the main kitchen, sauces, gravies, *jus* and stocks were brought to life. In a city with the most overheated real estate market in the world, where a recent survey by Bloomberg calculated that it would take someone on Taj wages 308 years to save for an average-sized apartment in swanky South Mumbai, the hotel put its employees up in cheap accommodation all around, including the crumbling four-storey Abbas Mansions for single men, opposite the south wing of the Palace, the women residing in nearby Rosemont Court.

From now until the early hours, Chef Oberoi would glide through the kitchens with a spoon in his breast pocket, dipping into plates as they flew out of the pass, pulling them back with a cry: 'Not as described on the menu!' Over two decades, the chef, who came from a Punjabi backwater that snuggled up to the border with Pakistan, had turned his childhood memories of local tastes into international favourites. The star attraction at Masala Kraft, an Indian restaurant on the ground floor marble axial passage that connected the Tower lobby to the Palace, was a modern take on his mother's *atta*-chicken, the whole bird marinated in spices before being roasted *en-croûte* in a *tandoor*.

When Oberoi, the son of a stationmaster, had started to travel, the collecting became obsessive, comforting plates from the canteen of a trundling sleeper car turning into the inspiration for bestselling restaurant dishes. The further he went, the more ambitious he became. Mumbai's first real Japanese food was served in Wasabi, on the first floor of the Palace, in 2001, inspired by Oberoi's meeting with the US celebrity chef Masaharu Morimoto. Oberoi also opened Souk, a Lebanese-themed restaurant on the top floor of the Tower, after a stint in the Middle East. Paul Bocuse, the French grand master of *nouvelle cuisine*, gave him the idea of opening Zodiac Grill, to reach out to Mumbai's 'Ultras', the super-rich who could afford to pay Bocuse-style eye-watering prices.

Oberoi lived for cooking. Behind his office door was a set of fresh whites, in case he had to work the night through. His wife, who lived just around the corner, complained she never saw him. He inspired a devout loyalty from his 200-strong Kitchen Brigade, his star chefs immortalized in a bold group photo that hung in the chefs' dining room, their faces grinning, their weapons of choice held aloft: a knife, a pepper grinder, a spatula and a tomato. 'We stay because of the Tatas,' Oberoi would observe, wryly referring to the family that still owned the hotel. 'We certainly don't do it for the money.' A Taj restaurant manager earned £300 a month, while a competitor in Mumbai might pay them twice as much.

By 6 a.m., in draughty Abbas Mansions, the noise of the day shift rising disturbed the night shift just bedding down. Amit Peshave, the 27-year-old baby-faced manager of the hotel's twenty-four-hour coffee shop, Shamiana, pulled a thin cotton bedsheet over his head in a vain attempt to block out the din. At this time of year, the chilly mornings took some getting used to. Today he felt exhausted. The Shamiana job (which also involved managing Aquarius, the pool-side café) was his first senior position, and he had only been in it for a few weeks. Located on the ground floor, on the corridor linking the Tower lobby to the pool and Palace gardens, Shamiana was where all-night drinkers and insomniacs ended up. Everyone agreed it was among the hardest jobs in the hotel.

Today Amit needed to catch up on a report he was writing about an Italian food festival he had hosted the previous weekend. He had been working on it until 2 a.m. and had still not finished. The last couple of days had been doubly gruelling, since Chef Oberoi had also asked him to look after Sabina Saikia, a notoriously picky restaurant critic who was reviewing the new 'Chef's Studio'. She had been rude and demanding, but he took it in his stride. 'Only two more days,' Amit told himself, rolling over. Friday was his long-awaited 'off-day', the first since taking the promotion. Maybe he would drive his motorbike to Juhu Beach, in the north, catch a game of snooker, or ogle the college girls at Pizza by the Bay, a cool, all-white restaurant on Marine Drive.

When Amit had joined the Taj seven years before as an industrial trainee, working under Faustine Martis at the Sea Lounge, the older man had got him running around balancing trays, 'seeing how fast I could go before dropping everything'. By 2006, he was Faustine's boss. 'But that was just the way it is: I was a graduate and he wasn't.'

Amit dozed off again. When he woke, he was late. He leapt up, showered and jogged around to the Time Office. Changing into his black manager's suit, he felt for the 'Taj Values' crib sheet in his breast pocket. 'Embrace *Talent* and harness *Expertise* to leverage standards of *Excellence* in the *Art of Hospitality*.' Every day he would gather Shamiana's waiters and test them on it, too. It was one of the first things Faustine had drummed into him. Recite the Taj Values. Learn them by heart. Everything else will follow. The cards had changed a lot since Faustine had begun work and now also encapsulated the Tatas' ambitious financial goals, reminding everyone how from one hotel they now controlled a global empire of 112 outlets in twelve countries, with 13,629 rooms, and a goal of turning over $2bn, or £650m, by 2016.

When he reached Shamiana, which was decked out like an Indian wedding tent, with diaphanous ceiling drapes and twinkling chandeliers, it was packed. The head waiter, Rehmatullah Shaukatali, who had been at the Taj so long some colleagues called him 'the heirloom', was run off his feet. Amit greeted him and his young sous-chef, Boris Rego, manning the display kitchen. Rego's father was the most famous chef in Goa, and had trained at the Taj in the seventies, becoming friends with Oberoi. 'The Indefatigable', Amit called Rego Jr. The smiling chef shouted over the hubbub. 'What d'you want for supper, Boss?' For days, Rego had been promising to make his manager a special pizza. 'Tandoori chicken, lot of capsicums, extra mozzarella cheese and a hell of a lot of onions, Chef,' Amit hollered back. Rego saluted: 'It'll be ready by 9.30 p.m., sir.'

The Shamiana manager checked the noticeboard in the kitchen where Chef Oberoi pinned updates at dawn. Several VIPs and MPs were due. Always a nightmare, Amit thought. They drank too much, bullied the staff and tried to skip the bill. There was a big Sindhi wedding tonight, three banquets and a birthday party booked for 8 p.m. It would be hectic. He saw that the swimming pool terrace supervisor had called in sick. His assistant would have to run the poolside barbeque tonight. He called Adil Irani, one of Aquarius's up-and-coming waiters, asking him to muck in, too.

By 7 a.m., out in the Tower lobby, Karambir Kang was on the prowl. With a walk that his friends joked looked like a shark carving up a pod of seals, the hotel's General Manager began his first tour of the day, appraising everything, as the rising scent of beeswax mingled with freshly cut Night Queen.

Karambir's competitors working for other hotel chains regarded him as the Taj's attack dog. But among his staff who flitted about buffing and polishing, brushing down the cantilevered Grand Staircase that dominated the central atrium of the Palace, the blue-eyed General Manager was seen as affable. At thirty-nine he was also a youthful 'captain of the ship', as he described the GM's job, someone who led from the front, the visible face of the Taj on the hotel's bridge, a man who inspired his team and claimed he was 'always the last to leave'. Doing his rounds, he stopped every now and then to crack a joke, or ask about a family problem, making it his business to know guests and employees alike. Up on the mezzanine, the half-landing before the first floor, he also took a moment to make a private *namaste* to the black bust of the hotel's founder. A Tata man through and through, Karambir admired those who had started it all.

He was as particular with his attire as he was about the hotel: a navy suit, crisp cotton shirt, matching silk tie and handkerchief, usually chosen by his wife, Neeti. Today it was orange and gold check, a bright note to lighten a hard day as the high season was upon them, with all of its associated stresses. Up on the Palace's third floor, his deputy Food and Beverage Manager was conducting a morning stock-take in one of the hotel's alcohol stores, hidden behind a false door, marked as room 324. On the fifth floor, in a flower-strewn room, the hotel's 'public areas' florists constructed towering assemblies. Today it was roses from the north-east arranged around a base of shocking pink chrysanthemum and hibiscus flowers from Kerala.

He strode out of the Palace lobby and into the Taj's poolside cloister, pressed with vitrine mosaics and topped by onion cupolas, giving it the appearance of a *hammam* installed in a Florentine boarding school. Architects grandly call this the Indo-Saracenic style, a cocktail of Indo-Islamic, Gothic Revival and Neo-Classical styles, in the way that India was also a blend of Islamic, Hindu, Sikh, Christian and Buddhist values. For Karambir, the Taj was part Kew Gardens and part haunted *palazzo*. Around him came the swishing of palm frond besoms as groundsmen removed the overnight leaves. They earned 6,000 rupees a month (£70), and were gone to their *chawls* by the time the guests emerged. His circuit done, he went back to his office behind the Tower reception area to leaf through the roster of the day's events.

He could have done this on his laptop or his BlackBerry. Everything was set up to digitally assay the days and weeks ahead. But Karambir liked to feel his way with his fingertips. The Taj deserved this kind of intimacy. For him, the hotel was a special case, so needy that he lived here too, up on the sixth floor of the Palace, in a stunning suite overlooking the Arabian Sea that he shared with Neeti and their two boys, Uday, twelve, and Samar, five. Located in the top southern corner, it was surrounded by some of the hotel's most exclusive apartments.

The son of a Sikh major general who had fought Pakistan in 1965 and 1971, Karambir found his metier in the sales department of the Taj group soon after graduation from Fergusson College in Pune, moving into sales. When he was posted to New Delhi, he transformed the flagging brand into the city's most popular hotel in under a year. He was sent to Lucknow to establish a new Taj out of nothing – his friends joked that the group's owner, Ratan Tata, would tell Karambir to take a morning flight to a new city and, when he got there, advise him that he was taking over. Given how much of his life was spent in five-star hotels, it was fortunate that Karambir loved everything that went with them: good company, a glass of wine and an expensive cigar. After his mother came to terms with the fact he was never going to join the army, she joked that her son had become so hospitable he should have been a housewife.

When Karambir met Neeti Mathur, a North Indian girl with rook-black hair, at a Taj conference in 1994, he told his father she was the one. Neeti gave up her job to become a full-time mother. Uday, their elder son, was calm and stoic like his father, and Samar was peppy like his mother. Neeti got used to couriering her husband's clothes to the next hot location and talking to him mostly on the phone. Somehow he always made it back home for parents' evening or school plays, often slipping in late. The family was delighted when Uday won a place at Mumbai's Cathedral School, one of India's best.

After seventeen years in sales, in 2006 Karambir was given his first hotel to manage, the stale Taj Lands End, Bandra, a fashionable district to the north-west, loved by Bollywood stars. 'It was putting me in the deep end,' he recalled. His boys were delighted, hoping they would get to see more of him. And he out-performed himself, more than doubling occupancy in under a year. In November 2007, he was given the Tatas' jewel, the Taj Palace and Tower on Apollo Bunder, becoming General Manager and Vice-President. Neeti was excited to be back in the heart of Mumbai. But the Taj proved demanding, with the family complaining that they saw less of Karambir than before, as he was always on call.

Today was no different. His planner showed that most of the hotel's 20,000 square feet of conference, banqueting and function rooms – located on the first floor of the Palace – were booked. The indents and event sheets presented by Chef Oberoi listed the Sindhi wedding in the Crystal Room, a favourite location for society functions, which, when fully opened, stretched the length of the pool. The board of Hindustan Unilever, one of the hotel's most powerful clients, was also expected, with thirty-five French, Dutch and Indian executives and their wives coming for a luxurious dinner in the Prince's Room, an intimate private dining space in the southernmost corner of the hotel.

A large European Parliament party was arriving imminently, with trade commissioners and Members of the European Parliament (MEP) from Britain, France, Holland, Spain, Italy and Germany. Also checking in was a committee of Indian MPs. The Taj would soon be hosting several international cricket stars, including Shane Warne and Kevin Pietersen, who were launching the new Champions League Twenty20, and their advance team were landing in the hotel today. Sunil Kudiyadi, Karambir's security chief, was up in his fifth-floor office, finalizing the hotel's security plan. Over in the modern Tower, there was no let-up. A visiting Korean trade delegation of more than a hundred had booked Rendezvous, a function room on the top floor, next door to Souk.

This morning would be especially frantic as Karambir had to leave the hotel after lunch. The chairman of the Indian suit manufacturer

Raymond's, a Mumbai 'Ultra', was throwing a bash in the Taj Lands End and Karambir was on a three-line whip to attend, with the Formula One driver Mika Häkkinen making a guest appearance. It was an hour or more each way, so he and Neeti might not see each other until the morning. In his absence, Grand Executive Chef Oberoi would take charge.

Before leaving, Karambir had one especially sensitive task to attend to. The hotel was mollycoddling Sabina Sehgal Saikia, the most powerful food writer in India. While professional kitchens across India were male dominions, Sabina had levelled the playing field by becoming their chief surveyor. Having her in the hotel was a double-edged sword. On good form and in the right company, her words could turn a new restaurant into a money-spinner. But she was as famous for her vicious tongue-lashings. Nowadays, suffering from diabetes and general ill-health, she was increasingly bad-tempered. Sabina was feeling down and had not yet recovered from the death of her father in February. When the Taj first floated the idea, she had not wanted to come.

She only said 'yes' when she realized the trip coincided with a society wedding in Mumbai. Instantly, she had regretted it and rang a close friend in Delhi, Ambreen Khan, who was also heading to Mumbai. 'My life is out of control – I am so stressed out,' Sabina had complained, telling Ambreen she was under pressure to stay in Delhi for a niece's pre-wedding party on the night of 26 November. 'What should I do?'

She had met Ambreen when the latter was doing PR for the Oberoi hotel. 'Be careful or she'll eat you alive,' Ambreen's boss had warned. But Ambreen found Sabina 'easy to deal with', telling a confidante: 'She is sweet and wants affection.' There was a price. Once Ambreen was inducted into the inner circle, Sabina was demanding, on the phone 'every day, all day, and hard to decline'.

Sabina had come to this game by chance, starting life as a classical musician, before joining *The Times of India* to manage its 150th anniversary celebrations. It was her otherworldliness that caught everyone's attention and often made for the best stories, told by her with her unnerving frankness. In the nineties, a PR working for the Dalai Lama's exiled government had called with an enticing offer: 'Richard Gere is in town and wants to throw a concert for Tibet. Can you organize?' Sabina had not heard of Gere, but agreed to meet him in the InterContinental's coffee shop, worrying immediately that 'this good-looking man' would annoy her boyfriend, Shantanu Saikia, 'an Assamese hothead', who was waiting outside in his car.

Gere never stopped talking, she told everyone. 'The longer it took, I knew the more pissed off Shantanu was getting,' she recalled. 'I kept wondering why these other diners on tables were staring at Gere. "Can't these Indians see a good-looking Caucasian and leave him alone?"' Then his phone rang. He apologized, saying it was his girlfriend, Cindy Crawford. Sabina had not heard of her, and all she could think was: 'OK, your girlfriend is calling and I have my boy-friend waiting outside. Is this business or what?' Finally, Gere thanked her and gave her his card, with his private number. When he offered to walk her to the door, she declined. 'You stay inside or I'll have some explaining to do.' That weekend, Sabina and Shant-anu rented a video, *An Officer and a Gentleman*. 'Mii gawd,' she shrieked, scrabbling through her bag for Gere's card. She had lost it.

In 1998, dabbling again, Sabina had tried a food column. It was a huge success. But these days she had fallen out with *The Times*, although she could place her pieces wherever she wanted. 'She either trashed places or lapped up their hospitality,' said Ambreen, who warned her friend, 'You're mean and hard on people. Bad will come of it.'

Now Sabina was dilly-dallying over the Mumbai trip and Ambreen was unsympathetic. 'What's the matter with you?' she asked, inter-rupting her friend's monologue. 'The whole of Delhi is going to be at the Mumbai wedding.' At this thought, Sabina perked up and committed to come.

She had touched down in Mumbai on Monday, 24 November, to be met by a chauffeur-driven Jaguar sent by Karambir. Sabina had been stunned, calling Savitri Choudhury, another strong-minded freelance hack, who lived in Mumbai and worked for the Australian Broadcasting Corporation among others. 'Sabi, they are launching a Chef's Studio. Hemant Oberoi is doing a special dinner for *me*.' Pause. 'I want you and Vikram to come. Let's make a party of it. OK?'

At the Taj, Karambir had shown Sabina up to the Sunrise Suite. With marble floors, a magnificent ribbed wooden ceiling, a lounge, a bedroom and a dining nook, it filled most of the hotel's southern-most cupola and was next door to Karambir's family's apartment. There was champagne on ice when Savitri and her husband called round at 8.30 p.m. Feeling exuberant, Sabina pulled them through the door. 'Come on, let's jump on this huge bed.'

Oberoi's Chef's Studio was an idea imported from the US and Europe, where he had eaten at several Chef's Tables – intimate set-tings placed inside the kitchen of a star cook. For Mumbai he had to refine the idea, as no 'Ultra' was going to sit in a kitchen and pay 125,000 rupees (£1,500) for a dinner for six people – excluding wine. 'Sabina, you're on top form,' Savitri told her, as they ate from Ver-sace plates, served by Amit Peshave. 'The food is amazing.' They kept bringing more. 'It was the first time I had Kobe beef. With Sabina, they went overboard. Typical Taj.'

After eight courses, Sabina went up to her suite, feeling groggy. She called Shantanu, who was now her husband. 'They are really laying it on,' she told him. But he was busy at the family wedding party in Delhi. The whole family was nonplussed at her flying off to Mumbai for somebody else's celebrations. The needy Sabina did not get it and was hurt. 'You don't know what you're missing,' she said, cutting the line. She called Ambreen: 'You *can't* believe this suite. Please come over.' But Ambreen was working. As General Manager of the *Indian Express*, she needed to attend a conference. Sabina spent the night alone in a bed fit for a king.

26 November 2008, 4 p.m. – the Palace lobby

Karambir Kang was in Bandra, Chef Oberoi was studying orders in his cabin, Amit Peshave was still not done with his Italian food festival report, and out in the Tower lobby holidaymakers and businessmen stood three deep before the reception desk. Along the marble axial corridor, beside the Grand Staircase, was the calmer Palace reception, where VIP guests sat in wing-backed chairs, waiting to check in. Will Pike and Kelly Doyle were among them, dressed in flip-flops and beach gear, catching some stares from the doormen.

They had just flown in after two weeks in Goa and the ride in from the airport had been a baptism of fire. 'My first experience of real India,' Will murmured as their cab was circled by salesmen at every traffic light, wielding books, phone rechargers and dusters. 'It's mental.' Now in the perfumed calm of the Taj, he felt himself relaxing. 'Good afternoon, Mr Doyle,' said the receptionist, using Kelly's surname as everything had been paid for on her credit card. Will grinned, a smile that stayed on his face as they were shown to their sea-facing room, up the Grand Staircase on the third floor. He was two years younger than Kelly *and* her junior at work, with his salary a fraction of hers. He joked that he was permanently emasculated.

When they entered room 316, the panorama of the Arabian Sea hit them. What a view. Opening their bags, spilling sand and wet clothes on to the floor, Kelly headed for the bathroom. Will tried a window, but it was double-glazed and would not budge. He perused the TV channels and the hotel restaurant list. After two weeks of Kingfisher beer, grilled fish and *malai kofta*, there were too many choices.

As he lay back, contemplating the ruched silk curtains, he felt he had been away from London for weeks. The whole holiday plan had been a chaotic, seat-of-the-pants scramble, with Kelly booking flights but forgetting about visas, leading to an embarrassing scene at the airport and a humiliating return to work. They eventually made it out on 10 November, a week late, but it had been worth it, with a memorable fortnight spent on Goan beaches, riding trains and in a yoga retreat.

It was Kelly who suggested the last-minute splurge. Will, who had spent two weeks smoking *charas* (hashish), was not so sure he could acclimatize, or even that he wanted to. The Taj might be the most famous hotel in India, the kind of place where Gregory Peck and

Duke Ellington had hung out, steeped in history and refinement, but it was not his scene. They had to come through the city to catch their flight home, Kelly argued, so why not?

When it opened in December 1903, the Taj had been a disaster. The British did not like it and it was too expensive for Indians. Broken-hearted, the founder, Jamsetji Tata, had set sail for Europe and died the following year from heart disease. He was buried at Brookwood cemetery, Surrey, in the Tata family mausoleum. But slowly maharajas and *nawabs* began to treat the hotel as a second home, coming with retinues of servants. By the time the Prince of Wales and Princess Mary landed on Apollo Bunder for a state visit in November 1905, the Taj was turning a corner, awash with indigenous royalty.

As India changed, the hotel kept pace, the old aristocracy eased out by the well-off figureheads of the independence movement, including Muhammad Ali Jinnah, who proposed to his wife, Rutti, in the sea-facing Ballroom and would lead the new Pakistan in 1947. Sarojini Naidu, a child prodigy and poetess, who became the president of the Indian National Congress, spoke at the hotel. After the Partition of India eventually was declared, it was from the Taj that the first eulogies of independence rang out. When the British staged a formal departure, it was from the Gateway of India, built to commemorate the 1911 visit by King George V and Queen Mary. Once the bastion of colonialism, the Taj had effortlessly realigned itself as an emblem of self-reliance.

The next three decades saw Hollywood come to love it, too, with Frank Sinatra and Sophia Loren rubbing elbows with world leaders, entrepreneurs and tycoons. In 1973, the over-subscribed hotel doubled its occupancy, with an American-designed Taj Tower. A new lobby was created at its base, on the harbour side, with a private club located above it and named after the hotel's architect, William Chambers.

While the public areas were streamlined, the service areas became more labyrinthine with each renovation. The kitchens had moved down from the top floor to the first floor in the thirties and a new sixth floor had been added to the Palace in 1969. After the Tower was built, new service areas straddled it and the Palace but they did not quite line up. All over the place stepladders led up to storerooms hidden in otherwise inaccessible ceiling cavities. Windows became doors, panels swung round to reveal service lifts. Extra staircases were built but not added to the architectural blueprint. Interconnecting corridors developed irregular angles.

Will had taken some working on, and during their penultimate day in Goa Kelly kept at him. He needed to make his mind up. Her London salary meant they could afford a more expensive package, which included a free airport pick-up, a butler and a heritage room with a sea view. Kelly was already thinking about the king-size bed, the flat-screen TV, the bath and fluffy towels, a first-class treat after two weeks barefoot on the beach. 'There's only so long you can be a hippy,' Will said, wondering if that was actually true. With his mind half made up, they had packed for the Taj, lured by a night of extravagance before real life kicked in on Monday morning, in London, where the forecast was for drizzle. The line of least resistance was one he had travelled for most of his life, although that was changing.

The Indian trip was the culmination of two great years. 'This is my moment,' he had said to himself, before leaving. His work had been going well. He was in a relationship with 'a really cool girl and we are going to be together for ever and ever'. He had turned the corner early in 2007, after flunking his degree and spending several years managing Soho bars. One night a customer had offered him a job as a runner at Bare Films, a London-based TV production company, where he had first spotted Kelly. From then on everything had clicked into place.

Precise, pretty and high-octane, Kelly was an up-and-coming producer. She was also married. But Will – with his floppy hair, footballer's physique and laid-back demeanour – made an impression. One night they went out for a drink and 'things just developed'. He had woken the next morning, struggling into his jeans, feeling like he was an embarrassing indiscretion who had just lost his job. Three weeks later it happened again. Soon they were embroiled in a relationship that should never have happened but that neither of them could stop. Kelly's energy was infectious. 'You just know that if you follow her you're going to have a really good time,' Will told his friends. The only time he had felt anything like it before was when he was sixteen and had fallen in love with a girl at school. When that relationship had ended, he had 'cried for a week'.

Kelly left her husband. Early in 2008, she and Will rented a 'cool flat' in Camden Town. From now on, they spent their weekends driving about London in Will's red MG coupe or browsing Camden market for 'quirky bits of furniture that didn't fit into the minuscule flat'. They both liked to entertain, cooking paella for a dozen friends, or hosting a fancy dress party. Will DJ'ed in local clubs, styling himself 'LazyPike (the Jungalier)'.

Work began to move, too, with a vague advertising idea Will had had for Pret A Manger coming together after he had submitted it via the 'comments' section of the company's website. He wondered, as he posted it, if anyone read this stuff. The chief executive called soon after and asked Will to meet him in January. Planning was not Will's strong suit. 'And yet here it was all happening without me doing anything.' The summer highlight had been a long, lazy weekend of music and camping at the Big Chill festival surrounded by friends and family, including Kelly, his little brother Ben, his sister Rosie, and their über-chilled father, Nigel, a retired advertising executive.

It was Kelly who had suggested an autumn trip to India, a chance to take a breath before Will's Pret A Manger pitch. They also needed to think about where they were headed. They spent most of the holiday in the southern Goan resort of Palolem, where the array of palm-shaded bars and cheap guest houses attracted a large contingent of stoners, Will skinning up while reading and listening to music.

In his rucksack was a biography of the tortured father of computer sciences, Alan Turing, and *A Mathematician's Apology*, G. H. Hardy's requiem for his own fading career. An armchair obsessive,

Will got immersed in things. When he wasn't reading, he kicked a football around with local kids on the beach or filmed sunsets, train journeys and markets with an old Super 8. He bought Indian versions of the Ken and Barbie dolls, with plans to use them to film a stop-animation short. Will and Kelly were cruising. 'We were really good at doing fuck all,' he told his brother.

Wednesday, 26 November 2008, 6 p.m.

A ten-minute drive across town from the Taj to the Trident–Oberoi, which Karambir Kang liked to call 'the second-best hotel in town', the Deputy Commissioner of Police (DCP) for Zone 1, Vishwas Nangre Patil, was having a gruelling day. He calculated that he was still only halfway through an eight-hour security review conducted by the Special Protection Group, ahead of a visit to the city by the Prime Minister, Manmohan Singh, on 28 November.

He reminded himself, as he stifled a yawn, that this was a small price to pay. Policing Zone 1 was all about the glory. It covered the city's smartest hotels, apartments and villas, Mumbai's historical heart, as well as the central backpacker district of Colaba. Zone 1 also came with a filing cabinet full of drawbacks: VIP visits (like the Prime Minister's), foreign dignitaries jetting in, and mouthy well-to-do residents. These were people who earned in a day what a dishonest policeman could acquire in a career, and what a straightforward copper would never earn.

With the sleeves of his well-pressed shirt precisely rolled, Patil sported a tidy moustache and a square, stubborn jaw. He had been a surprising choice for Zone 1 when he got the job five months before. A native Marathi speaker from isolated Kokrud, a village of temples and farmers some 220 miles to the south, he had risen above his upbringing as a country boy. In a subcontinent where names mean everything, the Patils were traditionally landowners and warriors, and Vishwas Patil, the son of a renowned weightlifter, spent most of his childhood thinking he would join the army. He had been 'crazy about uniforms' since he was a boy, joining the National Cadet College in his teens, winning a gold medal for shooting. But having topped his class, he defied the expectations of his father to gain a Master's degree before sitting the elite civil service exams in 1997. He joined the Indian Police Service, his first posting in a rural spot where he understood the people like they were his family.

The boy from Kokrud had assumed he would not get so far. The force in Maharashtra and elsewhere was led by privileged officers like Mumbai's Commissioner Gafoor, the city's police chief, the son of a *nawab* from Hyderabad. But in a little under a decade the outsider Patil had got himself noticed, shaking things up with high-profile campaigns, challenging privilege and appeasing conservatives, being promoted to the cherished DCP position in South Mumbai in June 2008. And now he was here at the top table, alongside the most senior cops in the city, including Commissioner Gafoor and Rakesh Maria, the legendary chief of Crime Branch.

As he sat listening to his seniors, Patil was becoming deeply worried. What gnawed away at him was how little attention anyone was paying to a number of warnings that had been staring him in the face since he started here, and that, if taken seriously, would surely have put the city on a war footing, irrespective of whether the PM was coming.

He had received the initial tip-off in his first week, a report that the Leopold Café, a popular tourist hangout near the Taj, was on a terrorist hitlist. Over the following days, looking through intelligence chits, Patil had discovered a disturbing pattern of warnings that were frequent and detailed. His predecessors had received dozens of classified bulletins about potential terrorist strikes on the city. But, as far as he could see, the intelligence agencies and the police had ignored them.

The first gobbet had arrived in August 2006 and stated that Lashkar-e-Toiba, an influential Pakistani jihadi organization that had cut its teeth sending Muslim insurgents to fight the Indian security forces in divided Kashmir, was 'making preparations' for a major assault on Mumbai. Several five-star hotels were mentioned as targets, including the Trident–Oberoi and the Taj. Since then there had been twenty-five further alerts, many of them delivered by the CIA to the Indian government's external intelligence agency, the Research and Analysis Wing, and passed on to India's domestic Intelligence Bureau.

Patil had pondered the origin of the information. When he examined the detail, it seemed clear that the US was tapping into a significant source, the welter of leads drawing a picture of someone right inside the notoriously closed Lashkar, an outfit that everyone believed was funded by Pakistani intelligence.

It was not as though terror was new to Mumbai. Over the last few decades, the city had witnessed a dozen serious attacks in which more than 500 had been killed and almost 2,000 injured. After the most recent carnage in July 2006, when a series of train blasts had killed 181, the Maharashtra government had constituted a study group. Late by many months, it had still not filed any recommendations.

Patil could see that all previous incidents consisted of concealed bombs left on bicycles and scooters, abandoned in market places and outside prominent buildings. Some of the materiel was home-made, derived from potassium chlorate purloined from textile mills, where it was used as a colour fixative. Other blasts relied on *black soap*, as locals called the sticky military explosive RDX, smuggled into the country from Pakistan or the Middle East. But the more recent intelligence suggested Lashkar was plotting something new, a live raid on the city. Three warnings specifically mentioned the use of *fidayeen*, meaning guerrillas armed with grenades and AK-47s who fought to the death, inflicting heavy casualties before being overcome. Lashkar had deployed this strategy in Indian-administered Kashmir to deadly effect.

Eleven warnings suggested the plan would involve multiple simultaneous attacks. Six warnings pointed to a seaborne infiltration, which would be a first in India. Zone 1 lay at the narrowest part of the city peninsula and was accessible from Back Bay to the west and the harbour and docks to the east. Patil had contacted the coast guard and asked what was being done to beef up security. 'Nothing,' he was told. He called the DCP responsible for the port, who confided that he was so short of funding that he did not have a single high-speed boat to chase waterborne suspects. He had taken to hiring fishing vessels using his own money to get around his patch.

Unsure of how to proceed, Patil sought advice from one of his close friends on the force, DCP Rajvardhan Sinha, the deputy in charge at SB2, the wing of Special Branch responsible for monitoring foreigners. Patil and Sinha, who was known universally as Rajvardhan, had both graduated into the police service as batch-mates in 1997, although their career paths had taken them in different directions. Rajvardhan had been born in the fractious northern Indian state of Bihar, and his first superintendent posting was among the toughest any policeman could imagine: Gadchiroli, a town in the wild east of Maharashtra. It was part of the so-called Red Corridor, a stronghold of Naxalite rebels. Named after a village in West Bengal where the movement started, the Naxals had purportedly taken up guns to overthrow corrupt landlords, protecting local tribes from exploitation and stopping land grabs by corporations. The police were caught in the middle, with some officers enraged at what they saw as having to do the government's dirty work, while others took the opportunity to become combat-ready.

Rajvardhan, who had a dramatic duelling scar running diagonally across the top of his nose, was in the latter camp. 'You get that killer instinct when you are in the jungle,' he joked with his colleagues. In his first week his convoy had been hit by an IED, trucks and jeeps spun on to their roofs, the men hosed down with bullets in an ambush as they fled into the forests. The cool-headed Rajvardhan had led them to safety on foot, without losing a man. His advice to Patil when he learned about the massing intelligence in Mumbai was to take the warnings seriously. 'If the shit hits the fan,' he told his friend, 'you'll be the one who has to deal with it.'

Patil had started nightly meetings for his brightest officers, giving them specific tasks in key locations. He personally visited several places named as targets. In July 2008, he began focusing on the unregulated fishermen's colony at the southern end of Back Bay called Badhwar Park. It was close to the World Trade Centre, the Trident–Oberoi and the Taj hotel. Patil wrote to the Commandant Coast Guards, Western Region HQ, warning: 'If anti-social/terrorist/ anti-national elements desire to attack by rocket launcher, these boats can be used.'

Then, the Intelligence Bureau had received two more date-specific warnings about the Taj. One concerned a possible attack on 24 May and the other on 11 August, both prompted by tip-offs from a source in Pakistan said to be inside Lashkar. A more political officer might have avoided taking on the country's most glamorous hotel, steered by one of the subcontinent's most powerful industrialist families, the Tatas. Patil piled straight in, demanding a meeting on 12 August and spending nine hours with the security chief, Sunil Kudiyadi. In his subsequent report to Commissioner Gafoor, the Zone 1 DCP concluded: 'Overall, the management has done very little to adapt the hotel to the changing security environment in the city.'

Patil was not a hotelier, and had no idea about the need to beguile guests. What he saw was a historic building ringed by a large number of unsecured, undefendable entrances and easily assailable porous walls. There was CCTV but it was ambiguously labelled and poorly organized. There was an alcohol *godown* (store) on the third floor, which was prohibited because of the fire risk. The systems in place to detect weapons and explosives being smuggled into the hotel were slapdash. No blast barriers or screens were installed, meaning the Taj remained vulnerable to a drive-by or drive-in suicide bomber. Patil told Kudiyadi: 'Don't think about what has happened in this city. Think about what they've *not* yet done. If they have set charges on motorbikes, look up to the skies.' Patil wished to create a fortress, while the Taj needed to remain a theatre.

After the 12 August meeting Patil had decided to make things official. He issued written advice to Kudiyadi, copying in the General Manager, Karambir Kang. Given the building pattern of US-supplied warnings, he recommended that the hotel install blast barriers, armed police pickets and snipers on the roof. The advice was politely rebuffed: guests wanted to be greeted by brightly uniformed *chobedars* (doormen), not a SWAT team that would undermine the hotel's luxury image.

He made some progress after 20 September 2008, when a massive truck bomb devastated the five-star Marriott hotel in the Pakistani capital of Islamabad, killing more than fifty people. As grim scenes from the blast site were broadcast across India, Patil secured a meeting with the Taj management. Over the next few days, he drew up twenty-six emergency measures, including police gunmen overlooking the main porch and the deployment of between six and nine armed officers below. He recommended a security grille for the glass-fronted Northcote side door at the southern end of the Palace, automatic locking for other entrances and the permanent closure of the Palace lobby doors overlooking Back Bay. All staff, guests and visitors should enter the hotel through one choke point, the Tower lobby, where there would be metal detectors, bag checks and pat-downs. By the second week of October, the Taj had implemented many of these suggestions and Patil went on leave, with the hotel pledging to complete the rest.

Now at the security meeting Patil recommended something similar be done at the Trident–Oberoi, where the PM would be speaking. 'The city is ripe for an attack,' he warned. The intelligence services knew it too. One recent warning from the CIA commented that 'Lashkar is equipped and ready to launch a broadside against the city.'

7 p.m. – room 316, Palace wing

Back in the Taj, Kelly was still in the bathroom, 'doing girly things', as Will watched the darkening sky turn purple. He banged on the door. 'We won't have time for shopping and a beer.' She emerged in a strapless maxi-dress and sandals, with blood-red nails and lipstick to match. Perfect.

They set off for the shops of Colaba Causeway, a crowded strip two blocks behind the hotel. They were here for such a short time that they wanted to sample it all. But after the reverie of the beach, and the sterility of the hotel lobby, it was far too manic, and seeing a free table inside the Leopold Café they dived in. A Mumbai institution, it looked like a cross between a Victorian dispensary and an ice cream parlour, and had been in the hands of the same Parsi family since 1871.

It was happy hour. 'Lets have beers and jalapenos,' Will suggested, loving the buzz. They drained a couple of pints, talked about eating there and then ruled it out, sticking to the plan of an elegant dinner at the Taj. Meandering back, they came up Best Marg and entered the pristine hotel through the Northcote entrance. 'No security here,' Will ribbed Kelly. 'If you wanted to raid this place you would come this way.' Walking along the chilled marble corridor towards the Palace lobby, passing empty boutiques and a display case of illustrious former guests – Neil Armstrong, Yehudi Menuhin and Gamal Abdel Nasser – they stopped at the poolside bar, and had another drink, served by an amicable steward, Adil Irani.

For a few moments they chatted with him about Goa. He had been there once or twice and a cousin ran a bar. But soon he became distracted by the noise of firecrackers and shouting out in the street, and called over his manager, Amit Peshave. 'What's the kerfuffle?' Amit shrugged: 'It's nothing.' The manager was still fretting about his Italian report. When was he going to file it? He rushed off to see what was going on in Shamiana, at the rear of the main lobby.

Kelly and Will paid up and went to check in online for their flights home. Will sent a quick email to his father and siblings too. He was looking forward to a beer, some music and a game at the Arsenal. 'Fancy coming over for a curry on Sunday?' he signed off. 'I'm cooking.'

Up on the sixth floor of the Palace, the critic Sabina Saikia was in her suite, dressed in a beautiful sari, a large Hindu *bindi* on her forehead and with her hair pulled into a tight bun on top of her head. She had made it out to the society wedding in Parsi Hall only to beat a retreat back to the Taj, her head spinning, her kidneys aching. After three days of eating and drinking, her body had revolted, and when her butler had come over to help, she had vomited on his shoe. Unflappable, he got on with clearing up the mess, asking if she needed a doctor. Mortified, Sabina sent him out for medicine, needing to be on her own.

She texted Ambreen Khan for advice, sounding addled and upset. 'Throw on your track pants,' Ambreen suggested, adding that she would call round as soon as her function at the Trident–Oberoi was over. Sabina looked out of the window at a sleek yacht gleaming in the harbour. It looked like a party was going on. She texted Ambreen again: 'Come over, I've lit candles, there are flowers and dinner. I'm waiting for you.'

A few paces away, in their sixth-floor apartment, Karambir Kang's family was back after an afternoon shopping trip. Elder son Uday was busy working on a school project and Samar was preparing for his Cathedral School admission interview on 3 December. The boys seemed so happy and full of life, so Neeti made a snap decision to get new portraits taken as a surprise for her husband. She called down to the photographers in Taj Memories, a studio on the first floor. Pearl Dubash, the manager, arranged for someone to come at 8 p.m. Neeti called Karambir for a catch-up. The traffic had been grinding as expected, but he had arrived at the Taj Lands End party. They were putting on quite a show, he said, and there was a rumour that Bollywood top-draw Shah Rukh Khan might turn up. He promised to slip away as soon as he could. Neeti said she had something for him. 'Well the kids do,' she confided. The photo would be their surprise.

9 p.m. – the Tower lobby

Suited visitors and wedding guests in saris and gowns filtered in, heading for the Crystal Room reception or dinner, walking across the white Italian marble and apricot silk rugs. Guests sat in the lobby's scooped-back chairs sipping *nimbu pani* (lemonade) from heavy crystal glasses that rested on nests of onyx tables.

Outside on the steps, a scrum of noisy MEPs and their staff spilled out of their bus, greeted with marigold garlands. Propping up the check-in counter were six burly ex-commandos who worked for Nicholls Steyn & Associates, a South African VIP protection company that had many lucrative contracts, including providing security advice to the annual Oscars ceremony in Los Angeles. Hired by the Board of Control for Cricket in India (BCCI), they were part of the advance team for the forthcoming Champions League Twenty20 cricket tournament and had arrived off the back of another job in Dubai. It had been a late night – fireworks and a performance by Kylie Minogue – and they were feeling groggy.

'Go and dump the luggage,' Bob Nicholls, the British-born boss, told his men. He had been in town for a couple of days already, meeting with Sunil Kudiyadi, the Taj's security chief, Karambir Kang, the police and the BCCI. 'Let's eat and have a few beers.' The new arrivals wanted Chinese. But the only available table for seven was up in Souk, on the top floor of the Tower. 'More goat,' one of the commandos muttered, as they went to freshen up.

By 9.15 p.m., the sleek, glass-walled Souk, in the crow's nest of the Tower, with its big views out over the Gateway of India and the Arabian Sea, was filling up with diners. Nicholls and his team sat hunched in conversation around one of the glass tables by the windows. Mumbai police were taking their time to embrace the security needs of the forthcoming cricket tournament and over the next couple of days they would have to pile on the pressure.

Across the room, Ravi Dharnidharka, a 31-year-old US Marine captain and fighter pilot of Indian descent, took a table against the far wall. He was with his brother and their Indian relatives. It was the San Diego-based Ravi's first time in Mumbai since coming over with his father as a teenager. After his father had died unexpectedly young, Ravi had lost touch with the Mumbai side of the family and had not seen his grandfather for thirteen years. For a long time, he had 'wanted to reconnect', but he had got enmeshed in two rough tours of Iraq, including flying combat missions during Operation Phantom Fury, the ferocious battle for Fallujah that began in November 2004. Led by the Marine Corps, more than a hundred US soldiers had been killed along with thousands of Iraqis. Ravi, who flew Harriers to soften up insurgent strongholds, had 'literally hit the ground running'. When he eventually got home, he took a while to readjust.

Now he had found the time to make it over to India, and the past ten days had been a whirlwind of old and new relatives. Wrapped up for the past four years in America's 'war on terror' as he had been, mixed feelings about his own foreign-ness and Asian roots swam around his head. Earlier this evening, he had gone to meet a cousin who lived close to Badhwar Park, off Cuffe Parade, and she had shown him the view from her window over the fishermen's huts lining a small inlet where brightly painted boats were anchored. As he watched the sun set and the fishermen mend their nets, he had felt truly relaxed for the first time in years. Now he was looking forward to a good dinner and a catch-up with another cousin. Later, they had plans to meet up with relatives who were eating at the Trident–Oberoi hotel. His cousin pointed to it through the Souk windows, all lit up like a lighthouse at Nariman Point. 'What an amazing view,' he commented. 'It's like sitting in fishbowl on top of world.'

Down in the Tower lobby, a calm was returning as the diners and wedding guests dispersed. Moreno Alphonso, the Taj pianist, finished off 'Always'. Six nights a week, this balding music teacher, whose father had played violin here in the thirties, manned the grand piano to the right of the main glass doors. 'Al' had worked at the hotel almost all his life; his earliest memories were of sitting with his brother on little wooden stools, their names inscribed under the seats, accompanying their father. He looked at his watch: 21.36. It was time for his mid-evening break. Al put down the lid and slipped out through an unmarked staff door.

2.

Prince David

When David Headley walked into the Taj for the first time in September 2006, he had been so impressed by its easy opulence, by the graceful staff and convivial regulars, that he wondered if he would be able to plot its demise. The grandeur reminded him of his own aristocratic antecedence, of his family's great wealth and influence, stories he had learned on the lap of his mother.

The *chobedars* hollered greetings as they threw back the doors, saluting as if they were posted especially for him. The citrus and talcum smell of frangipani in the Tower lobby, not to mention the view through the Sea Lounge's windows that made the crowded Gateway of India look like a well-crafted diorama, almost convinced Headley that the hotel was something secular and precious that was worth saving.

Headley found this city of insomniacs invigorating. He greedily ingested its history, how the archipelago of seven islands had been a gift to King Charles II as part of the dowry from his new wife, Catherine of Braganza, in 1661, although up until the nineteenth century it was predominantly inhabited by Koli fishermen. Then Parsi migrants like the Tatas built empires (and the Taj) out of the saline swamp, and transformed the city into the busiest seaport in Asia and the capital of the Bombay Presidency, one of the most prosperous and peaceful regions in British India. Headley was impressed by the Tatas' determination. He loved the frenzy of Mumbai with its sharp-elbowed, entrepreneurial spirit. It was just the *idea* of India – the land of his paternal forefathers – he despised. And he used this hair's-breadth chink, between the city and the country, between the people and what he described as 'their Hindu rulers', to justify his covert project to bring death and mayhem.

On his first visit, he could not afford to stay at the Taj, since his work had just begun and the budget was tight. But here, like most places where he had grafted, appearances were everything. He found himself a Grade-A address, a private rooming house in the upmarket Breach Candy neighbourhood four and a half miles away, bandying it about the Taj, where he became a fixture. Waiters, managers and guests saw him regularly quaffing a glass of Dom Pérignon in the Harbour Bar or entertaining someone he would introduce as 'a client' up in Faustine Martis's Sea Lounge, telling his companions in his loud American voice about his 'cool Breach Candy bachelor pad'.

Headley was unmissable: six foot two, his blond hair scraped back in a ponytail, broad-shouldered like a prop and with a fair complexion, dressed in crumpled Armani jeans and shirt, a leather jacket hung over his shoulder. He carried himself like he might be dangerous, with a £10,000 Rolex Submariner poking out of his cuff. But he mingled easily and in the Starboard Bar, in the Taj lobby, and in the Aquarius, by the pool, Mumbaikers argued over who knew him best, and told stories about the women who fawned over him. David would listen to your troubles and high-five you. 'Yeah, no problem,' he'd say. 'Whatever you want.' David was cool. 'I can help you.' He was resourceful and generous. 'Let me get that.'

But anyone who knew him as David – an American entrepreneur from Philadelphia – only had half the story. To his sister Sherry and half-brothers Hamzah and Danyal, to his wives Portia, Shazia and Faiza, to his cousins Farid and Alex, his Uncle William, his best friend, Tahawwur Rana, and to Major Iqbal, a spy employed by the ISI, Pakistan's pervasive Inter-Services Intelligence, he was Daood Saleem Gilani – an American of Pakistani descent.

This mixed heritage and muddled ancestry that had got him to India in the first place, doing reconnaissance for a terrorist assault, was strikingly represented in his mismatched eyes: one blue and one brown.

Daood's father, Syed Saleem Gilani, was a renowned Pakistani radio broadcaster from a well-connected Lahori family. Serrill Headley, his mother, was an heiress and adventuress from Maryland. Her great-aunt had been an American philanthropist and maverick who funded women's rights and even Albert Einstein's research. But Serrill's privileged childhood was struck by tragedy in 1952 when her father, a former college football star, died after being hit by a bullet while trying to break up a bar fight. Serrill's mother and her four children made a fresh start in neighbouring Pennsylvania, buying a large farm in the Main Line, an affluent suburb of Philadelphia. But Serrill, who was thirteen when her father died, became uncontrollable. When she met Gilani, who was on secondment to Voice of America, she was a nineteen-year-old undergraduate at the University of Maryland and it had been like 'two flints striking'. Gilani, cultured and sophisticated, was famed in Pakistan as a connoisseur of traditional ghazals and he wooed her with music. After Daood was born in 1960, in Washington DC, Serrill agreed to move to Pakistan, excited by the prospect of an adventure. But what had worked on the East Coast, in a Federal-era town house, fizzled out in the gated Abbas House in Lahore, Gilani's ancestral home. In 1966 they divorced, and Serrill married an aged Afghan insurance executive, leaving Daood to be brought up by Gilani's second wife, a well-connected Lahore heiress.

Feeling rejected, Daood became as uncontrollable as his absent mother had once been. To straighten him out his father enrolled him at a cadet college in a small town in the western Punjab, popular with military families. Although Gilani was not an officer, he shared their milieu. He was a *mohajir*, a migrant from India, his family originating from Kapurthala in the Punjab, from where they had been forced out in the pogroms kickstarted by Partition. Its bloody spectre hung over the Gilani dinner table, while hostilities with India were also framed in the cadet college classroom and re-enacted on its parade ground.

Like his American mother, Daood was reluctant to buckle down, and was constantly reminded of his foreignness by his Pakistani family, which was soon augmented by two new brothers, Danyal and Hamzah. At the first opportunity, when he was sixteen, Daood flew to the US to be reunited with his mother. Serrill had moved back to Philadelphia after her Afghan husband had died and bought a former speakeasy on Second Street near Chestnut, in what was then a rougher part of town, transforming the place into the Khyber Pass Pub, rigging a Pakistani *shamiana* (wedding tent) in the garden. She was, however, distracted by a new man, a reporter with the *Philadelphia Inquirer*, and left her long-lost son to the care of pub regulars, who tagged him 'the Prince'. Daood, a conversative Muslim teenager living above a pub, struggled with his new life. His Uncle William, Serrill's brother, recalled that he spent most of his time transfixed by *Happy Days* on the pub TV, waiting for his mother to come home. But eventually he embraced what America in the seventies had to offer. A local TV channel came down to make a programme about the pub and filmed Daood with his crewcut grown out and his hair to his shoulders, his long legs flapping in flares, Serrill resplendent in a full-length fur coat. Within two years he had moved to Manhattan, using family money to rent an upmarket apartment on the Upper West Side, opening a video store.

Daood also developed rich tastes, and when the family cash ran out he reflected on what he could do to stay afloat. He could speak the languages of two countries and travel freely to chaotic places Americans were precluded from visiting. In 1984 he contacted his best friend from college, Tahawwur Rana, an introverted A-grade student who was training to become a military doctor in the Pakistani army. Daood was coming back to Pakistan and asked the medic to accompany him on a road trip to the tribal areas, Rana using his military connections and his ID card to get them around a sensitive part of Pakistan – ignorant of the half-kilo of heroin Daood had purchased from local smugglers, concealing it in the boot.

Back from the Af–Pak frontier with his stash, Daood blew it in Lahore. Hitching up with a woman, he gave her a taste without understanding the purity of the gear. She overdosed, and the police busted him. Through his father's connections he was extricated, and the case file was quietly disposed of. But from that point on Daood's father became remote, urging his sons to 'keep away' from their half-brother.

Undeterred, Daood tried it all over again. He headed back to Peshawar, the gateway to the Khyber Pass, and became a regular visitor, frequently abusing Rana and his jeep. He also decided to try his hand at the export business, smuggling the heroin to the US in his luggage and selling it through his Manhattan store, Fliks Video. Occasionally he would turn up in Philadelphia with a huge suitcase of VHS tapes with which to impress his American cousins. 'He was charismatic and charming. But we had no idea what he was really up to,' said one.

When customs officers caught up with him four years later at Frankfurt airport en route to Philadelphia with two kilograms of heroin in his case, Daood faced a lengthy prison term and his father disowned him. Handed over to the US authorities, and on his own now, he offered the Drug Enforcement Administration (DEA) a deal: his American co-conspirators. They were jailed for between eight and ten years, while the turncoat Daood started working as a paid DEA informant, with instructions to infiltrate the Pak–US heroin trafficking networks. He translated hours of telephone intercepts, while coaching agents on how to interrogate Pakistanis. He also refused to stick to the rules. One DEA agent complained that he disappeared while on business and set up meetings that were not monitored. But his product was so compelling, the information so accurate, that when he came back online he was forgiven.

Daood could talk himself out of anything, a former DEA agent recalled. Hardened drug investigators found themselves excusing his defects because he took them to places they could not reach. His American mother, Serrill, idolized her son from afar, and while she saw little of him face to face, she had a giant laminated photograph of him on her living room wall. Others on the American side of her family were not so sure. Daood was only ever interested in himself, they warned, arguing that his selfishness was born out of his lack of a sense of self: a young man with a grievance against his mother and alienated from his father, with several blurred identities, none of which properly fitted. 'We would joke he had a Koran under one arm, and a bottle of Dom Pérignon under the other,' said his Uncle William.

While the DEA was locked on to biting chunks out of the heroin trade on the eastern seaboard, their star informer, Daood Gilani, returned to Pakistan and began to hang out at a mosque known as the Four Pillars, a vast seminary and prayer hall that occupied most of a historic crossroads in a frenetic part of Lahore. The Jamia Qadisiya was the realm of Lashkar-e-Toiba, the jihad organization that had made its name in Indian-administered Kashmir. From the mosque's speakers came Lashkar's message of liberating Kashmir from India. Banners strung outside the mosque announced 'jihad', a holy war in service of the Koran. In Pakistan, a country in free fall, without a reliable health service, emergency services or public education, the socially committed Lashkar was often the first to respond, especially after any kind of calamity. That made it attractive to many.

Daood, well versed in his father's stories of Partition, was drawn to the anti-Indian crusade, and to the romantic idea of becoming one of Islam's commandos. He also sensed a commercial opportunity: the possibility of trading up from drugs, with heroin on the decline, to procuring sensitive information about an entirely new threat that was beginning to worry his paymasters back in the US. When Daood got busted again, this time in New York in 1997, he tested this idea, coming up with a deal involving his proximity to radicals. A letter put before the court showed its effectiveness, as prosecutors conceded that while Daood might have supplied up to fifteen kilograms of heroin worth £947,000, he had also been 'reliable and forthcoming' with the agency about 'a range of issues'. Sentenced to fifteen months in the low-security Fort Dix, New Jersey, while his co-conspirator received four years in a high-security jail, Daood was freed after only nine months.

In August 1999, he returned to Pakistan, his ticket paid for by the US government. It was one year after hundreds had been killed in simultaneous Al-Qaeda bomb attacks on American embassies in Dar es Salaam, in Tanzania, and Nairobi, in Kenya, and the reprisals from Washington saw seventy-five cruise missiles slamming into five Al-Qaeda training camps in Afghanistan. He remained attached to the DEA, but American counter-terrorism outfits were also now interested in him, as Washington woke up to the forces of extremism operating from the Af–Pak border.

Back in Lahore, Daood acted as if he were plotting a textbook infiltration. He bedded down, marrying Shazia Ahmed, a conserva-tive Pakistani woman, and settled in an enclave beside the Lahore canal, the so-called lovers' waterway, although his father, who was now Director General of Radio Pakistan, and his brother Danyal, who was sitting his Civil Service Exams, kept their distance. In late 2000, shortly after Al-Qaeda attacked the American destroyer USS *Cole* in Yemen, Daood donated 50,000 rupees (£600) to Lashkar's jihad fund, buying himself entry to a private lecture given by Hafiz Saeed, *amir* of Lashkar's parent organization, Jamaat-ud-Dawa. Saeed, a man who wore his beard Barbarossa style, bushy and hennaed red, was already on the US radar. After the talk, Daood asked the *amir* if he could enlist, but his request was 'very politely declined', he recalled. Half American and with white skin, Daood was treated with suspicion. He would have to work harder to gain acceptance.

He returned to the US and his other careers. He moved a new girlfriend, Portia Peter, a Canadian makeup artist, into his Upper West Side apartment, telling her nothing about the wife he had left in Pakistan. Until 9/11 happened, he seemed to her like a red-blooded American. But on that day Daood was glued to the TV and she recoiled when she caught him appearing 'to gloat', telling her in a fit of rage that America deserved to be attacked. His immersion in the world of jihad was showing through.

Horrified at his attitude at this moment of national crisis, Portia repeated Daood's comments to a friend in a New York bar, who reported him to the police. The FBI questioned Portia. On 4 October, two Defense Department agents working for the Joint Terrorism Task Force (JTTF) quizzed Daood in front of his DEA handlers. 'You think I'm an extremist,' a defence official who reviewed the notes recalled Daood saying. 'But you should check, as I'm working for the US government.' He also played a game of chicken, claiming that he was related to the deputy director of Pakistan's ISI spy agency, suspecting, correctly, that no one in the US would be able to quickly work out if that was true. By February 2002, five months after 9/11, Daood was once more in Pakistan, asked by the US government to redouble his efforts to get inside Lashkar, many of whose cadres were now also orbiting around Al-Qaeda, including Daood's new best friend and neighbour in Lahore, Pasha.

Pasha's full name was Abdur Rehman Hashim; an ex-army officer in the 6th Baloch Rifles, he was handsome and battlefield savvy, and had resigned his commission after refusing an order to fight against Osama bin Laden in the Tora Bora Mountains, when the Pakistan military signed up to the Americans' 'war on terror'. Daood was transfixed by Pasha's war stories, the former soldier revealing how he had joined forces with the Afghan Taliban. Under Pasha's influence, Daood went from spending less than a month a year in Pakistan prior to 2001, to spending the better part of the year there.

He dressed in *shalwar kameez* (traditional dress). He told friends that he had renounced alcohol, TV and his mobile phone. He lodged at Lashkar's headquarters in Muridke, a vast campus outside Lahore, even converting to the severe Ahl-e-Hadith sect that underpinned the outfit, a conservative Salafi strain of Sunni Islam, governed by the sayings and deeds of the Prophet. He also tried his hand at the arduous three-month paramilitary course, taking the bus into the mountains of Pakistan's portion of Kashmir, to reach Lashkar's secret training centre, the dramatically named *Bait-ul-Mujahideen* (the House of the Holy Warriors). It was under the control of Zaki-ur-Rehman Lakhvi, the outfit's *amir*, co-founder and military commander, who was known by his students as *chacha* (uncle).

At forty-two, Daood was more than twice the age of most recruits. He failed the course and at the end of 2002 returned, humiliated, to New York. For the moment, he had nothing to trade with anyone and over the following months chafed against an American life, refusing to see anyone except his closest relatives. He had grown an unruly beard, as all *Hadeethi*s were required to do, and spent much of his day praying, his hands crossed over his stomach in their severe and distinctive style. His mother Serrill and girlfriend Portia were alarmed by his transformation, with Serrill confiding her worries to a friend who ran a local coffee shop. 'He is attending training camps in Pakistan and talking about how much he hates India,' she said. Serrill's friend reported Daood to the FBI.

What she did not know was that the FBI had already investigated him, as had the JTTF. The official view on Daood was that he might be an erratic source but he had massive potential, according to one of those who read his file. Accustomed to running agents deep under cover, they had higher tolerances than relatives and girl-friends. All deeply embedded sources were imperfect, hostile even, and hard to cajole, motivate and discipline. The nature of never belonging meant that their personalities were pulled out of shape, as were their lives, which were stretched between different cultures and commitments. The FBI's training manual told agents to assume that deep-cover informers only ever served themselves. As one vet-eran FBI agent, who worked in the JTTF for two decades, put it: 'The best a handler can hope for is that the source's goals, at some point, coalesce with those of the outfit running him.'

Slowly Daood began to settle down, and his family put his out-pourings to one side. After a few weeks he won Portia back, proposing to her in Central Park, flying her off to Jamaica, where they married in December 2002, with no mention of the two young children he had fathered in Pakistan with his first wife, Shazia.

For the next two and a half years, Daood flitted between the US and Pakistan, keeping his two lives separate but failing to get any real purchase on Lashkar. His personal life flared up again in August 2005 when Portia, who was frustrated and suspicious about her hus-band's frequent trips to Pakistan, called up his father in Lahore, only to discover the secret family over there. Outraged and humiliated she confronted Daood in Fliks on 25 August, complaining to the police afterwards that he had turned violent, beating her. She also called the terror tip line, repeating everything he had told her about Pakistani training camps and Lashkar – which had been added to the US list of banned terrorist groups in 2003. The JTTF interviewed her three times but then she heard no more after Daood once again convinced the US authorities that everything he did was part of his covert life that was now well documented. He offered the Americans unique insights, not only into Lashkar, but the cadre within it who leant towards Al-Qaeda, choosing now to reveal his friendship with Pasha, who 'knew Osama bin Laden'. Six years into the hunt for the Al-Qaeda leader, Daood was classified as 'significant' in counter-terrorism circles, one of the only American passport holders who could claim, with any credibility, to be moving in the same circles as America's Most Wanted.

In January 2006, after the United Nations Security Council added Lashkar-e-Toiba to a list of sanctioned organizations, freezing its leaders' assets and instigating a travel ban and arms embargo, Daood decided to go out on a limb. He called up Pasha, suggesting an unauthorized road trip to meet contacts from his drug-dealing days, who 'might be able to use those routes to smuggle weapons into India'. Surely this would open up Lashkar. But since 9/11 the landscape had drastically changed. West of Peshawar, the gateway to the Khyber Pass, the two men were arrested. These border areas were especially sensitive, as the West accused Pakistan of concealing Taliban refugees and Al-Qaeda's leadership there. The Pakistan military had swamped the region with spies, agents and scouts, and foreign passport holders like Daood Gilani were banned from travelling there.

Pasha whipped out his military ID card, and after a night in the cells he was allowed to make one call. The ex-serviceman rang an old friend in the Khyber Rifles. Pasha and Daood were taken to an army camp, where an officer introduced himself as Major Ali. He saluted Pasha, the Lashkar cadre, and apologized for their treatment. Pasha whispered to Daood that 'the Major was a spy', an agent of the ISI, the intelligence agency run by the military that distributed funds and weapons to jihad factions fighting against India.

Dressed like a bank clerk, with a clipped moustache and dyed-black hair, the Major did not look like Daood's vision of an ISI agent. Pasha explained that there were many different types of ISI men. Those on full-time deployment to the jihad mission became like their clients, often voluntarily submitting to conservative religious organizations too. The Major, on the other hand, was on short-term Lashkar duty, co-opted into Joint Intelligence North, which meant a two- to three-year cycle dealing with jihad outfits, after which he would be moved elsewhere in the kingdom of spies.

Daood did what he always did when his back was against the wall: he offered the Major a deal. He hoped it would play as well in Pakistan as it would back in the US, if he ever were allowed home. Breaking into a mid-Atlantic accent, he revealed that he was actually only half Pakistani and that he also held an American passport, and was keen to help in the jihad against India. The Major seemed startled, but Daood pushed on, suggesting that he was their man. 'Why not use a clean skin to do the reconnaissance for a spectacular attack on a great Indian commercial hub like Mumbai?' He was even willing to legally change his name to make it sound more Western.

Over dinner, Daood used his father's name and reputation to ingratiate himself and revealed that his brother Danyal was working for Yousuf Raza Gilani, a rising political star and former speaker of the Pakistan National Assembly. 'Some people will be contacting you,' the Major said, eventually allowing Daood and Pasha to return to Lahore. Soon after, a 'Major Iqbal' rang, directing Daood to an address in the Lahore Army Cantonment, on Airport Road. Major Iqbal was the same type as Major Ali and Daood had no doubt that he was also an ISI agent. The Major talked around the Mumbai idea, as intrigued by it as his colleague up on the border. But such an audacious plan made everyone nervous and the meeting ended without any firm commitment.

It was a month before the Major was in touch. Daood's family connections had checked out and he had good news, offering to pay for Daood to return to the US and apply for a passport with an anglicized name. Daood chose David Coleman Headley, borrowing the last two parts from his American grandfather, who had died so tragically at the age of thirty-seven. He formalized the documents that month, telling his American relatives that he was tired of being stopped at immigration because of his Pakistani name. One, who was in the US military, became suspicious. 'I had a really bad feeling and considered reporting him to my superiors.' But he did not and Daood's actions alerted none of the US authorities that might normally have been expected to challenge an application from someone with a criminal record who had been investigated several times for supporting terrorism. This was an aberration or the authorities were a party to the move, as they had been to so many other things in Daood's chequered career as a US government agent provocateur and super-grass.

On Daood's return to Pakistan, Major Iqbal assigned an army officer to train the freshly minted 'David Headley' in a condensed version of the ISI's two-year field course on surveillance and counter-intelligence. If he was to scout Mumbai, he would need to know how to record his findings, what to look out for and how to ensure that he was not being observed. Major Iqbal gave him what he described as 'classified Indian files' that he said had been obtained from within the Indian police and army and which 'revealed their training and limitations'. The Major boasted they had a super-agent at work in New Delhi who was known as 'Honey Bee'. The Major revealed that while he would guide Headley, the Mumbai operation was to be run by Lashkar.

Headley was in. Within days he received a message to meet his newly appointed Lashkar handler at the remote House of the Holy Warriors camp. He travelled on the hairpin road to Muzaffarabad, the capital of Pakistani-administered Kashmir, and walked up into the densely forested Chelabandi hills, 7,500 feet above sea level. The camp sat in a bowl-shaped plain and consisted of a large mosque, several hostels and a well-stocked munitions store. Recruits in khaki *shalwar kameez* could be seen exercising on three sandy parade grounds, Uhad, Tabook and Qadisiya (all of them named after legendary Islamic battles from the epoch of the Prophet). Sajid Mir, Lashkar's deputy chief of foreign operations, greeted Headley and took him to his office, which was clinically clean, fiercely air-conditioned and filled with computers, satellite phones and maps. Camp comrades had nicknamed it the 'Ice Box'. Mir's brood of children spent so much time in there trying to avoid the summer heat that everyone referred to them as the 'polar bear cubs'.

Mir told Headley they would call his plan Operation Bombay. He was to scout for targets that Lashkar commandos would then assault. He would need a cover story. Headley immediately came up with a suggestion from his drug-dealing days. He could use his old friend Tahawwur Rana, who had left the Pakistani army and now lived in

Chicago, where he had established a thriving immigration business helping South Asians migrate to America. In June 2006, the ISI paid for David Headley to fly back to the US to meet up with Rana. Without explaining the back-story, Headley asked if he could set up a branch of Rana's immigration business in Mumbai. Friends and family were commodities in Headley's mind, to be cashed in and exploited. 'He could persuade just about anyone to do whatever he wanted,' said one. Arranging the paperwork, Rana, who would later claim that he suspected nothing, went to the Indian consulate with Headley's new passport and applied for a one-year business visa, while Portia, Headley's estranged wife, applied for permanent residency in the US under a law for abused spouses. On her petition, she accused her husband of violence, and also of espousing hate crimes, attacking Jews and Hindus, and praising suicide bombers.

Her allegations were filed away, the FBI later insisting that privacy laws prevented the immigration department from reporting their concerns. However, by then the JTTF had interviewed Portia, Headley's mother, and several other family members, as well as family friends who had tipped off the authorities, which either made for a grievous series of intelligence failings, or, as Serrill and Portia were becoming convinced, compelling grounds to believe that David/Daood was informing on Lashkar for the US intelligence community (and vice versa).

In the autumn of 2006, David Headley used £15,000 he had been given by Major Iqbal to open the Immigration Law Centre in Tardeo A/C Market, a commercial district close to Mumbai's upmarket Willingdon Sports Club. He put adverts in local papers – 'Guaranteed work visas to the US and Canada for skilled and unskilled Indians' – and hired a secretary who staffed the office alone, wondering why Headley had no fax or international phone. She also thought it strange that he never asked her to make his travel arrangements. But then he *was* a foreigner.

In reality, Headley had another office his secretary knew nothing about: the Reliance cyber café near Churchgate railway station, where he maintained a vigorous email exchange with Tahawwur Rana, Sajid Mir, Major Iqbal and Pasha, whose online pseudonym was Scorpion 6. Mir used the codename Wasi and two email addresses – rare.layman@gmail.com and get.me.some.books@gmail.com – while Major Iqbal, who addressed Headley as 'My dear', wrote from the email address chaudherykhan@yahoo.com. Headley, who sometimes signed off 'Dave Salafi' and was ranger1david@yahoo.com, always found time to report back on the local talent. 'Girls here are really hot,' he wrote in one email to Rana. 'Just the both of us should come here minus our girlfriends to have a good time.'

Now he needed to bed in. He joined a gym called Moksh (Salvation) close to his apartment, where minor Bollywood stars worked out, and he befriended a fitness trainer, Vilas Warek. They chatted about the movies and crashed Bollywood parties. Warek was impressed by Headley's ability to pull women and they toured Bandra's late-night bars, driving around on Warek's motorbike. 'We're brothers from another mother,' Warek bragged to the girls.

One night, he took Headley to Shivaji Mandir, a theatre and temple complex, to see a bodybuilding show. There, Warek introduced him to Rahul Bhatt, the son of Mahesh Bhatt, one of India's most acclaimed film directors. Soon Headley, Warek and Bhatt were inseparable, the Indians calling their new friend 'David Armani' because of the clothes he wore. To keep things smooth, Headley referenced some of his American life: the bar in Philadelphia that his bohemian mother ran, the tragic story of his grandfather and how his American forefathers had built the first oil well in New York State and knew the Rockefellers. He also picked up the tab for their frequent meetings in the Taj, especially at Sea Lounge, where Faustine Martis supervised high tea. The Pakistani side of his family was never mentioned.

One thing that set Bhatt wondering was Headley's encyclopaedic knowledge of weaponry. He gave a running commentary about ambushes and raids by the security forces throughout the world. He could describe the calibre and capacity of most weapons. But one time, when Bhatt called him Agent Headley as a joke, he exploded.

'Stop *that*.' He was touchy about the strangest things, Bhatt thought, and on more than one occasion a little wild. He told his friends he wanted to take them to see the Af–Pak border. Bhatt shook his head laughing: 'I am too afraid,' he said. 'I'll be murdered like Daniel Pearl.' Headley laughed. 'No one will touch you if I'm around. You should change your names.' He looked at Bhatt and said: 'Maybe you should become Mohammed Atta!' Everyone knew the 9/11 conspirator. 'There's safety in the blindingly obvious,' Headley told them, laughing in their faces.

When he was not with Warek or Bhatt, Headley often visited the Taj alone. In his mind it was already emerging as the number one target. Drinking with a well-connected local businessman, Sunil Patel, he got himself invited to a Bollywood party in the Crystal Room and bought a Mont Blanc pen from the hotel shop. He browsed in Nalanda's. He loved the Taj and its lifestyle, and observed it minutely. On at least two occasions, he joined the Friday Tour, a paid walk-and-talk tour popular with tourists, which he also filmed, recording on one of those videos the hotel layout and its history. He read up on its founder, Jamsetji Tata, whose family, originally priests from Gujarat, had emigrated to the city, sending their boy to London in 1858 on a voyage of discovery.

Everything was research material. Headley taped the guide explaining how the scion of the Tata dynasty had returned from Europe with a plan to open cotton mills, building an industrial empire based on personal loyalty. Jamsetji Tata also purchased a rectangular block of reclaimed land overlooking the harbour at Apollo Bunder, envisaging a hotel that merged Mughal, Rajput and Oriental aesthetics backed up by Colonial standards.

In a hotel pamphlet, Headley underlined passages about the Taj's design, how the industrialist Tata had hired a dynamic Indo-European team led by the great Victorian master builder of Bombay, Frederick Stevens, who had constructed the Royal Alfred Sailors' Home (later the state police headquarters), as well as Victoria Terminus (later renamed Chhatrapati Shivaji Terminus) and Churchgate station.

The pamphlet described how Stevens had created a U-shaped

structure out of hard-wearing grey basalt, turning in from the harbour, with spacious galleries running the length of the building, along each wing and from the second floor up to the roof: a great net to catch the evening breezes. Headley walked with the group down these galleries, videoing all the way, sketching the route afterwards, as visitors were told how Stevens had planned to lace these galleries together with Gujarati trellises and balustrades interpreted in an Edwardian style.

As Headley fathomed the complex layout, drawing detailed sketches of wherever he had walked, he also learned about the hotel's history of innovation. He highlighted passages in guidebooks that explained how the positioning of the hotel back-to-front also enabled the greatest number of guests to have a sea view. Like Victoria Terminus, the Taj had cupolas on each corner and a grand central dome covering a cantilevered central staircase. The cellars contained a refrigeration plant, the ground and first floors would be shops and restaurants, while the bedrooms would be on the second to fifth floors, with a roof garden crowning the building. When Stevens died suddenly in 1900, his successor, William Chambers, added a Florentine Renaissance theme. Jamsetji splashed out 26 million rupees – the equivalent of £200m today – for thirty private apartments and 350 double and single rooms with electric lights, fans, bells and clocks, along with four mechanical passenger lifts imported from Germany. The hotel had its own power plant, a chemist's shop and a Turkish bath. Adding to the city-state atmosphere, a post office was opened. Upping the technological ante, the residents were cooled by a carbon dioxide-powered refrigeration system that also provided ice for Bombay's first licensed bar. With an English manager and a French head chef, the Taj was half finished in 1902 when Jamsetji embarked on a grand tour of Europe and the US, sending back Belgian crystal chandeliers and spun steel pillars from the manufacturers of the Eiffel Tower.

By 14 December 2006, all of Headley's memory cards were full, his bag stuffed with tourist maps and booklets on the hotel and the city. He told his new friends he was returning to Philadelphia to spend Christmas with his mother, but instead caught a flight to Lahore. He went straight to Major Iqbal and handed over the footage. A couple of days later, he travelled to the Ice Box in the Chelabandi hills, where he screened his Operation Bombay footage for Sajid Mir. But there were others in Lashkar whom Headley needed to impress. He was given a private audience with *chacha* Zaki, the military chief, whom he had not seen since failing the *mujahid* training camp. Military chief Zaki offered Headley milk and saffron as a gesture of respect, but maintained his distance. Mir reassured Headley afterwards that *chacha* took time to win over. 'It is hard to sell the plot but we are trying,' Mir said. 'The most important thing is that you are in his sights.' From now on Headley should be assured that Lashkar was seriously looking at how to attack all of the targets he was reconnoitring, including the city's police headquarters, a tourist hangout called the Leopold Café and the Taj.

Back in Lahore, Headley stewed at home with Shazia, his Pakistani wife, who was eight months pregnant with their third child. He was no good at waiting, and when he received a call from Chand Bhai, an old acquaintance from his drug-dealing days, he raced over to see him.

CB, as Headley called him, ran a bric-a-brac shop and poker den in Lahore's Muslim Town, and he told Headley he had found someone he would like. A young Moroccan medical student, Western, liberated and voluptuous, Faiza Outalha had come to Pakistan to train as a doctor, but after a year she had had enough of human dissection. Well-educated and fluent in English, Arabic and French, Faiza had swapped her middle-class Moroccan upbringing, playing sports and piano, for what she now had concluded was 'a Third World hell'. Doctors had diagnosed her as suffering from hypertension, and prescribed a course of injections that made her woozy and confused, drugs she feared were contaminated. Faiza wanted to go home, and filled her time smoking joints at CB's place, which was 'full of spiders, dust everywhere'. When Headley strode in, she was playing cards at the back of the shop.

Staring up at him, with his broad shoulders, laconic, Western manner and captivating smile, Faiza instantly felt her luck was changing. 'He was exchanging that look with me and a voice inside me told me, "He's the one, I know I'm going to marry him",' she wrote in her diary.

After tense months spent wooing Lashkar and pleasing the ISI, plus the stressful scouting trip to Mumbai, the beautiful, vivacious and irreverent Faiza was a tonic. Within a week they were 'married' and Headley had moved her into a rented apartment, some distance from his wife, whose existence he kept to himself. The new couple went for candlelit dinners overlooking Badshahi mosque and she whirled around the ancient lanes of Lahore on the back of his motorbike. When he asked her to wear a hijab, she agreed. 'My Dave was this handsome man, with one brown, one blue eye, so cute, shy, intelligent, good-hearted,' Faiza wrote. 'Sometimes he was innocent, sometimes a baby. He used to say to me: "Honey, you know what, I have you in this world and the hereafter." Like he found me in two worlds.'

The honeymoon was cut short, however, when Headley suddenly announced that he had to go abroad. He'd received an email reminder from Major Iqbal that they expected him to complete his reconnaissance for Operation Bombay, regardless of *chacha* Zaki's reservations: 'hi, how are you no contact what is the progress on the projects please update me.'

He flew out of Pakistan on 21 February 2007, leaving Faiza upset and suspicious. She rifled through Headley's phone bills, ringing around, discovering the existence of the heavily pregnant Shazia, and her two children. Both women called Headley in Mumbai, distraught. Worried that his complicated love life might upset the operation, he put everything on hold while he flew back to Lahore. It took him five days to calm Shazia. His new wife, Faiza, who dismissively described her rival as 'a covered creature', referring to her conservative Islamic appearance, took longer.

Headley returned to Mumbai on 20 March 2007. Faiza insisted on coming along, describing the trip as 'our honeymoon'. Headley had a different view: 'I was not interested in getting her to India. But she insisted.' He mugged along, splashing out, booking a room at the Taj for the first time. At last he would be able to record all of the labyrinthine hotel's nooks and crannies that were only open to guests, like the corridors of the exclusive fifth and sixth floors in the Palace. But the minute he walked into the lobby, he realized his mistake. Having once been the model of liberation, smoking *charas*, gambling and drinking, Faiza now refused to take off her hijab.

Headley's Taj drinking pals spotted him immediately and rushed over. What was their godless American buddy doing with a veiled Muslim woman? 'Oh, she's a client,' he improvised and for the next few days, he used Faiza as an excuse to tour the Taj, taking hundreds of photographs of her, all the while wondering how he was going to get her back home. A few days into their trip, Shazia called, adding to the pressure: she had just given birth to a son.

Headley booked Faiza a return ticket to Lahore, but she refused to go, fleeing instead to her parents in Morocco, with the growing feeling that all of Headley's life was a lie. 'He told me he worked in an immigration office but there was no evidence of any real business,' she wrote in her diary. First, Headley had to settle Shazia, who had flounced off to Dubai to her maternal relatives. He met his new son, suggesting, without irony, that they name him Osama. Cousins in the US were alarmed when Headley announced the news at a family get-together in Philadelphia, describing the new addition to the clan as 'my little terrorist'. Leaving the Faiza situation hanging, he returned to Pakistan and promised Lashkar's Mir and the ISI's Major Iqbal that he would complete the surveillance. Without it, the entire operation would be scrapped.

In mid-June 2007, Headley returned from Mumbai with new surveillance material and there were some immediate responses. Everyone wanted to know the identity of an attractive young woman in many of the shots. Headley conceded he had married again. Lashkar's concern was theosophical. 'Sajid blackened Faiza's face in the computer.' The military commander, *chacha* Zaki, insisted on digital hijabs being placed over the faces of all photographed women. Major Iqbal's concern was tradecraft. How did the new wife affect Headley's cover? To make things simpler Headley decided on a code. In all future communications, he would refer to Shazia as M1 (Marriage 1) and Faiza as M2. No mention was made of the estranged third wife back in the US, Portia Gilani.

*

In July 2007, unforeseen external events forced *chacha* Zaki to upgrade Headley and Operation Bombay. Millions of Pakistanis became transfixed by one of the country's first significant live broadcast events, footage of a standoff between police and jihadis at the Lal Masjid or Red Mosque in central Islamabad. Its grey-haired *maulvi* (Islamic scholar) had become an outspoken critic of the military dictatorship of General Pervez Musharraf, criticizing him for assisting the West's war against Al-Qaeda. The cleric's students had also formed vigilante patrols that attacked video stores and hairdressers, accusing both of being un-Islamic or brothels.

On 3 July, Headley and Zaki both watched live footage of government forces trading shots with jihadis outside the Red Mosque, kicking off a wild gun battle that left twenty dead. Five days later, Musharraf's commandos raided, killing the *maulvi* and dozens of religious students, news that sent the Islamic Republic over the edge. Mourners and Al-Qaeda declared a holy war against the Pakistani establishment.

Waves of suicide bombers, many of them children, were directed against the police and military. That December, the violence claimed the life of Benazir Bhutto, the former Prime Minister, who had returned from exile to canvass for impending elections. Headley was with Pasha, the diehard Lashkar man, when news came through of the attack and he 'prayed Bhutto would die soon'. They were also together when Lashkar was assaulted, the state-backed jihad outfit dismissed by pro-Red Mosque radicals as 'a tool of the army'. Within hours, government forces were deployed outside the Qadisiya mosque in Lahore, while ISI agents rode shotgun with *amir* Hafiz Saeed. Government gunmen guarded Lashkar's secretive Muridke training complex, too, with plain-clothed agents, hair cropped, cradling machine guns, patrolling the faux Greek villas of the movement's leaders.

Under pressure from the jihadis, a sizeable faction inside Lashkar, Pasha included, argued that the outfit should dump its ISI paymasters, join forces with Al-Qaeda and shift its theatre of activity from fighting Indian forces in Kashmir to launching attacks against coalition forces in Afghanistan.

Chacha Zaki called Headley to the House of the Holy Warriors and conceded that he 'had serious problems in holding Lashkar together and convincing the outfit to fight for Kashmir'. He was also worried that if Lashkar spurned the military, it would lose its ISI shield and come under attack from all sides.

Major Iqbal called Headley back to Lahore, admitting that the ISI 'was under tremendous pressure' to stop Lashkar falling apart. The outfit needed to pull something out of the hat, an operation that would bind everyone together. He told Headley that Zaki was now 'compelled to consider a spectacular terrorist strike in India' that would sate the desire of some factions to attack the enemies of Islam – Americans, Israelis and Europeans – as well as India. Operation Bombay was the perfect plan, he argued, targeting India and also the city's international guests.

By September 2007, Headley was back in Mumbai, surveying the Taj's 'entries and exit points' and the jewellery shop, data that he was told was now being mounted in an operations room in the House of the Holy Warriors, where a huge schematic of the hotel and its environs had been prepared using Google Earth.

Headley was now so busy he needed to simplify his life. Somehow he had talked M2 (Faiza) back to Lahore in August 2007, no doubt cutting a deal with her, just as he had done with everyone else. Delighted, Faiza wrote in her diary: 'I've been with all his faces, and that is the most beautiful of it all, to know that this person didn't have to act that much when he was with me.' But when Headley visited her next, it was to ask for a divorce. She had not seen that coming. During the furious argument that followed, he punched her before returning to Shazia, whom he armed with a gun. 'Could you believe that he thought I would go and kill that woman with his kids?' Faiza wrote, dismayed. 'These things made me cry, made me sad.'

Faiza wanted revenge. She talked her way into the heavily fortified US embassy compound in Islamabad's Diplomatic Zone, where she accused Headley of being a jihadi. 'I have seen all of his personalities,' she told the officials. 'David, James, Daood or Dave.' She knew about his life as a drug-dealer, and had come to love him despite this. But since their hasty wedding in February 2007, she suspected he was up to far worse.

The embassy official asked her to meet a 'regional security officer', who arrived with 'an inch-thick file' about her husband. As she told them about Headley's activities, they nodded as if they already knew. When he was around Lashkar, he acted as a devout Muslim who went by the name Daood and publicly lambasted the US for its wars in Iraq and Afghanistan, she said. At home he was 'Dave' who watched *Seinfeld* and Jay Leno. His closest friend was Pasha, who was allied to Al-Qaeda, yet at home he listened to 'the Boss' and knew all the words to 'Born to Run'. She was 'scared and confused'.

She was most worried about his frequent trips to Mumbai. Her husband was back and forth to that city, she said, even though at home he cursed India and its government. She had photos to prove it, including copies of all of those shot inside the Taj, in April and May 2007. She got them out. That was supposedly 'our honeymoon', she explained, but she had been introduced to his friends as a 'business client'. Was he planning something over there? No response.

The officials ended the meeting, and before she knew it she was outside, blinking in the bright sunshine. The US embassy later categorized the incident as a 'domestic row'. Faiza wrote in her diary: 'I told them, he's either a terrorist, or he's working for you. They pretty much told me to get lost.'

A few days later, Headley turned up on the doorstep, furious. 'Why did you go to the embassy?' he demanded. She wrote in her diary: 'How did he know?'

Family, wives and friends were not the only ones ringing the bell about Lashkar. In 2007, President George W. Bush's National Security Team at the White House had received a hand-delivered dossier. European investigators brought it to Washington DC, having discovered a worrying development. A new terror axis was emerging, the dossier warned, with Pakistan's Lashkar identified as 'wrestling with its old remit as a regional jihad outfit'. The file suggested that a section of veteran Lashkar members were starting to look further afield, to India and beyond, citing evidence gathered in the UK, France, Germany and Australia. Sajid Mir, Headley's handler, had been trailed across Europe and the Gulf, where he worked as a recruiting sergeant and fundraiser, leaving behind Lashkar sleepers with whom he kept in touch using codewords. The UK was central to his plans, with England designated as 'West 1'.

In Washington, the dossier was politely rejected. The message that went back to British investigators was simple: 'President Musharraf is our best bet in Pakistan. Lashkar *remains* his judgement call.' US officials added that priorities were 'disrupting Al Qaeda', and 'developing all intelligence and human assets that might lead to the capturing of Osama bin Laden'.

In January 2008, Serrill Headley died in Philadelphia aged sixty-eight. Years of living life to the full, and five tempestuous marriages, had finally caught up with her. David Headley, who had always kept in touch with his mother by letter when he was abroad, was devastated. But there was no time to grieve; Operation Bombay was moving apace. Days after he had attended her funeral in Philadelphia, his cousins recalled that Headley flew back to Pakistan. There he was invited to a secret Lashkar conclave that met in a safe house in Barakahu, a notorious jihadi hangout on the eastern fringes of Islamabad. Sajid Mir welcomed him, introducing him to a face he vaguely knew from the House of the Holy Warriors, Abu Qahafa. Despite his preacher's beard, Qahafa, the big-bellied number two to *chacha* Zaki, was known as 'the Bull' because of his strength. A Punjabi from·Bahawalpur, he was a legendary field commander. He would be handling the military components of Operation Bombay. Qahafa had news to share. Lashkar had decided to resurrect an idea that it had been toying with since 2006: a seaborne assault on the city.

His head befuddled by grief and excitement, Headley was ordered to return immediately to Mumbai to find a landing spot. 'Sajid provided me with an old used Garmin GPS.' Qahafa taught him how to use it and gave him 40,000 Pakistani rupees (£300) for expenses. Before leaving, Headley met up with Major Iqbal, who gave him a bundle of counterfeit Indian rupees, and a suggestion. 'Honey Bee', the ISI double agent who had provided the classified Indian training manuals, had come up with a potential landing area, in Badhwar Park, a fishing colony in South Mumbai, reporting that it was only patchily patrolled and was shielded from the road. He should check it out.

Headley touched down in Mumbai in early April 2008 and on his first night boarded a tourist boat in front of the Taj, taking a round trip to the Elephanta Caves on the far side of the harbour. The quay-side was brightly lit and crawling with tourists, security guards and police. No one took any notice of him as he photographed and took GPS readings.

The following day he took another boat, this time leaving from Marine Drive at 8.30 p.m., forewarned by Qahafa the Bull that this might be the time the attackers would land. It was frantically busy. The next day he took a taxi down to Cuffe Parade, sticking to the coastline until he reached Badhwar Park. Chatting to a boatman, Headley persuaded him to take him out at 3 a.m. the next morning. They went almost three miles to sea. Before returning, Headley noted that the landing point was, as promised, dark and chaotic, sheltered from the main road. He returned the next day, spinning the fisherman a line about 'college students [who] would contact him for a boat ride soon'.

Headley flew back to Pakistan, driving five hours to the military cantonment of Rawalpindi to deliver the GPS coordinates for the landing site to Sajid Mir. When he arrived, he was shocked. Lashkar's deputy head of foreign operations had undergone plastic surgery in Dubai, although to Headley's eyes Mir still looked like Mir, 'perhaps slightly Chinese'. If Mir was preparing to vanish, Operation Bombay was surely now a certainty.

A CCTV photograph of David Headley in the immigration queue at Mumbai's airport on 1 July 2008 revealed an exhausted-looking traveller, his pale blue polo shirt stretched and faded, a turquoise baseball cap covering a greasy ponytail. His carry-on bag hung heavy on his left shoulder and contained the cameras he would use on what Lashkar had advised him was his last surveillance mission.

As well as scouting out the Taj, the Trident–Oberoi and CST, Headley began documenting a late addition to the target list: Chabad House. The Jewish welfare centre, which was located in a densely populated Colaba side street, was staffed by an American rabbi and reached out to Israelis who worked or holidayed in India, many of them fresh from military service. The suggestion to attack it had come from a team of sixteen Indians whom Lashkar had recruited in Mumbai to produce lists of potential targets. A disparate squad, in Muridke they were referred to as *chohay* ('the Mice').

This target was an example of the tough backroom deals being struck to keep Lashkar together. The old guard wanted to rule out Chabad House as it strayed too far from the outfit's brief and attacking it would result in Lashkar becoming a global pariah; the hardcore, pro-Al-Qaeda lobby, who had the upper hand and even the ear of *chacha* Zaki, now pushed Jewish targets as Lashkar's 'new direction'.

When Headley returned to Lahore, Mir called him to the House of the Holy Warriors right away. Headley had barely slept, and by the time he arrived at the camp, clutching a sweaty chit stamped with Lashkar's double scimitars over a burning sun, he was ragged. The emotional toll of his mother's death, coupled with the energy he had exerted in maintaining dual lives, was draining him. Wearily, he delivered the GPS waypoints for the new targets, accompanied by hours of video footage and annotated maps, the data overlaid on the ever-growing schematic of the Taj and its environs. That night Headley collapsed, sick with fever. When he woke the next day, he found Mir at his bedside, confiding that Operation Bombay was about to be discussed at a special planning session organized by the outfit's *sura*, its ruling council.

Headley readied himself to enter the outfit's core. But Mir was grim-faced. Although *amir* Hafiz Saeed, *chacha* Zaki, Qahafa the Bull and other senior figures would be attending the *sura*, Headley was not invited. Mir made some excuse about not wanting to expose him before new faces.

What he could not say was that at an earlier caucus *chacha* Zaki had revealed that Major Iqbal had sent warning that the ISI believed Headley to be 'playing them all'. They still needed him for Operation Bombay to succeed and they were in a quandary. Zaki had proposed: 'Keep him at arm's length and let the operation run.' If Headley was betraying them to the CIA or another Western agency, they could still use him. Zaki believed that whoever was handling Headley in the West was so greedy for information that they would leave him in play up until the last minute, which would give Lashkar the leeway to launch. 'Just keep him away from the *sura*,' Zaki said. 'And we must hold back the date.'

After the conclave, Mir came to find Headley, and managed to cajole him into going back down the hill with one juicy titbit. The attack team had already been recruited and Operation Bombay was now officially a *fidayeen* mission. The *mujahideen* they had selected would seize targets in the city, taking hostages and extracting live media time, before executing their captives. Then they would set fire to Mumbai's most famous landmarks, and martyr themselves in a spectacular final shootout.

3.

Salaam Alaikum

Wednesday, 26 November 2008, 6 p.m.

A bronzed Andreas Liveras, his silver hair swept back, his linen shirt open at the neck, stood on the sun deck of his super-yacht *Alysia* and contemplated the sea-stippled Taj. He had just returned from an afternoon's shopping in Chor Bazaar, Mumbai's famous thieves' market, accompanied by his good-natured Indian cruise director, Remesh Cheruvoth, who managed his fleet and also carried his bags, bulging with carvings and papier-mâché. Andreas had last visited this city with his wife, Anna, going to the Taj for 'a memorable curry' in Masala Kraft. A few months ago an aggressive cancer had killed her, and tonight Andreas, seventy-three, intended to return to the hotel, in memory of Anna, in search of 'another famous curry' and to get away from the boat.

His British friend and yacht broker Nick Edmiston was borrowing the *Alysia* for the launch of a new Indian venture: his first foray into yacht sales and charters in the subcontinent. Andreas was not in the mood for socializing, which was unusual for him. A rambunctious Greek Cypriot exile, he normally loved to brag of the *Alysia*'s luxurious dimensions: an imposing 280-foot hull, with eighteen state rooms, eighteen suites, a jacuzzi, a helicopter landing pad and a temperature-controlled wine cellar. It took a team of liveried crew to get it sailing. 'I'm the king of yachting,' he told people, explaining his simple formula: 'The bigger the boat, the more expensive, the busier [we] are.' Built in 2006 at a cost of £70m, the *Alysia* was listed by *Forbes Magazine* that year as the most expensive ever and it had represented a high-water mark in Andreas's mercantile life.

One of nine children born to impoverished Cypriot farmers, in the sixties he had migrated to London, where he had started as a baker's delivery boy in upmarket Kensington, West London, before building up the hugely profitable Fleur de Lys patisserie and catering chain. After selling the business for £130m, Andreas, in his rose pink suit and thick gold chain, embraced the high life, buying jets and luxury homes all over the world, including Monaco, where he befriended Prince Albert and became a member of the Royal Yacht Club, through which he met Nick Edmiston, another Monaco exile from London.

Andreas and Nick had bonded on a ten-day retreat to the Meteora monasteries in Greece, a backdrop to the James Bond movie *For Your Eyes Only*, both of them sharing a passion for super-yachts, and making good money from private charters. The *Alysia* cost £500,000 a week to hire; Wayne Rooney, the Manchester United striker, was one of Andreas's most recent customers, celebrating his wedding to Coleen on board in June, while it was anchored on the Italian Riviera. But Andreas never forgot his humble beginnings and all those who worked on the *Alysia*, Remesh especially, thought of him as an attentive, generous boss.

To get his Indian venture started, Nick had hired the socialite and entrepreneur Ratan Kapoor, a Delhi-*wallah* from an affluent family of carpet traders, whose winning pitch had been that when there was blood on the floor, Indians started spending. 'Appearance is everything,' Kapoor had told him, when they met earlier in the year, as Nick and Andreas's London- and Monaco-based yacht businesses were lashed by the global financial crisis.

Kapoor had cut his teeth tempting Irish investors to the subcontinent before the Celtic Tiger became extinct, and he gave Nick a crash course in the city's elite, pointing out the most significant mansions. 'If the most important six couples in Mumbai get interested, then the whole city will follow,' Kapoor promised. He had had to work harder on Andreas, who disliked his constant bragging and sent a string of characteristically direct emails: 'I don't want street people on the boat.' Put out, Kapoor had mailed right back: 'I don't *know* any street people.' He had reeled off the list of 'Ultras' who had already bought into the yachting life, including Vijay Mallya, the Kingfisher beer and aviation tycoon, who owned the boat that Richard Burton had given as a present to Elizabeth Taylor in 1967 when she won an Oscar for *Who's Afraid of Virginia Woolf*.

Kapoor's idea was a simple one: the *Alysia* was a glamorous advertising hoarding anchored off the Taj. It would also provide the backdrop for a series of exclusive functions. There had already been a press lunch for magazine editors, hosted by Indian *Vogue*, and tonight Ratan and Nick would throw a lavish dinner sponsored by Moët & Chandon. The sister-in-law of the Bollywood legend Amitabh Bachchan was hosting tomorrow's 'ladies' lunch', while on Friday night the megastar Shah Rukh Khan had agreed to show his face, which would lure hundreds on board.

There had been a few last-minute snags. The *Alysia* had turned up late, dropping anchor 500 metres from the Taj just two hours before the lunch started. Almost immediately a flotilla of Indian officials had streamed on board. Despite filling in every form, paying bribes to the police, the navy and the port authorities, Kapoor was still worried. The anchorage limit of 100 guests would be well exceeded and, since they were in a navy-controlled waterway, severe restrictions on music and the consumption of alcohol would also be disregarded. When Commissioner Gafoor, the city's police chief, finally accepted an invitation, everyone breathed easier.

Now, as the crew changed into red T-shirts printed with the Edmiston logo, Andreas took Nick to one side. 'It's your boat tonight,' he said to his friend. 'I'm going to grab a quick curry at the Taj and then I'll be back.' At 7.30 p.m., he set out in the *Alysia*'s tender for the Gateway of India slip, accompanied by Remesh and two Filipino girls who ran the on-board spa. A queue of lacquered Mumbai 'Ultras' chugged in the opposite direction, ferried to the *Alysia*, where foie gras was on the menu. 'This is going to be some party,' Nick said to his son Woody. 'The boat looks great. The location is wonderful.' The notoriously volatile Arabian Sea was calm and the Taj was bathed in a golden light.

*

Line Kristin Woldbeck, a Norwegian marketing executive and sea-
soned traveller, looked at her watch. It was 7.45 p.m. and she and her
boyfriend, Arne Strømme, were stuck in traffic, creeping along
Marine Drive towards Colaba. She tried to block out the racket by
staring out to sea. They had flown in from Gujarat for just one night
to meet up with a new Facebook buddy Meetu Asrani, a 26-year-old
Mumbaiker. For Line it was their last stop on a month-long spiritual journey and Meetu was coming into the city centre specially
to see her, meeting them at the Leopold Café, a stroll away from
the Taj.

But three lanes were now six, the cars so close together that they
were grinding the paint off each other's doors. Line's phone whirred.
It was Meetu. 'Sorry, hun. I'm 45 mins late.' She was caught in
the same traffic jam, heading in from the north-western suburbs.
'See you at Leo's, mwah.' Line panicked. In the morning she and
Arne had to catch a flight to Delhi to make their connection back
home. If they did not make this rendezvous, she would never get to
see Meetu.

When they finally reached the café shortly before 9 p.m., it was
buzzing. Red-shirted waiters bustled about and Line recognized
Meetu from her Facebook profile. Excited, they found a table for
three near the far wall, Meetu telling Line that she had just landed
her first Bollywood job, as a creative director for Balaji Telefilms, the
most prolific TV hit factory in South Asia. She would be working
on a TV soap opera that had just been named 'show of the year'.
She also showed Line photos of a wedding she had attended a few
days back. 'Look,' she said, laughing. 'My first sari *ever*.' They stared
at each other. Line was dressed in a loose *shalwar kameez*. Meetu
was wearing skin-tight jeans and T-shirt. Laughing at each other,
they felt like old friends. When the waiter came over at last, Line
took charge. 'Let's order pasta and bruschetta,' she said.

Outside, the traffic was thick and the air was filled with the noise
of hawkers. Sachin Sorte, a security guard manning the doorway of
the Benetton store opposite, was watching the crowds of tourists
glide by when he caught sight of two young men in their early

twenties emerging from a yellow cab, weighed down by bulging rucksacks, as if they had come back from college. He had just logged the time, 9.43 p.m. precisely, in a small exercise book. They looked like clean-cut local kids, the kind who grazed nightly in well-to-do South Mumbai. They stood for a few minutes, looking through the café windows, then he half caught one of them saying, 'Come on, brother, let's do *Bismillah*' (in the name of God the Most Gracious, the Most Merciful). The two then delved into their sacks and pulled out matt-black and cherrywood assault rifles. What were they up to? As they entered the café, hurling something into the crowd of diners, a flash temporarily blinded Sorte. The thunderclap that followed made his ears whistle, as smoke poured out of the Leopold, followed by a blast wave that smacked him down on the pavement, glass and debris shredding his shirt as the sound of automatic gunfire – *ack, ack, ack* – rose up.

When the smoke cleared, he could see the two men were drilling rounds into the crowd inside the café and out in the street. Hair-raising, wild screams filled the air as bullets flew all around, some slamming into the metal shutters behind his head. He crawled, moaning, for cover, and put his hands over his ears. They were bleeding and his face was lacerated.

Inside, Line could not move. 'Oh God,' Meetu said, standing up, dazed. Arne also staggered to his feet: 'What the hell?' Coming to her senses, Line grabbed both of them by their wrists and hauled them under the table, as another blast upturned tables and diners. Then the *ack, ack, ack* came at them again, in short controlled bursts. 'Keep quiet! Don't move!' whispered Line, hugging Arne and Meetu who lay on either side of her.

'This can't be real,' she kept saying to herself. The *ack, ack, ack* drove channels into the tiled floor, throwing up cement chips. There were cries followed by more short bursts. Were they executing diners? Right now the gunmen were on the other side of the room, but moving over. Meetu was shaking. 'Play dead,' Line whispered. 'Lie still!' A gunman was beside them now. She felt hot bullet casings clatter down. She turned to Arne. He was ashen. 'I love you,' she mouthed, as everything was drowned out by the thrum of the firing.

A sweet ferrous smell pricked Line's nostrils: blood. It was unmistakeable. Meetu shook and Line kept hold of her, as short convulsions surged through her body. To Line, it felt as if Meetu were radiating a peaceful wave of energy. She rolled over to Arne, recoiling as she saw that he had been shot in the face and hand. 'Meetu's dead,' she whispered, holding on to her tears and hugging her friend as her body went limp.

Two hundred metres away from the café in Colaba police station, the duty inspector heard the rounds tumble and fizz, wondering if they were from an AK-47. Running down to investigate, he left the TV and the one-day international between England and India and put a mark in the station incident log at 9.45 p.m. His lodgings were on the first floor of the police station and he was certain the firing came from the direction of the Leopold.

At the station gate, nervous-looking constables gathered in a huddle while pedestrians ran by screaming. The inspector walked a few paces and was certain he could see bodies lying ahead in Colaba Causeway. It looked like a bomb had gone off: advertising hoardings had been ripped off the buildings, car sirens were wailing and the streetlights had blown out. He grabbed a subordinate's walkie-talkie and called South Control. '21.48. Police Colaba Walkie-Talkie: Send Colaba 1 to Leopold hotel.'

The inspector buttonholed two constables armed with standard issue .303 bolt-action rifles. They were so antiquated that they were no longer in production in India, making repairs difficult and spare parts scarce. At most city police stations these and bamboo *lathis* (canes) were the only weapons available. Behind him was a mobile unit of five men, Colaba 1, armed in a similar way. 'Let's go,' he urged them, clapping his hands, as if he were driving hens. Whatever was happening, it was chaotic and bloody. He strode ahead, approaching the café, stepping around the injured. The *ack, ack, ack* was now softer, as if the attackers had moved off.

After a few minutes, he spotted a face everyone knew: Rajvardhan Sinha, the chief of SB2, galloping over. Relief washed over him. The Special Branch Deputy Commissioner was like a tank, rolling over whatever came in his way. A veteran of many skirmishes, he would know what to do. Rajvardhan had been at home in the police station campus on VT Road with his family when he got a call from the state's deputy intelligence chief, who suspected this was a scrap between Russian and Israeli gangs who ran drugs in Goa. The inspector shrugged. All he knew was that his men said there were two gunmen, carrying assault rifles, who had shot up the Leopold and were running towards the Taj.

Rajvardhan strode inside. Beside the door were three bodies, two of them Westerners. He estimated that fifteen or sixteen more were dead among the jumble of badly injured. In one corner, a blood-stained waiter was calmly sweeping up, as if a tray had simply fallen. Rajvardhan glanced up to the mezzanine, and saw a diner had been shot dead, falling against the glass, his grimacing face peering down. A constable would have to haul that body back. He blocked out the hysterical weeping and screaming, focusing on the evidence trail. Explosions had ripped large chunks out of the concrete floor. Grenades, he concluded. He followed the flurries of shrapnel pockmarks up the walls. Then, he spotted two empty AK-47 clips taped together on a tabletop and recognized this as a classic combat configuration, allowing a quick change around. This was no *goonda* (hired thug) drive-by. It was not Russians or Israelis. He wondered if the two gunmen were operating with others or on their own.

He grabbed a passing wireless operator. 'Where's the backup?' he shouted into the handset, already worried that the gunmen who had fled the scene were part of a much bigger operation. The force needed to mobilize. 'All police patrols operating within a one-mile vicinity of the area should come immediately.' There was no response from the Control Room. He called it in again. '21.49. Police Colaba Walkie-Talkie: Send help, send help.' This time South Control responded, calling in a pitter-patter of men. Rajvardhan counted. Four units. That meant two dozen officers at best, which was nowhere near enough.

He did a quick tour of the walking wounded, asking for descriptions. He stared at a woman hugging another female diner, who was clearly dead. It was Line Kristin Woldbeck, who stammered that she had seen two or three shooters, young and clean-shaven. Another Westerner described how one gunman was dressed all in black, while the second, who was taller and bulkier, wore black combat trousers and a long-sleeved grey T-shirt with some pattern on the front. South Control called, asking about casualties. The DCP hedged his bets: possibly sixteen needing hospitalization, with a dozen dead. 'Is the one who opened fire held or did he escape?' Rajvardhan listened to the now distant shooting. 'The firing is still on, near Taj hotel.' South Control called it in: 'Striking 1, come to Taj hotel immediately.'

Striking 1 consisted of a Bolero jeep, carrying six men. Rajvardhan sighed. They were not going to win like this. The force needed to pull its finger out. He ran off down Nowraji Ferdonji Road, following the *ack, ack, ack*, working through what he had seen inside the café. 'It's the fucking Pakis,' he said, under his breath. 'Come to piss in our backyard.'

Manish Joshi, a Taj computer operator, had come off duty at the Taj's office in Oxford House, on Nowraji Ferdonji Road, when he heard 'wedding crackers' at 9.46 p.m. Going outside, he saw something lying in the road. He walked over and found a foreign woman, shivering and bleeding. She had been shot, she stammered, and the gunmen had run on. She pointed towards the Taj. Horrified, and unable to understand what was going on, Manish dragged her inside, and propped her up, while he reached for his mobile phone, ringing colleagues inside the hotel: 'I think gunmen are coming for you. Get out.'

A Taj security guard on the Oxford House terrace saw two men carrying assault rifles running along the road and he also rang ahead to warn his colleagues inside the hotel: 'Lock down the hotel. Gunmen are coming.' The message was relayed up to the Taj's security chief, Sunil Kudiyadi, on the fifth floor, who knew five entrances were open: the main Tower lobby through which Bob Nicholls and

Captain Ravi had arrived; the Palace entrance facing the sea, where the critic Sabina had checked in; the south-side Northcote door, the route Will and Kelly had used returning from the Leopold; the Time Office staff entrance; and another staff door at the rear of Taj Tower.

Out front, Puru Petwal, a young security officer on duty in the Tower lobby, one of Kudiyadi's so-called 'Black Suits', dressed in sombre, well-tailored jackets and trousers, got the message to lock the doors just as a tsunami of guests, diners and passers-by surged through the security barriers and walk-through X-ray machine.

In the crush was Sajjad Karim, a Labour MEP for Blackburn, England, who was part of the EU delegation. Moments earlier, he had spotted another guest carrying a half-conscious, bleeding woman through the main gates, shouting that he had come from the Leopold Café, which was under attack, many drinkers from there having fled to the five-star Taj, assuming it would be safer.

Petwal waded into the torrent, as a second scrum of passers-by – chauffeurs, taxi drivers and policemen – attempted to get inside. 'Slow down,' he screamed, panicking. 'People are getting trampled.' The MEP Karim allowed himself to be carried through the lobby past the Harbour Bar on his left, then the reception desks and towards Shamiana in the top left-hand corner. 'I have no option,' he said to himself.

Back out on the main steps, unnoticed by Petwal, two young men with backpacks also slipped in with the current of people, seen only by the hotel's CCTV. Inside, they stood for a few seconds, overwhelmed by the opulence. Then one, dressed in a red T-shirt and red baseball cap, calmly turned left towards the Harbour Bar, while the other, dressed in a yellow T-shirt, headed straight on for Shamiana. They knew exactly where they were going.

As if on cue, they set down their bags and pulled out assault rifles.

Up on the second floor of the Palace, Florence Martis was in the Data Centre when she heard what sounded like a lorry dropping a load of freight. It came from the direction of the lobby. She glanced at her computer: 9.48 p.m. Mumbai was a city of ruckus, she told herself. But tonight she felt unsettled. Tonight she was alone on the night shift, and she hated it. She tried singing her favourite Bollywood film tune but it did not help. Half an hour earlier, she had popped down to the Palm Court, one floor below, looking for her father Faustine, but he was nowhere to be seen. She had tried his phone: no answer. She wasn't too worried about that, though, as the family had bought him a new handset for his birthday and he had still not got the hang of it.

Florence pulled her thin cardigan tighter. Manish Joshi, who worked with the hotel's computers, had got her going a few days back by spinning ghost stories about long-dead guests coming back to haunt the Palace corridors. What she needed now was a bright memory. Something came to her. To celebrate her new job at the Taj, the family had gone on its first holiday, to Mount Abu, a hill station in Rajasthan. They had hired local costumes and got their photos taken. Her father had been invited to a 'gents' party': a few beers and one or two pegs of whisky. Tomorrow he was having a day off, to celebrate his wedding anniversary. She looked down at the smart white plimsolls that he had given her as a present that morning and smiled. Then her desk phone rang. 'Florence, terrorists have come.' She knew the voice: Manish, the office prankster. She wasn't falling for it again. 'Just stop it,' she hissed, cutting the line.

One floor up in the Palace wing, in room 316, Will was flicking through the TV channels, waiting for Kelly to finish getting ready, when he heard fireworks or gunfire. He went to the window but there was nothing to see. 'Kelly, did you hear that?' he called through the bathroom door. 'What?' she asked, coming out, wrapped in a towel. 'I heard shooting.' She pulled a face. 'Don't be ridiculous. This is a five-star hotel. We're going for dinner.'

Ack, ack, ack. This time Kelly, dripping water on the carpet, heard it too. It was hard to say where it was coming from, but it was near by. 'What the hell's going on?' she asked, drying her hair. *Ack, ack, ack.* That burst was inside the hotel. The shots were echoing. Was it the Grand Staircase? They were fifty paces to the left of it, and three floors up. 'Let's see,' Will urged. Kelly did not want to go but she did not want to stay on her own. Opening the door, they ran along the silent corridor in bare feet, keeping their heads low, 'like people did in the movies'. The hotel no longer smelled of freshly cut flowers and expensive perfume but of fireworks, and when they reached the staircase, they gingerly poked their heads over the banisters to see smoke coiling up towards them. 'Look at *that*,' Will said. Kelly had no idea what she was looking at. It smelled of autumn in the park.

Across the staircase they spotted a blond Westerner, who had had the same idea as them. They exchanged nods, their eyes drawn to two young Taj staffers who ran up from below. Will waved at them, but they kept going to the fourth floor then disappeared. 'Some rescue party,' he murmured.

The bang-bang started again. This time there was no doubt that these were gunshots. The man opposite ran off and Will and Kelly scurried back, too. Should they hide or try to get out? 'We don't even know where the fire escapes are,' Will said, starting to panic, looking for a map on the back of the door. 'Look, the hotel will protect us,' Kelly reasoned. That is how it went, right? The hotel's security team would chase the gunmen out and then come for them. That's what they did in *Towering Inferno*.

They locked the door, turned off the TV and lights, wedged themselves between the bed and the bathroom wall, and took each other's hands.

From the top floor of the Taj Tower, in the sleek, glass-walled Souk, the orange flare from the city's streetlights unfurled below like a fine silk carpet. Captain Ravi Dharnidharka, the US Marine captain, was no longer looking at the view but worrying about the great wave of text messages and calls crashing across the room. One of his cousins received a call: 'Gang fight in Colaba, a couple of blocks away.' An aunt rang next. 'A crazy man is waving a gun around behind the Taj.'

'Told you,' Ravi said to himself, recalling earlier misgivings about security in the hotel's main entrance. When he had walked through the security cordon half an hour back, a metal detector had beeped, but no one had stopped him. That had really got him going. Why did people have systems and then pay no heed to them? Who else had got through unchecked? He hoped that his paranoia was simply the prolonged repercussion of battle fatigue.

Across the room, Bob Nicholls, the VIP security boss, was sharing a joke with his commandos when the people at the next table leant over: 'Do you know what is going on downstairs?' Bob shook his head. 'Our friends are trying to get in and they're saying there's shooting.'

Everyone heard the explosive growl from deep inside the hotel reverberate up through the floor. One of the commandos got up, but a waiter asked him to return to his seat. 'Two men are shooting at each other in the lobby, sir,' he confided. Bob gathered his men around. 'If it gets any more serious, I am going to have to do a *Die Hard* and bust us all out of the hotel,' he said, raising a laugh. Bob was great at settling people down. Stout, with copper hair, he was the anti-Willis.

Down in the Crystal Room, on the first floor of the Palace wing, the names of the bridal couple, Amit and Varsha Thadani, were picked out in gold writing on a noticeboard by the door but they had not yet made their grand entrance. Some guests were grumbling as it was already 10 p.m. and the wedding reception was supposed to have started at 9.30 p.m. But this was a city of latecomers. There was also the fatigue. The wedding was into its fourth day, having started the previous Sunday afternoon with a *sangeet* (music) party and culminated with rituals the previous night at a Sindhi temple. Tonight's reception, a buffet for 500, was a chance for the bride and groom to entertain a wider group of friends and family.

The Crystal Room shone with money, elaborate pink and grey table decorations, and frothy centrepieces. A journalist, Bhisham Mansukhani, thirty years old, dressed all in black, had been one of the first to arrive. An old school friend of the groom, he had reluctantly brought his mother along, hoping he would not have to mind her all night. She had wanted to stay downstairs and sit around in the lobby, people-watching. But he had persuaded her to come up, hoping to score a large Bloody Mary after he heard the host had paid for a free bar.

Out of the corner of his eye, he saw a friend of the family, a consultant anaesthetist at Bombay Hospital, and wandered over, trying to park his mother with her. 'It's typical Bombay style, everyone coming late,' he remarked, as what sounded like firecrackers fizzed down below. The guests gave each other a look. 'How gauche. Did the groom set that up? An indoor display?' Seconds later, a dozen Taj staffers rushed in and the anaesthetist turned to her daughter, pulling big eyes: 'It looks like the couple has decided to *make an entry*.' But they began bolting the doors. She grabbed a passing waiter: 'What's going on?' He looked shaken: 'Ma'am, please stay calm. We don't know.'

At 10.05 p.m., down by the hotel's poolside café, the manager of Aquarius, Amit Peshave, was serving a bottle of wine to a Canadian couple, chatting about their holiday in Goa, when he heard an explosion in the main lobby that could not have been part of the wedding celebrations. Instructing his waiters to escort the Aquarius guests inside the smaller Palace lobby, from where they could exit on to the street, Amit raced a hundred metres across the pool terrace towards Shamiana, where dozens of guests were seated for dinner. Shamiana overlooked the main lobby and he feared for their safety.

Adil Irani, in charge at the Aquarius, was in the middle of shepherding people away from the pool when he saw the glass doors separating the terrace from the Tower slide open and a man cradling an assault rifle step out. It was one of the two gunmen who had entered through the front and, seeing the huddled guests ahead, he aimed and let loose with cold, clinical bursts, felling single guests, before finding another target, aiming and firing again.

Adil's heart thumped so hard he felt it might burst. Guests were scattering, some diving ahead into the Palace lobby, others back into the bushes around the pool. Trying to corral them, he saw out of the corner of his eye that the silver-haired Canadians were still at their table. Trying to get their attention, he screamed: 'GET OUT.' Before he had a chance to grab them, another waiter shouted from inside that all the street exits had been locked, meaning they were trapped. As the two waiters began ushering guests up the Grand Staircase, Adil realized he still had a tray with two empty glasses on it in his hand. 'Keep moving up,' he urged, worrying for the Canadian couple outside.

As the guests climbed, a deafening burst of automatic fire rang out. Adil spun round and saw the gunman close behind him. Panicking, he jumped over the banister and pelted off along the ground floor corridor towards La Patisserie and the Northcote side exit, drawing the gunman away. *Ack, ack, ack*. As he ran, his shoes slapping against the marble floor, he felt a rush of bullets flying past, nicking his clothes and kicking up plaster and marble. He charged for the door as the gunman turned back towards the guests on the staircase. 'Open up,' Adil shouted at the Black Suits ahead of him, who were locking the exit. 'We need to get out.' As they looked up, confused at the sight of a staffer running at them, holes punched through the door from the other side. More attackers were outside in Best Marg, trying to get in. Adil and the two Black Suits turned on their heels, heading back down towards the Palace lobby seconds before the Northcote door was shattered and two men burst through it, one wearing black, the other in grey. It was the two gunmen who had shot up the Leopold Café and they gave chase.

Adil, followed by the two Black Suits, dived into the hotel's Louis Vuitton shop, halfway along the corridor, the waiter remembering that it had a service lift at its rear. As he banged the buttons, he could see the gunmen entering the shop: 'Shut, shut, shut.' The gunman in black lunged for the doors, trying to get a boot in to stop them closing. Adil watched him raise his gun, just as the doors slammed and the lift juddered upwards. He slumped down in relief, expecting to exit on the second floor from where he knew a way out. But when the doors opened, he found himself on the exclusive sixth floor, where Karambir Kang and his family had their apartment. The Black Suits motioned: which way? He didn't have a clue and they ran off, leaving Adil rooted to the spot, listening to the sound of firing moving up the Grand Staircase towards him.

Behind the hotel, DCP Rajvardhan had grabbed a police walkie-talkie and was shouting into it. Where was the backup? It was 10.10 p.m., almost twenty-five minutes since the first attack, and he could hear shooting coming from inside the Taj. He cautiously peaked through the rear wall of the hotel into the gardens and pool terrace, overlooking the Aquarius. Nothing. *How many are dead already?*, he wondered, hearing a duet of assault rifles spraying rounds. For the past ten minutes his radio had relayed reports about other incidents too. '21.56. Marine Drive 1: Hearing firing sounds near Oberoi.' That was the Trident–Oberoi, where Rajvardhan's batch-mate Vishwas Patil, the DCP of Zone 1, had spent the day, discussing the impending prime ministerial visit. How many gunmen were out there? The police were in the process of setting up checkpoints across the city. '21.58. South Region Walkie-Talkie: block all the roads.'

Rajvardhan ran round to the Northcote side entrance in Best Marg to see that it was wide open. He entered cautiously, noticing that the boutiques along the marble corridor had all been strafed with bullets. When he reached the Grand Staircase, he could see a dead security guard slumped by the lifts beside a prone dog. It was the hotel's sniffer dog team and they had been shot at point-blank range. Ahead was a sound so intense he could also feel it. Someone was strafing the lobby with an AK. He turned around, exiting the way he had come in, and shuffled along the front wall of the Taj, towards the Gateway and the main Tower lobby, where an agitated crowd had gathered at the now locked main doors. They were still trying to get into the hotel, terrified by the reports of a gun battle in Colaba, not yet understanding there was also shooting inside the hotel. A bellboy lay on the steps, his white uniform drenched in blood, the corpse buffeted by the terrified crowd, while hotel security guards linked arms, trying to keep the scrum back. The Black Suit Puru Petwal was there, holding the line, shouting: 'There is firing inside too. It is not safe. Move back.'

For the next ten minutes, Petwal and his colleagues stared through the glass, watching helplessly as two gunmen picked off anything that moved as they gradually cleared out the lobby. Petwal watched as one of the apprentice chefs, a friend who had recently been accepted on to the Taj's management trainee scheme, led a group of diners out of the Zodiac Grill to the concierge station near the front doors, before returning for a second sweep. Petwal was silently cheering him on when he saw one of the gunmen turn around. Petwal banged on the glass and screamed out, trying to attract the chef's attention, before watching in agony as he was shot in the head.

Rajvardhan was at Petwal's side now, pressing his face against the glass, his radio buzzing with reports of firing at Chhatrapati Shivaji Terminus (CST), the central railway station, used daily by Florence and Faustine Martis and several million others. 'South Control: send help to CST.' Two gunmen had stormed the concourse, spraying gunfire into crowds of commuters, killing many. Then, another message: firing at Chabad House, the little Jewish hostel, around the corner from the Leopold. 'South Control: come immediately. Firing is on. We need help immediately.'

As far as Rajvardhan could tell, at least four separate incidents had been called in and casualties were rapidly mounting. Just as he wondered if it could get any worse, a taxi driver from the Gateway rank ran over, wide-eyed. 'I saw two gunmen placing a bag over there,' he said, pointing. Another officer walked with him and peeked inside, seeing a mess of wiring and tiffin tins. 'Call the bomb squad,' Rajvardhan screamed into his radio set. 'We need *nakabandis* [roadblocks] and backup. Send maximum *bandobast* [cordon].' The bag bomb had a timer inside it and was set to blow.

*

1. The Taj hotel, Mumbai, overlooking the central dome and the Arabian Sea.
Taj Mahal Palace Hotel Collection

2. The Taj from poolside.
Taj Mahal Palace Hotel Collection

3. Jamsetji Tata (*third from right*), who built the Taj Mahal Palace hotel, with his family.
Taj Mahal Palace Hotel Collection

4. Indian princes forming a guard of honour to welcome the new Viceroy, Lord Willingdon, on his arrival at the Gateway of India, 1931. Photograph taken from the Taj.
Taj Mahal Palace Hotel Collection

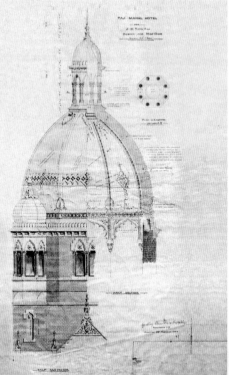

5. Original architectural plan for the central dome of the Taj.

Taj Mahal Palace Hotel Collection

6. Faustine Martis (*left*) in his early days working as a Taj waiter.

Florence Martis

7. Portrait of the Taj chefs that hangs on the wall in the kitchens, with Nitin Minocha (*far left*) and Hemant Oberoi, holding a tomato (*centre*).

Ian Pereira

8. Kaizad Kamdin, one of the chefs who died during the aborted evacuation of Chambers, in the Taj kitchens.

Kamdin family

9. The Chambers Club, where many were trapped.

Taj Mahal Palace Hotel Collection

10. The Crystal Room, where Amit and Varsha Thadani
were due to hold their wedding reception.

Taj Mahal Palace Hotel Collection

11. Amit and Varsha Thadani on their wedding day,
25 November 2008, the day before the attacks.

Amit Thadani

12. Uday and Samar Kang photographed in the Taj Memories Studio just an hour before the hotel came under attack.

Taj Memories (courtesy Sarosh Engineer and Pearl Dubash)

13. (*Left to right*) Florence Martis, Faustine Martis, Precilla Martis and Floyd Martis.

Florence Martis

14. (*Left to right*)
Ambreen Khan
and Sabina
Sehgal Saikia.
Ambreen Khan

15. Andreas Liveras in Monaco.
Remesh Cheruvoth

16. Kuttalam Rajagopalan Ramamoorthy, who was held as a hostage, with his granddaughter.
K. R. Ramamoorthy

17. Remesh Cheruvoth, cruise director for Andreas Liveras, with the super-yacht *Alysia* in the background.
Remesh Cheruvoth

18. An early shot of Daood Saleem Gilani, before he changed his name to David Headley, and his mother, Serrill Headley, taken before they moved to Pakistan.

Author archive

19. This photograph of David Headley was his mother's favourite. She had an enormous print of it laminated and hung it on her wall.

Author archive

20. A youthful David Headley.

Author archive

21. Faiza Outhala, David Headley's Moroccan wife.

Author archive

22. David Headley entering India for his last surveillance operation in July 2008. This picture was taken by a CCTV camera in the immigration queue at Chhatrapati Shivaji International Airport, Mumbai.

Mumbai immigration authorities

Inside the Harbour Bar, to the left of the main entrance, Mike Pollack, a New York financier, was crouched under a flimsy table, alongside his wife Anjali, Mike's college friend Shiv Darshit, and his wife Reshma. They had arrived a few minutes before the firing began and while they had been able to hear everything, they could see nothing. All of them had their heads down, listening to screams, footsteps and deafening ricochets, drawing their own pictures of mayhem.

The Pollacks had a special affinity with the Taj. Anjali, originally from a wealthy Mumbai family, had partied here in her teens. She and Mike had married in the Crystal Room in 2004, following Anjali's family tradition. An American hedge funder, Mike had clicked with her at a party in New York, but she surprised her family when she brought the six-foot, clean-cut Wharton business school graduate to India. These days the Pollacks lived in New York and had a two-year-old son and six-month-old baby. As a co-founder of Glenhill Capital, a global investment fund that Mike had helped grow into a $2.5bn business, he was overworked, while Anjali missed her family. They were over for just a week, squeezing in as many friends and family as they could. Tonight they had had a special pass as her parents were babysitting. Waiting for a table to become free at the Taj's Golden Dragon Chinese restaurant, the last thing they had expected was to end up cowering from a terrorist attack.

Mike looked around, taking in the bar. It was open plan and furnished with rickety aluminium tables and leather sofas. There was no cover; that much was clear. 'We have to get out,' he urged, as he grabbed a table and attempted to hurl it through the window. It bounced back. They had all been glazed with toughened glass after a bomb exploded at the Gateway of India in 2003.

A hostess emerged from behind the bar. She had served them ice-cold Kingfishers earlier and now she motioned for them to stay put while she stood as a lookout by the door, feeding back whispered snapshots. 'A man carrying a machine gun is shooting everything,' she said. 'I can see a body.' The hostess had an idea. She ran towards the back of the bar, signalling for them to follow her. They ducked behind a thick concrete pillar that concealed a spiral staircase. It rose to the first floor, and they came out in the Japanese restaurant, Wasabi. 'I'll take you into the kitchens,' the hostess said. 'No one will find us there.'

Moments after they had departed, CCTV footage showed the gunman dressed in red looking into the Harbour Bar. Seeing it was empty, he carried on along the marble corridor, stopping outside Masala Kraft. Its door was locked and the restaurant was in darkness. He shattered the glass anyway and pumped in some rounds. The restaurant was packed, diners beneath their tables, dazed and tearful, listening to the bullets smashing into the banquettes above them. Among them was the *Alysia*'s owner, Andreas Liveras, who was putting on a brave face. Remesh, his cruise director, was beside him, comforting the terrified Filipino spa girls from the yacht. *Ack, ack, ack. Wump.* Gunfire and a grenade. Glass smashed all around them. The room glowed with sparks kicking off the metal serving trolleys as bullets bounced around the restaurant. There was a pause and Remesh sat up. He caught a glimpse of a man dressed in a red T-shirt, 'running with a gun past the glass doors'. He urged his boss to hide in the kitchens. But Andreas was livid. 'I haven't even eaten yet.'

Grumbling, he got up and they all squeezed into a small store, diners standing shoulder to shoulder. A woman whispered that she had been held hostage two years back in Kabul. 'How could it happen to me twice?' she said, stunned. 'Pull yourself together,' Andreas snapped. The tension made him unforgiving. Then he walked back out into the firing zone of the restaurant to grab one of his two mobile phones, which he had left on the table. He was in the middle of a deal to build the biggest yacht in the world, a 395-footer, and a gunfight was not going to get in his way.

Stuck in southbound traffic from Bandra, Karambir Kang was frantic. It was 10.15 p.m. and he wondered how long it was going to take him to reach the Taj. His mobile phone rang constantly. His family was still up on the sixth floor, the hotel's CEO was trapped on the second floor of the Tower and Chef Oberoi had shut down all of the restaurants and bars, sealing the guests inside. The Taj's group head of security was at home. Ratan Tata, the owner, was on his way over. As the public face of the hotel, Karambir needed to get back.

Neeti got through to him. Should they come outside? Stay where you are, he advised, the shooting is downstairs. 'It is a huge hotel and you are very remote.' He was sure the security forces would neutralize the gunmen before they got a chance to come up. 'You will be safest in your room.' The hotel was a maze these criminals could not navigate. Karambir sounded so confident that Neeti didn't doubt him.

Next, he called his security chief, Kudiyadi, for an update. The figures were chilling. More than 500 staff were on duty, with records showing 1,200 guests and diners trapped inside. 'No police response,' Kudiyadi texted. The first priority was to organize Kudiyadi's Black Suits. They would have to step up and begin a stealthy evacuation, starting in the lobby. 'Get the switchboard girls back to their desks and call everyone,' he texted the security chief. 'Guests must stay in their rooms.' Kudiyadi's response sounded panicked. Karambir reassured him: 'Remember, you know the hotel, they don't.'

The Sunrise Suite

Sabina Saikia was huddled by the door, listening to the sound of gunfire and thinking back to a conversation she had had earlier in the day with her friend Savitri, who had brought her daughters over to sample the Taj's five-star luxury. While the girls had eaten chocolate cake and watched TV in the lounge, Sabina and Savitri had lain on the vast bed, talking.

The two women had met each other in the dying years of the eighties, in a dive of a hotel in Varanasi, on the banks of the Ganges. They had clicked after Sabina found out Savitri was Assamese, like her boyfriend, Shantanu.

Luxuriating on hand-stitched cotton sheets, they had chatted this afternoon about a recent bombing in Assam that had killed more than seventy people. 'A friend of mine almost died when the bomb blasted right in front of him,' said Savitri. Sabina nodded: 'Assam is a real basket case.' Then she checked herself. 'Here we are lying in the lap of luxury in the most exclusive place in Mumbai being so smug about it.'

Now, six hours later, she wished she had taken up Savitri's invitation to stay at her place tonight.

Sabina's phone rang. 'Hey, it's Nikhil, are you OK?' It was her younger brother, calling from Delhi. He and the rest of the family were at the pre-wedding dinner and had been nipping in and out to the TV lounge all evening to catch the cricket. In the last few minutes the match had ended and someone had switched channels to find news of the attacks in Mumbai. Nikhil expected to find Sabina still out at the Parsi wedding. 'No, I was sick, I came back early,' she whispered. 'I can hear gunfire but the switchboard just rang and told me to stay here. What should I do?'

10.20 p.m. – Shamiana

Down on the ground floor, Amit Peshave stood frozen in the centre of his restaurant, having just spotted a gunman hovering outside. The man looked no older than him and was wearing a grey long-sleeved T-shirt over a black polo neck, with a bulky blue cricket bag thrown over one shoulder. Amit could see writing on it: 'Changing the Tide'. The manager knew that if he ran, he would draw the gunman's attention, but if he stayed put, he would certainly die. Behind him, more than fifty diners sat waiting for him to make the call. He ducked down and scurried towards them, urging them to get underneath the tables. Some ran out via a fire exit, and a quick head count showed that thirty-one remained crouching on the floor. He had an idea. Behind a curtain at the rear of Shamiana were two private salons. Hiding in there might buy them time but some of the guests were very drunk. Could he gather them together?

'Move, move,' he hissed, herding them inside. Turning round, he saw Rehmatullah, the head waiter, emerge from the kitchen, carrying a plate of biryani. Amit waved his arms wildly. 'Rehmatullah!' The gunman had spotted him too and squeezed off a burst, catching the old man in the chest, throwing him on to his back, the tray clattering to the floor, rice flying around the room. For good measure, he then bowled a grenade towards the buffet counter, just as Amit's assistant manager emerged to see what the noise was about. 'Run,' Amit screamed, as the grenade detonated, shattering the crystal chandeliers, throwing the room into a jagged and choking darkness as his assistant rolled out of the way. Stunned by the sheer noise of the blast, Amit lay motionless for a moment. What about his chef, the 'Indefatigable Rego'? Desperate for a way out, Amit scanned the restaurant and his eyes came to rest on the 'dead door'. Normally a live band played in front, but he remembered it led into the gardens beside the pool terrace. Hidden in the shrubbery was the hotel's transformer room from where another door opened out into Merriweather Road: a secret door to the street. It was a long shot but their only chance. Amit ran to the door, tugging and charging it. He kicked and kicked, tumbling out into the night air. He was out. For a few seconds he lay there, looking up at the stars. 'Amit, save yourself. Run for your life.' Could he live with that decision? He thought of his parents in Pune, philanthropic GPs who often worked for nothing. He could not. Amit got up and went back inside. 'Into the bushes,' he whispered, counting thirty-one diners out of Shamiana and into the undergrowth, hushing the drunks who giggled and growled.

Staring out towards the pool terrace, Amit spotted the gunman strolling towards the poolside café Aquarius, where the old Canadian couple he had served earlier were still at their table. 'What the hell?' He could not believe it. Was it stiff upper lip, resignation or insanity? Amit wanted to yell: 'Get out of there.' But that would have exposed his position. They were just two people.

The gunman could not yet see the diners, or they him. When he crossed the last pillar they'd be in his sight line. Amit willed them to get up but they kept on with their tête-à-tête. Now the gunman was at the pillar. In one stride, he was round it. He spotted them, pulled himself up and raised his assault rifle, shooting the elderly man in the back. As the injured tourist rose, bewildered, the gunman put a second round through his head. He swung the barrel over to the woman, and as she lifted her hands in horror he shot her in the chest. Amit felt his stomach flip as both guests crumpled dead to the floor.

Inside the locked Crystal Room, above the pool, wedding reception guests sat in silence, drinks untouched, candles flickering, listening to the gunfire that hammered down below, as the piped music continued to play. The hotel smelled like a burning *ghat*, the journalist Bhisham thought, wondering where the newlyweds, Amit and Varsha Thadani, had got to. 'How can this happen in the Taj?' he asked under his breath. He hoped it was some kind of drug war. 'They'll kill each other and that'll be it.' But for now no one knew anything. And they couldn't see anything either since the only view from the windowless Crystal Room was through a couple of portholes in the service doors at either end.

Suddenly, a screeching bullet pierced a partition wall, shattering a huge glass panel above the bar. 'My God,' Bhisham gulped to a financier friend beside him, as they all ducked under the tables. 'How can they be *inside* the hotel? People are saying there's a gang *inside*?' *Ack, ack, ack.* More bullets sliced through the walls. 'They *are* inside,' someone cried out from beneath a table. Bhisham was dismissive. 'This is stupid,' he said. He texted a friend at the Press Club: 'Siy, you check the news, heard gunfire. Bullets in banquet hall.' More rounds bored into the Crystal Room, ripping up swagged curtains. One woman was calling her husband's name. 'Shut up!' someone hissed.

Bhisham texted his friend again: 'I am at Taj, wedding. They're saying gang war.' Who was shooting? Muslim mob, Hindu zealots, drug gang? 'Al fucking Qaeda?' Siy sent word back. There was also shooting at CST and outside the Metro cinema. 'Multiple attacks,' Bhisham whispered to his neighbour.

Crack, crack. The Crystal Room doors shook. Was it another guest trying to get inside? Should they open up and help them out? *Crack, crack.* The doors shook. It was a gun butt smashing down on the handle. Bhisham stared at the doors. He could hear kicking and grunting. A gunman was trying to get in. The doors rattled, but held firm. He heard footsteps pattering along the service corridor and a snatch of foreign voices. Was it Urdu? Or Pashto? Were these Afghanis? The city had once lived in fear of an Afghan godfather, the city's don, Karim Lala, although nowadays it was the Taliban that easy-living Mumbaikers associated with terror.

The footsteps ran behind them in the service corridor. They were circling, trying to figure out how to get in. A face flashed past one of the porthole windows. One of the guests tried to snatch a picture with her phone, and a dazzling white light bounced off the walls as her flash flared. 'You are going to get us all killed,' someone whispered. The face reappeared, pressed up against the porthole glass, boring into the darkened hall.

Wednesday, 26 November 2008, 9.45 p.m. – Malabar Hill, Mumbai

Joint Commissioner Rakesh Maria, the head of Mumbai's Crime Branch, was in the shower at his residence off Nepean Sea Road. For once he had got out of work early, special dispensation as his son was going away that night. But the JC was distracted. A capable officer, one of the city's most famed, a cop who was practised at managing his own legend, Maria felt events were slipping out of his control. For several months, intelligence about a terrorist attack on Mumbai had been massing and no one in the force seemed overly concerned. In two days' time, the PM was also making an important visit, which meant an extra security headache.

This was familiar territory for Maria, the son of a Bollywood producer, who grew up sharing his father's passion for the enthralling power of a good story. He rose spectacularly in the police, from heading traffic to leading Crime Branch, after unravelling the bloody conspiracy behind a series of bomb blasts that killed 257 residents in 1993. Back then, Mumbai was still Bombay and gripped by D-Company, a Muslim syndicate headed by an exiled godfather, Dawood Ibrahim, who fixed things from Dubai, served by a Hindu henchman Chhota (little) Rajan. Maria had quickly spotted linkages, defining the blasts as one interconnected attempt to kickstart a religious war.

Life became more complicated when the Hindu Rajan – repulsed by the Muslim Dawood's crime – split with him, factionalizing the city. The thugs gunned for each other, even hitting enemies in the witness box, as well as targeting the authorities, leading Maria to deploy hard tactics to save Mumbai from becoming a Naples on the Arabian Sea. He formed a squad of unconventionals who squeezed the families of wanted men to get them in for questioning. There were allegations of sleep deprivation, near-drownings, mock executions, and electrocutions in secret holding pens. Maria's team were also accused of indulging in a series of staged encounters in which anywhere between 400 and 700 criminals were allegedly eliminated in ambushes that the police framed as legitimate shootouts.

D-Company was emasculated, and the Mumbai cops rose anew. The writer Jeet Thayil described them as 'Brown Crows', conjuring up the image of birds renowned for their adaptive intelligence, the consumers of information who ate anything, everything they came across.

Now, the sound of four phones ringing simultaneously drove Maria out of the shower, bringing him news of multiple attacks. Getting dressed, he sensed the red mist creeping over the city once more. He called up an inspector: 'Start at the Leopold. Find out what's happening.' Maria also called police headquarters. Had the Standard Operating Procedure been implemented, clarifying who was supposed to be where in an emergency? Where was the anti-terrorism chief? He called the Joint Commissioner for Law and Order, who, according to SOP, was to run the Control Room in the advent of an outrage. Finding him still at home on Malabar Hill, Maria offered to pick him up.

'Don't you worry,' he told his wife as he slicked back his hair. 'We will come in all guns blazing, and they will run.'

Three and a half miles south-east of Nepean Sea Road, Mumbai's neo-gothic police headquarters was frantic. Maria and his colleague arrived shortly after 10 p.m. and charged up the main wooden staircase, passing a gallery of former commissioners. The present office holder, Hasan Gafoor, only the second Muslim to lead the force in a city with a vast Islamic constituency, was nowhere to be seen. The two Joint Commissioners entered the first-floor Control Room, where civilian staff and anxious-looking police officers were milling around and phones rang off the hook.

More than thirty police units, patrols, mobiles and striking forces had already been deployed to the Taj, Chhatrapati Shivaji Terminus, Chabad House and the Trident–Oberoi, but the best-equipped police – the Quick Response Teams, stationed seven miles north – were stuck in traffic. 'What about the State Reserve Police Force?' Maria asked. They relied heavily on this 16,000-strong detail, but in recent days Commissioner Gafoor had dispatched many units on riot duty elsewhere in Maharashtra. The force available tonight was severely depleted. Maria raised his heavily lidded eyes to the ceiling, resisting the urge to make his feelings public. 'How about the anti-terrorist chief?' he asked. 'Sir, he is still in transit.'

Maria's mobile rang. It was 'King', the call sign for Commissioner Gafoor. 'Where are *you*?' barked the boss. 'Sir, I am in Head Office collecting weapons,' Maria replied, chaffing. 'We are heading for the Taj.' That was what the SOP dictated. 'No, stay in the Control Room,' Gafoor ordered. Maria asked if the Commissioner was sure, reminding him that emergency regulations stipulated the Law and Order Commissioner should assume the Crisis Management Command. Everyone knew Gafoor had had a long run-in with this officer and now it seemed to be getting in the way of crucial operational. decisions. 'Law and Order JC will go to the Taj. Maria is to take police Command.'

Maria, the whip hand, was grounded. Furious, he stared at three banks of horseshoe-shaped desks around which the police radio operators were gathered. On either side responders were answering a cascade of emergency '100' calls from the public. At the front, television screens were running live feeds, showing excitable reporters standing in front of various targets, feeding the news machine with half-stories and conjecture, as Maria saw it. He had been ready for a dogfight and was now stuck in the bunker. He took his place at the Command desk, his heart sinking as a pile of papers thumped on his desk.

The first call from Leopold had come in at 21.48 hours: foreigners killed and injured. At 21.54 hours firing at the Taj attack was reported and at the Oberoi two minutes later. The attack on CST was called in at 21.59 hours and reports arrived at 22.02 hours of the raid on Chabad House, the Jewish centre in Colaba. A few minutes earlier a taxi had blown up in Mazgaon, three miles north of the Taj, killing its driver and one passenger and injuring nineteen passers-by.

Maria focused on the nature of the attacks, scouring eyewitness accounts from Leopold that described two young, clean-shaven men dressed in sweatshirts and combat pants, carrying large rucksacks. It was the same story at the Taj and at CST, where almost sixty were believed to be dead. Two attackers had entered the station just after rush hour, pulling AK-47s out of their rucksacks. One, a six-footer, had thrown a grenade, while the other, barely five foot tall, had fired indiscriminately. And, Maria asked, how had India's finest responded? Several policemen had been caught on CCTV running away, while another had resorted to throwing a plastic chair after his thirty-year-old bolt-action rifle jammed. Right now station coolies were dragging bodies away on luggage carts, leaving the concourse criss-crossed with bloody skid-marks.

Reports of a second explosion started coming in, another taxi, this time on the western expressway at Vile Parle, in the north-west of the city, the force of the blast decapitating a passenger whose head had been flung into the basement of Golden Swan City Club. The old criminal order of fade-attack-fade was over, Maria muttered.

Fidayeen rules were in play, while the police were wrapping themselves up in red tape, and the state and centre appeared inflexible. 'They learn and adapt. We stagnate, squabble and steal from one another.' Maria wondered if this force of 40,000, protecting a city of 13 million – well below the UN recommended minimum – was even capable of getting a grip on the crisis.

He studied a printout of recent police calls and saw that Mumbai's front-line defences were already in disarray, with police units having been sent helter-skelter in the absence of the Commissioner. Armed units had gone to pick up the wounded while regular patrols had reported to the worst hotspots. So far there had been one moment of clarity: a call from a beat marshal at 22.27, reporting an unusual marine landing at Badhwar Park. Maria dispatched a team to talk to local residents and search the abandoned yellow dinghy.

The water. How many gunmen had come in? Wild estimates were being bandied about but in truth an army could have arrived from Pakistan for all Maria knew. Just then, his phone rang. It was one of his Crime Branch inspectors: 'Sir. They're heading your way.' The *fidayeen* from CST appeared to be making their way towards police headquarters. *Are they attempting to take out the police communication lines too, leaving the city blind?*, Maria worried. He called an armed Striking Mobile unit to take position outside the main gate and turned to his men: 'They are coming for us.' He broke out the last arms. He had to inspire them to stand and fight. He gathered everyone. 'It is down to you.' He sent men with firearms to reinforce the perimeter cordon, and to choke off the staircase. Then he went back to his desk, anger rising. At 22.40 he made an entry in the Control Room diary: 'I have spoken to the Chief Secretary. We need the National Security Guard or the army to help us deal with this.' This was the state's call and it was still dithering. Then Maria had a 1993 moment. This felt like a nation waging a war against Mumbai and in Maria's opinion Pakistan was the obvious candidate. But would the Islamic Republic take such a risk? Its foreign minister was presently in Delhi, staying at the Taj hotel, having come to India to participate in long-awaited talks. The newspapers had been full of it this morning.

Maria's wife called. Their son was due to take a bus to Ahmednagar, five hours to the east. 'Should he go ahead?' she asked. 'Let him go,' Maria told her. 'God forbid if this whole city is finished, we are all finished, then there is someone in the family who will be safe.'

Two miles south of police headquarters, inside the Taj, Amit Peshave was hiding in a thicket beside the pool, wondering how much longer he could keep thirty-one guests quiet. A few were stoic, and praying. Some were terrified, fidgeting and crying. He was most worried about a drunken party of Indian MPs, who were throwing their weight around, loudly taking calls and threatening people. It would only take one act of inappropriate clowning to draw the killers over. He had tried the door to the transformer room, through which he had hoped to exit on to the street, but found it was locked from the inside. Somehow, he would have to locate whoever had the key. Peeking through the shrubbery, he could see through the pierced cement wall the lights of Merriweather Road. It was eerily quiet. 'Where the hell are the police?'

An Indian couple quietly sobbed. Amit wriggled over. 'Sir, madam, how can I help?' The fretting husband explained: 'Our six-year-old boy is missing.' They had been dining in Shamiana and their son had gone to the toilet moments before the attack started. Now they were separated. Amit's heart sank. The toilet was opposite the Harbour Bar, which meant the boy was trapped or dead. The woman struggled up. 'I will go,' she said. Amit pulled her back. 'You will not. There are thirty-one lives here.' She tried to slap his face and he clasped her hands. She began to call out her son's name. 'OK,' Amit hissed. 'I will find him.'

Holding his breath, he stepped out on to the pool terrace and straight into the path of a gunman. Dressed in black, with a pudding basin haircut, he was different from the one Amit had encountered in Shamiana, and he seemed equally surprised to see the Taj staffer, his rifle momentarily slipping. In that split second, Amit pelted towards Shamiana, but the gunman recovered and loosed off three shots as Amit's foot caught the paving, tipping him on to the grass, the rounds *phut-phutting* close by. As he lay there, the gunman aimed again. Glass crashed all around.

He opened his eyes to see a spurt of bullets as the recoil dislodged the rifle, sending rounds smashing into glass windows and doors. Amit tried to get up. But the gunman pulled something from his bag, lobbed it and Amit heard it thud behind him. He rolled over and saw a matt-green grenade lying in the grass like a fallen coconut. He clutched his ears and stared, waiting for the explosion. But nothing happened.

For the next forty-five minutes, Amit didn't move, thinking maybe he was dead. He looked at the grenade lying innocently beside a hosepipe and gazed up into the sky, mesmerized by the carpet of stars but no moon. 'I pray for my parents and all of my family,' he whispered. He thought about the opportunities he had missed – past girlfriends and indiscretions. 'I *have* had a good life.' When he finally got his senses back and realized that the gunman had gone, he scrambled to his feet, and slipped inside the devastated Shamiana, telling himself that he was the luckiest man alive. The first thing he saw was Rehmatullah, lying dead. The waiter's skin felt like cold, pressed meat.

Bile rose in his throat but Amit pushed on, heading for the Harbour Bar toilets, as gunfire snarled. Two rifles shot up the corridor, grenades tossed to the right and left. The toilets were still way ahead, around the other side of the open lobby. Behind him thirty-one lives depended on him. He could not do it. Feeling like a failure, he turned and worked his way back to the bushes, rehearsing what he was going to say, crawling this time, hiding behind pillars and furniture, until he reached the silent poolside. As he slipped back into the thicket, he noticed one of his guests, a British man, was bleeding heavily from a gaping wound in his hand. His brow was beading, the colour leaching from his skin. He needed urgent medical attention. Amit had to find the man with the transformer room key.

First, he sought out the frantic parents. 'Sir, ma'am, I *have* tried.

But I can't get through. You said you believe in God. Now you have to pray that they won't kill an innocent child.'

Zone 1's Deputy Commissioner of Police, Vishwas Patil, had slipped out of the PM's security meeting at 9.10 p.m., with every intention of going back two hours later, when the group planned to complete its session. He had hot-footed it from the Trident–Oberoi to the cramped police apartment he shared with his wife and two young children, opposite the Brabourne cricket stadium, a few minutes' drive north-west of Colaba. At 9.25 p.m., he was eating daal and rice that his wife had fetched from a nearby takeaway, when his mobile had started ringing.

It was his boss, the Additional Commissioner (South). 'Vishwas, there's firing at Leopold's.' Three days before, Patil had visited the café on a follow-up inquiry, having discovered in July that an intelligence bulletin had named it as a potential target of a Lashkar attack. He had told the café's owner to hire extra security, and had registered more than ninety cases against illegal pavement hawkers who converged outside, forcing them to move so as to limit the potential carnage from any bomb. 'God sent me some signal,' Patil told himself as he picked up his Glock and an unopened box of forty rounds. By the time he got downstairs, the Director General of Police (DGP), the most senior policeman in the state, had called. 'Vishwas, go to the Taj,' he ordered, trumping the earlier call. One of the DGP's relatives and Maharashtra's Additional Chief Secretary were stuck inside the hotel.

As his Tata Indigo drove towards Apollo Bunder, a mile south, Patil loaded two magazines. He had applied for the Glock six months back. Now he had seventeen bullets in the clip, and a spare, with a few loose rounds in his pocket. He was thankful. A normal side arm for his rank was a six-shot revolver or ten-round pistol. His constables were protected even less well. After the bomb blasts of 2003, Mumbai police had raised the dedicated Quick Response Teams (QRTs), trained in commando tactics by the army. Though they were supposedly armed with AK-47s and 9mm pistols, Patil learned that not a single AK round had been purchased for three years and the QRTs had not done any firing practice since September 2007. The next tier of city defences was the optimistically named Striking Mobiles, teams of five or so, armed with rusty carbines and self-loading rifles, often without ammunition. It was well known they had to account for every round fired. After an encounter he would often see them on their hands and knees looking for the casings. The few who were issued with bulletproof jackets found they did not 'cover vital organs', with one classified report noting the plate design 'was defective'. Long before tonight, he had warned his superiors: 'Mumbai's battle readiness is in doubt.' And he had made the same point in the Oberoi hotel meeting earlier today.

As his vehicle approached the glittering Taj façade, he thought back to how he had driven past as a young student, worrying that he would never be part of the world inside. These days he no longer cared. Looking up he saw guests silhouetted in the windows, waving or talking into their phones. Taking a snap decision, he directed his driver down a side lane and called the Taj's security chief, Sunil Kudiyadi, hoping that the hotel's beefed-up defences had held firm.

Getting out in Merriweather Road, Patil was amazed to see that the Time Office entrance was still wide open. Worried, he headed for the swimming pool terrace, wondering what else the Taj had scaled back on, as keeping this entrance secured was in the long list of measures he had submitted to the hotel. He marched in, several feet away from where Amit Peshave and his group of guests still crouched, dashing off to the far side of the pool before any of them could call out. 'Alert everyone,' Patil whispered to his 21-year-old wireless operator, who radioed Rakesh Maria in the Control Room. Patil spotted Kudiyadi emerging from the Palace lobby and waved him over. As he approached, words tumbled out. 'Terrorists . . . are killing people.' His Black Suits had been deployed all over the hotel but they were unarmed and terrified. 'How did the gunmen get in?' Patil asked bitterly. 'Tower lobby and Northcote entrance, sir.' The last time they had seen one another had been at the security meeting in October.

Kudiyadi explained that two weeks earlier the armed police

picket had been dismissed from outside the Tower lobby. 'They had asked to be fed while on duty and the hotel grew irritated.' The Northcote side door had never been secured, despite assurances that it would be. Many of the agreed security steps had been dismantled as soon as Patil had gone on leave, the hotel arguing it could not be expected to sustain a war footing. Exasperated, Patil asked: 'Where are the gunmen now?' Somewhere on the upper floors of the Palace, said Kudiyadi. 'It appears that they know exactly where they are going, sir.'

'Take me,' Patil said and Kudiyadi led him into the bottom end of the south wing and up a service staircase to the first floor. Gingerly they opened a door to look down the wing. Everything seemed peaceful. Crouching low, his pistol drawn, Patil heard sobbing. Creeping along the wing, turning left towards the Grand Staircase, he saw two injured women writhing on the floor outside the Ballroom, their hands shattered by bullets. Horrified, he motioned for two of Kudiyadi's Black Suits to haul them back, while the radio operator called for medical assistance. Patil and Kudiyadi retraced their steps, taking the service stairs up to the second floor. As they poked their heads out, it also appeared deserted.

Close to the Grand Staircase, they edged around a pillar and spotted men armed with assault rifles ascending to the third floor. Patil counted three, possibly four. A few good shots might end this now, he thought, judging the distance between them at around thirty feet. He aimed his Glock and squeezed off some rounds. The gunmen ducked, before spinning around, directing a prolonged burst back towards them, chiselling into the marble. He was outgunned. These were no amateurs.

A few metres along, inside room 253, Amit and Varsha Thadani sat on the bed in their party outfits, clutching each other, listening to the volley of shots. They should have been enjoying their wedding reception in the Crystal Room but instead were discussing whether to create a bunker or make a run for it. Minutes earlier, Amit had opened the door, blustering about 'taking them on' and Varsha, his new, doll-like wife, had dragged him back. 'There's a strong smell,' he told her. She knew it was gunpowder and began to cry. She could not stop thinking about their friends and family who probably were downstairs in the Crystal Room and the lobby, including her brother. Were they hurt or trapped or worse? Where was Amit's mother? She was supposed to have brought up the wedding jewellery half an hour ago and wasn't answering her mobile.

Her new husband could appear lumbering, the way he shuffled his large frame around town; however, Amit was anything but. Friends knew him to be methodical and wily. He was also calm. He got up, turned off the lights and put both of their phones on silent. Varsha went into the bathroom and began quietly calling up relatives and friends, while he stared out of the spyhole, working out their options. 'Look, don't be so tense, this is just a small thing,' he murmured. 'Once it's over, our party can continue.' His phone whirred. It was his brother, telling them to leave. 'Too late for that,' he said. Amit went back to the spyhole and recoiled: 'I think I just saw a gunman walk by.' He raced over to the window, looking down to see if the police had arrived. The only thing that caught his eye was a brightly lit yacht, out in the water. 'Should have hired a boat,' he said.

Out on the *Alysia*, its gleaming white lines festooned with scarlet Edmiston Company banners, Nick the yacht broker and his son had been greeting guests when mobiles started to trill at 9.48 p.m. One of the guests had switched his on to speaker and everyone crowded round to hear a crackle and pop of gunfire. 'It's my chauffeur, parked outside the Taj.' They could hear the driver speaking: 'Sir, there's a gunfight. Can I move the car?' In the UK, the driver would have run and not called, Nick thought. Ratan Kapoor, the Delhi socialite, came over. 'Look, it's a normal kind of Mumbai thing,' he said. 'It's a heated city.'

Reassured, Nick went below deck to talk to the staff about serving dinner. The guests took another glass of champagne as an explosion echoed across the water and a ripple of excitement ran around the yacht. 'We've got the best seats,' one man joked, as the waiters put the finishing touches to a huge teak dining table with raw silk napkins, silver cutlery and Bohemian crystal. Nick was worried about Andreas, whom he knew to be a risk taker, and asked the captain to call him: 'Tell him we're sending the tender over' – as another explosion woofed throughout the city, and he felt the blast vibrate in his chest.

Undeterred, the guests sat down for dinner, taking calls and texts. 'Fighting inside the Taj,' one man whispered. 'Isn't that serious?' Nick asked. He stared at the shoreline. He was fond of this hyper-active city, but irritated by its lackadaisical attitude to security. 'Don't worry,' said Kapoor. 'Everyone on the yacht is feeling safe and lux-urious with lots of champagne and French food. You're the host. This is an important party.' The captain came over, frowning. 'Mr Liveras says he's fine and to tell you, "Enjoy the dinner." He'll be back later.'

Nick took Kapoor to one side. 'We might just get away with it,' said Kapoor weakly, as someone rang to ask him if Friday's party was still going ahead. 'Ya, sure. This will blow over and then you'll be here, dancing with me, cheek to cheek.' Nick went into the main saloon and tried to find *Sky News*. While the crew played with the settings, he read text messages from London. 'It's a terror attack.' And another: 'They've entered the city from the water.' He thought: *My God. We are sitting targets.*

By 10.50 p.m., the DCP Zone 1 was back down in the Tower lobby and his wireless operator was on the radio: 'Zone 1 Sahib is in Taj. He *needs* help.' After the exchange of fire on the Grand Staircase, they had lost the gunmen and Patil needed reinforcements to comb the vast, unfamiliar hotel. He grabbed two young constables, stand-ing idly by a State Reserve Police Force van. 'How many rounds?' he shouted. They had ten shots each. 'Not enough,' he said to himself, shaking his head.

A spatter of bullets ripped up the porch canopy. He was sure from the muzzle flash that the gunmen were shooting from a third-floor guest room. Patil spotted Karambir Kang, the hotel's General

Manager, who had just got back from Land's End. The two men knew each other from the Taj security consultations and Patil was tempted to have a go at him right there in the street, but now was not the time. Karambir, looked ashen. 'My wife and sons are on the sixth floor,' he said, walking over, his eyes red raw, his immaculate suit dishevelled. What could Patil say? 'Sir, we need hotel plans.' Karambir said he would hunt around. He tried the CEO, who was trapped in his office, and called Chef Oberoi. Between calls he kept glancing up at the southern corner of the sixth floor, where his family were waiting for him. He came back to Patil: 'The hotel blueprints are with someone who cannot be found. We are still looking.' The DCP was irritated: 'We can't think of evacuating until we have located the gunmen, and for that we need to know where we are going.' Karambir said he would ask Ratan Tata, the owner.

Clutching a bottle of water, Karambir contemplated how his family should not even have been here at all. A few months back they had decided to shift to a private apartment and Neeti had stocked up on interior-decorating magazines, excited to be moving out of the hotel. They were supposed to have been in at the beginning of the month, but the contractor was still not finished. Karambir cursed the delay, but tried to banish his darkest thoughts. He said to himself: '*You* are the face of the hotel. *You* are the representative of the Tata family.' Everyone was looking at him and what they saw needed to inspire hope.

On the lobby steps, Patil spotted his batch-mate Rajvardhan. He was just the kind of hard head he needed and Rajvardhan did not need any persuasion to enter the stricken hotel. Slipping into the now silent lobby, where bodies lay strewn about, he made his own thumbnail assessment. 'Random injuries, multiple head shots, a slew of ammunition.' He was sure his earlier gut feeling was correct: Pakistani *fidayeen*. He called out the first stages of a plan: evacuate the ground floor while the gunmen are elsewhere, set up an improvised command post beside the Shamiana, close and guard all the exits to stop them escaping and blockade the lifts. He commandeered a service revolver and nine rounds. 'Call me up when you are ready,' he shouted to Patil, vanishing down a corridor, the weapon gripped in both hands.

Up in the first-floor kitchens, straddling the Palace and the Tower, Chef Hemant Oberoi had had a plan. After his restaurants had been thrust into the front line, guests and diners scattering all over, many of them had been brought, or made it on their own, into the parallel world of the service areas. The American hedge funder Mike Pollack, his wife Anjali and their friends had locked themselves into the chef's store of Wasabi, on the first floor of the Palace, and Andreas Liveras was on the ground floor, eating lentils, spinach and cottage cheese on an upturned *handi* in Masala Kraft's prep room, keeping everyone's spirits up by cracking jokes.

Chef Oberoi realized that his Kitchen Brigade could, unseen by anyone front of house, probably utilize the hotel's labyrinth of service lifts, stairs and passages to move guests into one central and protected location. He called Karambir Kang, who was pacing outside the hotel, to sound him out. The hotel's invitation-only Chambers club was ideal, he argued. Consisting of a suite of rooms, a bar and a library, it occupied a large area on the first floor, between the Crystal Room and the kitchens, overlooking the Gateway of India. It was not marked on hotel brochures and only the most frequent Taj visitors would have noticed it at all, perhaps glancing at the discreet plaque beside the Tower's lift buttons as they headed up to Souk, although the stop could only be accessed by staff, or by using a club key. Karambir agreed. The Chambers was an invisible refuge. He suggested Chef Oberoi begin immediately, starting with the people who were nearest to the Chambers, the wedding reception guests in the Crystal Room.

Shortly after 10.30 p.m., chefs and waiters had guided a column of guests down a service corridor, popping out into the club's foyer, which Bhisham, the journalist, instantly recognized. He had been here once before, for a press junket thrown by Ratan Tata. Emboldened, he asked if staff could open the bar. Writing about food and drink, he regarded himself as a connoisseur. 'Look, you got the best, bring it out,' he teased. But the Chambers manager politely refused.

Bhisham mournfully texted his friend: 'Best single malt collection in the country and not a drop to drink.'

Another group of guests was led in, among them a huffing Andreas Liveras, accompanied by Remesh and the spa girls. They saw that in one of the smaller rooms a group was conducting a business meeting. 'Look, everyone's carrying on as if nothing is happening,' Remesh whispered to his boss. Mindful that many guests had not eaten, the kitchens produced trays of mint chutney sandwiches. Andreas asked Remesh to grab some extra rounds. 'Hide them in case the food runs out,' he said, plonking himself on a large chaise longue, fielding calls from his office and family in London, as well as the *Alysia*. 'Everything's fine,' he assured Nick. 'We'll sit tight until the army get here.' He rang his son Dion: 'It'll all blow over, don't worry.'

The mood darkened when someone switched on the television, blaring facts mixed with conspiracy theories: more than sixty terrorists were roaming Mumbai's streets, the police were overwhelmed and hundreds were dead. Footage of the bloody station concourse at CST stopped the chattering. Bhisham walked over to his horrified mother and took away her phone. An insensitive message would tip her over the edge.

More guests arrived, including Mike and Anjali Pollack. She was frantic. The normally cool financier looked agitated, too. A few minutes before, one of the gunmen had tried to get into their hiding place in Wasabi, prowling outside the locked service door. A chef had brazened it out, redirecting the gunmen, saying the room was empty, narrowly escaping with his own life. Now all that Anjali could think about was their two young sons, staying with her parents in another part of the city. 'We could have died,' she cried.

As Chambers filled up, Bhisham and his mother moved down the corridor to one of the smaller VIP suites, the Lavender Room, just as an explosion shook the floor. Had they been found already? The lights and TVs cut out. Sitting in the dark, Bhisham messaged a friend: 'Heard the blast. What is happening?' The friend replied that the top floor of the Palace was now ablaze. Bhisham panicked: 'Is it serious? Is the army inside the hotel?' He turned to his mother, who was praying. 'What a great wedding.' There were now 250 people locked in Chambers, and only six policemen inside the hotel.

Outside on the pool terrace, Amit Peshave was getting more anxious by the minute. It was 11.30 p.m., and despite the dozens of calls he had made nobody seemed to know where the transformer room keys were. The bleeding British guest was getting weaker and his shirt was soaked in blood.

Amit's phone buzzed. It was his old room-mate Hemant Talim, a trainee chef in the Golden Dragon. 'Amit, how's things?' he asked calmly, warned about his friend. 'Look, we're all in Chambers now. We need to know your exact location.' Amit explained his predicament. Call Chef Oberoi, his friend suggested. Amit got Oberoi on the third go: 'Chef, I've got a Brit guy here who's going to die, drunk MPs out of their minds and a missing boy.' Oberoi tried to calm him, saying he would contact maintenance people to bring the key. Then Amit noticed out of the corner of his eye that one of the MPs was staggering into the open, and over to a statue of a lion that he attempted to climb. 'I've got to go,' he rasped.

Thirty minutes later, he heard hollow knocking. Someone *was* now on the other side of the transformer room door. The guests jostled anxiously. Then the doors were flung open, and everyone pushed forward. Amit noticed a man jumping down from the top of the transformer room roof, a European guest, wearing a red bow tie and a dinner suit. He must have been hiding up there all the time and hadn't said a word. 'James Bond!' Amit said to himself, watching in amazement as the man hared off. Now he had to get the injured British guest to a hospital. He shouldered the man's weight and stumbled out into Merriweather Road.

Up in Souk, on the top floor of the Tower, Bob Nicholls and his South African commandos were in security mode. There were upwards of fifty people in the restaurant, including the wife of the Taj Group's CEO, feeding back updates from her husband, who was trapped in his office eighteen floors below. 'He says we are in the safest place,' she assured them. Bob had been receiving his own updates, from a Mumbai-born business partner, watching things unfold on TV back in Johannesburg, Bob's wife Melaney sitting beside him. 'There's firing all around the Palace but the Tower looks untouched,' the first message said. 'The whole city is under attack. Stay put.'

Across the room, the US Marine captain Ravi and his brother went through their wallets, taking out US dollars and driving licences. They needed to erase everything that identified them as Americans or connected Ravi to the US military. He stuffed some essentials, including his stars-and-stripes credit card, into a sock. He thought about ringing his girlfriend back home in San Diego but decided against it. When his sister called, he told her he was nowhere near the action. What could she do? From now on he would also stay apart from his Indian family, worried that if he were caught, he would contaminate them, too.

Coming from San Diego, Ravi and his brother planned to fake Spanish accents if they got singled out. 'I hope to hell we never get to that point,' he murmured. But there were some things Ravi could not change, especially the fact that so many years spent in the US Marines rubbed off on a person. Now his neck was as wide as his head, which was scalped into a distinctive buzz cut. Everything about the way he carried himself, and especially his sloping shoulders and lean frame, said military.

Ravi strolled over to the South Africans' table. He reckoned the gang of square-jawed, close-cropped men were from the same tribe. 'Look,' he said to Bob, without giving anything away about himself, 'I'd just like to help if I can. I have some *experience* in this kind of situation.' He didn't volunteer any more information and the South Africans didn't ask. Bob put him to work, accompanying one of the ex-commandos on a recce. They needed to find somewhere safer than Souk, with its wrap-around windows. If a bomb went off in the lift lobby, everyone would be cut to shreds by flying glass. Through the kitchens, Ravi found a conference hall that occupied the rear portion of the top floor, the Rendezvous Room. He threw back the door and to his amazement there, sitting quietly, were a hundred Koreans.

He tried to question them, explaining that they all needed to bed in together, but they spoke only a little English. They were badly spooked and could not be left alone. Ravi rushed back to Bob with the bad news. The Korean delegation swelled their numbers to 150-plus.

Ravi saw no sense in remaining in Souk now. 'Let's decant.' Rendezvous was far easier to secure. Once they had got everyone inside, Bob grabbed a mic from the conference podium and began addressing the crowd. Everyone here had a different reading of the crisis. Those from the city saw it in ways that Bob could not imagine. They had lived through communal riots and serial bomb blasts, watched coal kings become Muslim godfathers, creating an alphabet of crime gangs that held the city to ransom, sending khaki gunslingers like Maria to war. Only in Mumbai would the inequality within the criminal underworld become a pressing political issue, with Hindu chauvinists trying to undercut the power of Muslim godfathers, by falling behind their own saffron crime boss, a Hindu don, who operated out of his lair in a mill workers' slum. If you were going to get your throat slit, there'd better be equal opportunities for all criminals of every faith in the city of seven islands.

Bob was sure-footed, the Marine captain thought. There was something about his everyman demeanour that appealed, even though he actually had no front-line experience. 'Don't talk loudly on the phone,' he said. 'Don't tell people on the outside where we are. Keep close to the floor. Don't move around. Don't sit under the chandeliers. Don't talk to the press.' He circulated a piece of paper, asking everyone to write down names and addresses. He did not say it was a 'dead list'.

Now they needed to build a fortress. One of Bob's commandos climbed inside a false ceiling, above the lifts, ready to drop on whoever entered. Ravi disabled the lifts by jamming chairs between the doors, and then secured the restaurant entrance shut with wire. Inside, they began constructing barricades to block two outward-opening fire exits, piling up tables and parts of the podium, placing chairs either side, with which they planned to clobber any gunmen who tunnelled through. Ravi also quietly recruited waiters to sit by these exits, to act 'as canaries'. As far as he was concerned, this thing wasn't likely to end any time soon. They were bedded in for a long wait.

They all heard the explosion that rumbled up through the hotel. Ravi knew it was far too loud to be a grenade. 'I can see smoke,' Bob said, sounding worried for the first time, and peering down on to the sixth floor of the Palace, clearly visible below the Tower. He could see flames emerging from the roof. *How will we escape if the fire turns the Tower into an inferno?*, he worried to himself.

On the top floor of the Palace, at the opposite end to the Tower, Sabina Saikia heard the blast too. Horrified, she called her friend Ambreen Khan: 'What should I do?' Ambreen reassured her. 'Look, I'm on the way over. Call up the duty manager now.'

'I'll call Karambir Kang,' Sabina suggested. Ambreen said no. She had seen on the news that his family was also trapped. 'He will be busy. Call the duty manager.'

Sabina called back minutes later. 'Ambreen, I'm scared. There's shouting and footsteps outside my door.'

'Peep out. Make sure they don't see you.'

'It's men with guns.' She sounded shaky.

'How many?' Ambreen got her to focus on the details.

'Three. They are young and also have backpacks.'

Ambreen was horrified. 'You have to hide.'

A few minutes later Sabina rang her brother Nikhil in Delhi. 'A man is knocking, saying "housekeeping". Should I answer?' 'No!' She rang off and then called back: 'He's knocking again, this time saying "security".' 'Don't answer!'

Ten minutes later she was back on the line. 'I'm in the bedroom and smoke is pouring in. What shall I do?'

'Put wet towels around the door,' Nikhil urged.

Sabina started babbling: 'I need to speak to Shantanu. I need to speak to the kids.' There were her older sisters. And there was her mother. 'I need to speak to them!' They were together in Delhi at the niece's pre-wedding party, watching the Taj on TV, more than three hours away by plane.

She rang Ambreen again. 'Someone is talking in Punjabi outside. He's knocking on the door with something metal.' There were several dull thuds. '*Ambreen!*'

A mile away from the stricken hotel, out in the narrow lanes of Cuffe Parade, Colaba and Nariman Point, where police were facing standoffs with gunmen at Chabad House and at the Trident–Oberoi, and from the midst of the maelstrom of callers crying out for assistance, a Western intelligence agency plucked a single mobile phone number.

Isolating long-distance calls from local and putting these through a key-word sieve had left them with a stack of possibilities. Using linguistic search tools to work on this stack, looking for Urdu and Punjabi speakers, had further reduced that pool. Identifying key phrases, using equipment that was officially denied to exist, had eventually slimmed the list to one possibility, assigned to a local Bharti Airtel SIM: +91 9910 719 424.

The news passed to Indian external and domestic intelligence, the Research and Analysis Wing (RAW) and Intelligence Branch (IB), was that the caller could be a participant or even the ringmaster in the terrorist operation. The IB contacted the state intelligence chief, who contacted Crime Branch's boss, Rakesh Maria, in the Control Room, and the Anti-Terrorism Squad (ATS) headquarters. There, in the technical section, a veteran ATS eavesdropper, experienced at truffling in the digital world, would isolate the phone's unique identifier and apply for a warrant to listen in.

Maria called his Crime Branch number two, the pug-faced Additional Commissioner of Police Deven Bharti: 'Find the caller,' he told Bharti. If this phone led to those directing the terror, they could decapitate the assault on Mumbai.

Bharti, who was out at the airport on a gang-related operation, pulled back to South Mumbai. At police headquarters he met up with the Deputy Commissioner of the ATS and they both signed out portable direction-finding equipment, with which to home in on the phone's signal. He and the ATS deputy set out in their cars with their laptops open, waiting for someone to call or for that number to be called.

To get an accurate position, they needed to triangulate between at least three phone towers. From there, the number could be isolated inside a map grid, and then a building, where human muscle would come into play: door to door and room to room. Bharti, who had done this before, knew it called for perseverance. Splitting Colaba and Nariman Point into a lattice on a map, he got comfortable, earphones plugged in, laptop on his knees, waiting. He knew they had only the duration of the call, however brief, to lock on and map it.

At 11.30 p.m., +91 9910 719 424 was switched on. *'Salaam Alaikum.'*

4

A Goat, a Knife and a Matchbox

May 2008 – Pakistan

A party of Lashkar trainee fighters bumped along in a hand-painted bus that spluttered and lurched into the wooded mountains of Pakistan-administered Kashmir. Qahafa the Bull, the *mujahid* trainer, and *chacha* Zaki, the outfit's military commander, had selected them from a much larger pool of recruits, and from this group they intended to choose the final ten-man team for Operation Bombay.

Arriving at the House of the Holy Warriors, on the bowl-like plains high above Muzaffarabad, the men were frisked for cigarettes, opium and tobacco, before being photographed and fingerprinted. No one would be allowed to leave without an instructor for fear of contaminating the outfit, although none of them had any idea as to where they were being assigned. Anxious and exhausted from the bone-breaking 350-mile journey, the trainees were shown to their canvas barracks, sixteen in each tent, each one issued with a number to replace his real name.

They would be allowed only one monitored phone call a week. Qahafa the Bull and his instructors regulated sleeping, eating, washing and praying. Chatting about home life was discouraged. All of them did it anyway.

One of the thirty-two was Ajmal Kasab, who had no idea that he was on the way to Mumbai.

Born in September 1987 in Faridkot, a scrawny village hugging the highway on the poverty-stricken far eastern fringes of the Punjab, Ajmal's neighbours eked out a living in a landscape dotted with shrines and long-forgotten ruins dating back to the Indus Valley Civilization. This was a historic recruiting ground, with many levies drawn from here by the British, and for centuries before them by warring princes. But Partition had sent the Hindu and Sikh residents fleeing to India, while their homes were taken over by Muslim refugees, who barricaded themselves inside brick compounds to endure Pakistan's Year Zero. Physically closer to India than to any of the Punjab's great cities, villagers were raised on stories of loss, and grew up despising their looming neighbour. The mosque was the only communal meeting point.

Chacha Zaki, who came from Okara, Faridkot's nearest city, twenty miles away, had left the district to fight in the secret Afghan war of the 1980s, as did hundreds of thousands of others from the Punjab. Afterwards, he had joined up with a lecturer at Lahore's University of Engineering, Hafiz Saeed, who spun emotive stories of his family having lost thirty-six relatives during the Partition slaughter. In 1990, the fighter and the lecturer (who was also a cleric) formed Lashkar-e-Toiba to spread a message that those who fled and their descendants could take revenge by destroying India, piece by piece. They fed off the anger, destitution and sense of dislocation that permeated every household.

In Faridkot, Ajmal and his four siblings lived behind a turquoise tin door. The main street was a sump, strung with petrol pumps and mechanical repair shops that serviced passing trade. Once the family had been goat herders and later they had sold meat, giving them their surname, which loosely translated as 'butcher'. But the Kasabs had fallen on hard times and Ajmal's father laboured 150 miles away on the building sites of Lahore, earning 400 rupees (£2.50) a week. The family home had no toilet or electricity. They drew their water from a communal tap, threw their rubbish over the wall and slept nose-to-toe in the room where they ate, lit by a single kerosene lamp.

The home was ruled by Ajmal's mother, Noor Elahi, who fell pregnant during her husband's occasional visits, but otherwise lived a covered life inside the family compound. With his father absent, Ajmal, the second son, a boy whose name in Arabic meant 'the handsome one', was rebellious. Short and muscly, he grew his hair long, chewed tobacco and hung out at Faridkot's bus stand. But the district was changing, its mood lifting, mainly through the success of Lashkar, which had made its reputation taking on one of the largest security establishments in the world in Indian-administered Kashmir, supporting an insurgency that had exploded there in 1989.

Forlorn Okara sent so many soldiers on jihad it became feted as a 'blessed city' and Lashkar made sure everyone heard the message: free literature handed out after Friday prayers, the health checks conducted by Lashkar-sponsored doctors, lavish *tamasha*s hosted for every *shaheed*, or martyr. Lashkar volunteers would shower the community with sweets and his family with compensation before the deceased's testament was read aloud like a battle citation. Dying for jihad in Kashmir was the highest accolade one could strive for in a bitter landscape where the alternative was living for nothing and it brought respect and dignity to families who previously had none. Visiting commanders toured like pop idols. Posters of martyrs were pinned in doorways in Okara, where in other cities one would see Bollywood movie posters. Collection boxes filled up in the grocer's shop. Graffiti dominated every village wall: 'Go for jihad. Go for jihad.' Others attested to the new world order: 'Neither cricket stars nor movie stars, but Islamic *mujahideen*.'

Teenagers like Ajmal read stirring youth publications printed by Lashkar's media wing, which liberally used the testimonies of slain fighters to solicit new recruits, even penning a cartoon strip in one, which children nicknamed *Shaheed Joe*. The outfit knew what it was doing. 'Children are like clean blackboards,' declared a Lashkar provincial chief. 'Whatever you write will leave a mark on them for ever.'

Ajmal's turning point came in 1999, the year Pakistan and India went to war in the Kashmir heights at Kargil and his father Amir came home from Lahore sick with TB. From now on, Amir would earn about half of his construction wage, around 250 rupees (£1.50) a week, wheeling a handcart laden with fried snacks around Faridkot's dusty square. He fought with his son, whom he expected to make up his loss, eventually sending the thirteen-year-old to work as a labourer in Lahore. Up at 4 a.m., washing in public toilets, Ajmal grew bitter and exhausted, his ambition blunted, his fear and loneliness pricked at night. He missed his mother and resented his vicious father.

After six backbreaking years in the building trade, Ajmal met a cocky youth who worked for the Welcome Tent Service, a catering business based in Jhelum, a city on the road to Islamabad. He was recruiting cooks, and offering hot food, safety and more money. The hungry Ajmal moved to Jhelum and made a new friend, Muzaffar, whose name meant 'victorious'. He had his own ideas about surviving. Rolling *rotis* by day, he took Ajmal prowling at night, encouraging the smaller teenager to wriggle through bathroom windows, breaking into homes and offices.

With money in their pockets, Ajmal and Muzaffar went to the cinema and watched multiple showings of *Sholay*, a high-octane Bollywood thriller in which a veteran cop recruits two thieves, one of them played by Amitabh Bachchan, to catch one of their own. In November 2007, they headed for Pakistan's cantonment city of Rawalpindi to buy a gun, hoping to become fully fledged hoods.

The city was buzzing with a carnival-like atmosphere. Elections were coming, Benazir Bhutto was back in town after an absence of almost a decade and the streets with filled with festive *shamianas* and fairground rides in preparation for Eid. Wandering around the tents, Ajmal and Muzaffar met an elderly man, who bought them tea and persuaded them to visit the local Lashkar recruiting office. They were welcomed like long-forgotten relatives with plates of rice and mutton. 'They asked us our names, telling us to come the next day with our clothes and supplies.' When one of the men in the office wrote 'Daura-e-Sufa' on a chit, telling them to travel to an address in Muridke outside Lahore, they readily agreed. Ajmal could barely read but with those few pen strokes, they had, without realizing it, enlisted on a two-week Lashkar conversion course.

Within twenty-four hours, Ajmal and Muzaffar had reached

Lashkar's global headquarters in Muridke, thirty minutes outside Lahore, a place called *Markaz-e-Taiba* – the Centre of the Pure. Passing through a succession of checkpoints, they were frisked and relieved of their mobile phones.

Inside, they joined thirty more newcomers, all of them nervous and tired from long journeys across the Punjab, their possessions crammed into tin trunks. A vast site, the Centre of the Pure resembled an expensive private university. There were broad roads and flower-lined pathways, playing fields, gardens, classrooms and an enormous concrete swimming pool, close to the back gate. The grandest building was the Abu Harrera mosque, which could hold 5,000 and whose parade ground outside was strung with electric fans to keep the observants cool. There was even a girls' school, something that surprised village boys whose sisters never left the family home until the day they married.

The second day they were woken at 4 a.m., and the programme began with prayers, the first words in a religious immersion course. Unlike other groups that sent mercenaries into battle without any indoctrination, but who fought anyone declared as an enemy of the Muslim community, Lashkar rebuilt its recruits in its image to operate under strict religious, political and ideological guidelines. 'We were first converted from Sunni to Ahl-e-Hadith and we were taught the methods of the *Hadeethi*s,' Ajmal recalled.

At first, he struggled. 'Everything from *namaz* [prayer] to lunch to dinner happened with clockwork precision,' he said. 'The trainers were very strict.' He preferred the afternoons, when they played cricket, a game that since early childhood had enabled Ajmal to vent his hatred and anger towards India. In these dusty matches on the Muridke grounds, Pakistan was always the winner.

One week in, they were introduced to Qahafa the Bull, *chacha* Zaki's number two, and from the start the boys were in awe of his fighting prowess. After evening prayers, Qahafa gathered the boys in the main mosque to hear stories of sacrifice and triumph, screening film of successful *fidayeen* attacks on Indian installations in Kashmir. Qahafa and his trainers continuously distinguished between *fidayeen* and suicide missions. The latter were unthinkable. 'Suicide is to kill oneself in desperation after one fails to achieve that goal which has been set,' Ajmal was told. A *fidayeen* squad 'died trying to achieve a virtuous goal'. They fought to win, and if they died that was a victory, too.

Finally, *chacha* Zaki arrived, driven into the campus in a Toyota pickup packed with armed guards, dressed in his trademark Afghan pakul cap and raw woollen shawl. It was many years since Lakhvi had fought the Soviets, his prominent belly and the *zabiba* (prayer bump) on his forehead signalling that he spent more time these days in the mosque. Lakhvi welcomed the new recruits and introduced them to a roster of instructors led by Al-Qama. Originally from Bahawalpur, in the southern Punjab, his real name was Mazhar Iqbal, and until recently he had run Lashkar's Kashmir operation. From now on trainers like Qahafa and Al-Qama would become father figures to the boys, as they gradually relinquished ties with their real families.

Al-Qama had news. He revealed that he was looking to assemble a special team for a secret operation: 'We are readying to attack big cities in India. We shall start a war from within so that India is hollowed out.'

The recruits were electrified and terrified. Soon after, the outfit's *amir*, Hafiz Saeed, arrived in a convoy of saloon cars, protected by armed outriders. The students listened to his message. Plucking his red beard before resting his hands across his chest as if he were praying, the *amir* delivered a ponderous eulogy about duty and bravery.

He rounded off with a pledge that Ajmal would never forget. 'If you die waging jihad,' the *amir* said, inspecting the recruits, 'your faces will glow like the moon. Your bodies will emanate scent. And you will go to paradise.' *Chacha* Zaki stepped forward to drum it home: 'You are Muslims. India is not humanity. They have left you in poverty and they are ahead of you.' Be ready, he told them. 'Your time is coming.' From being nonentities the recruits were suddenly 'somebodies'.

By February 2008, the group had shrunk to twenty-four boys, including Ajmal and Muzaffar. They were driven eight hours to the north-west, and the town of Mansehra, in the snowy hills of what was then Pakistan's North West Frontier Province. Hidden here was another Lashkar training facility, just north of the Pakistan Military Academy and the town of Abbottabad, where Osama bin Laden would be killed four years later. From the Mansehra bus stand they hiked up into the hills, carrying boots and a blanket, reaching a track that eventually led to Battal, a stone and wood village.

If Muridke had been scholarly, Battal was backbreaking. Motivational songs blasted from loudspeakers strung in the trees and during the twenty-one-day *Daura-e-Aama* (General Session), the recruits got to hold their first AK-47, or 'Kalashan'. They also tackled a numbing obstacle course, crawling through icy pits, and what Ajmal lacked in stature, at barely 5 feet 3 inches, he made up for in sinewy determination, the trainers noted.

With basic training completed, the boys were ordered to take a break. What lay ahead was the *Daura-e-Khasa* (Special Session) that lasted two and a half months and took place in the House of the Holy Warriors, in Pakistani-administered Kashmir. As it cost Lashkar £1,000 per fighter to graduate them, the outfit had to be sure about every candidate it put forward. At the end of it, Al-Qama would make his selection for the secret mission.

Muzaffar's family came to collect him. No one came from Faridkot for Ajmal, even though he was homesick. He called his mother, but the line was down. He was forced to remain at the Lashkar offices, mentoring new recruits, until the list went up for the boys accepted to commence the Special Session. Ajmal's name was on it, but Muzaffar's was not.

May 2008. Poor and semi-orphaned boys, who had been made to feel like Special Forces by Lashkar, pitched their tents high in the Chelabandi hills, above Muzaffarabad, where Sajid Mir, Lashkar's foreign operations deputy, had his Ice Box. Ajmal gravitated to another recruit, Hafiz Arshad. A muscly six-footer, Arshad was originally from Multan, in the southern Punjab. His family had handed him over to an Islamic seminary as they already had enough children working in the sugar cane fields. Arshad only had one skill, which explained his first name: He was a *hafiz*, a rote learner of the Koran. But by the time he was a teenager, he knew nothing of Pakistan or what lay beyond it. He became a labourer on the railways until he was handed a flyer advertising a public rally given by *amir* Hafiz Saeed.

The next to wander over was Shoaib, the youngest recruit. He had been born in the far north-eastern corner of the Punjab, in Barapind village, Sialkot District, which had been shelled during the Indo-Pak wars of 1965 and 1971, and he could see the mountains of disputed Kashmir from his home. His father was a long-bearded lay preacher famous for championing the Ahl-e-Hadith cause. Shoaib had dropped out of school even younger than Ajmal, and signed up in his teens for training at Muridke, hoping 'to make India bleed'.

By the end of the first evening, there was a fourth member of their band, Naseer Ahmed, a self-declared 'skinny runt from Faisalabad'. Coming from the Punjab's second-largest city, he was more self-assured than the rest. Naseer lived in a lane close to the city's famous Masjid Mubarik Ahl-e-Hadith, a Lashkar-supporting mosque, north-east of the city centre. Around the mosque, shops openly displayed fundraising boxes for Lashkar's charity wing and its functionaries were local celebrities. Naseer had got swept along, working for Lashkar from an early age, recruiting poor boys from remote villages. Despite his slim frame and reedy voice, he was brave and fearless.

Ajmal, Hafiz, Shoaib and Naseer knuckled down. When the gruelling course neared its end they were told to assemble on a parade ground. A tall, slim, clean-shaven army officer was waiting for them. He looked out of place among the beards and pyjamas, but *amir* Saeed and *chacha* Zaki embraced him and Al-Qama introduced him: 'This is a Major General Sahib and we people are his men only.'

No one baulked. Everyone knew there were many Pakistani army officers in Lashkar. A colonel who claimed to have left in 2005 openly ran the organization's information department. Some were disaffected soldiers who believed the military no longer had the liberation of Kashmir in its sights. Others believed the army was appeasing the enemies of Islam. Most of these military men referred to themselves as retired. Whether they were or not, only they knew. Lashkar was a tangled ball of wool, creating cover for the machinations of the deep state.

The Major General Sahib clicked his heels, and set off on an inspection tour of the barracks before leaving as circumspectly as he had arrived. Afterwards, training became harder. Climbing into the thick forests above the camp, the recruits reached the remotest bases: Maskar-e-Ummalkura and the Al-Aqsa (named after the third-holiest site in Islam, the mosque in Jerusalem). They hurled grenades in live-fire exercises. They shot off rounds until their arms were numb. They climbed with packs into the icy night, as Qahafa the Bull and Al-Qama ambushed them, firing shots over their heads and between their feet.

Finally, towards the end of July, they were paired off into 'buddies' and trained in two-man commando operations. They learned to communicate using hand signals. In abandoned buildings, they were taught how to enter and clear a room, criss-crossing each other at the doorway. They watched Al-Qama shield doors from blasts by holding a mattress up against them. They role-played hostage taking, and were taught how to interrogate captives. Everything hinged on the final test: three days without food, water or maps in the woods, hunted by the instructors. Ten recruits ran away. But when Ajmal, Hafiz, Shoaib and Naseer emerged, emaciated and frozen, they were feted by Al-Qama.

They received a goat, a knife and a matchbox, and were told to prepare their own graduation meal.

Mid-August 2008. David Headley was now sure that he was being kept at arm's length by Lashkar and Major Iqbal, of the ISI, who had begun communicating with him on a mobile phone number with a New York City code – even though he was in Pakistan. The Major, who avoided all face-to-face meetings, explained that Inter-Services Intelligence had started using Internet telephony, hiring lines and numbers all round the world to put competing spy agencies off the scent.

Headley's private life added to his stress. M2 (Faiza) was making threats against him and M1 (Shazia), but he could not bring himself to shut her off completely. He needed a change of scene. He took Shazia and their now four children to the popular hill station of Murree, three hours' drive north of Islamabad, returning on 19 August, the day General Pervez Musharraf was finally forced to step aside, handing the reins to a civilian leader, Asif Ali Zardari, the widower of Benazir Bhutto, and the Prime Minister, Yousaf Raza Gilani, for whom Headley's brother Danyal worked as a press officer.

A message was waiting for him from Lashkar's Sajid Mir. Delighted, Headley set off for the Ice Box. When he got there, Mir's manner suggested that Operation Bombay was imminent. But, rather than revealing anything, Mir roped him into a slew of menial tasks that exploited his anonymity. Headley was sent down the hill with a shopping list: ten Chinese backpacks, one for each attacker. He chose ones with logos in English declaring 'Changing the Tide' – that seemed an appropriate tag line for a seaborne attack. He was dispatched to the Indian border to test Indian SIM cards procured by Lashkar's 'Mice'. Five identical Nokia 1200 handsets had been purchased, black and silver, one for each two-man team.

Headley seemed to know he was being used. Worrying about Lashkar and the ISI growing cold on him, he dwelt on his family's safety, too. On 8 September, he sent Shazia and his children to stay with his school friend Dr Rana's extended family in Chicago. He also drafted a will. Its executor was Rana, whose immigration business Headley had usurped to build a cover in Mumbai. Headley wrote to him, addressing the email, 'Dear Doc'. First he applied himself to the vexing issue of his fiery on-off marriage to Faiza. In case of his death, she was to be encouraged to leave Pakistan for Canada, where she would be out of everyone's way. 'Send her $350 a month thru Pasha.' That was all she was worth to him. 'Communicate with her thru him and don't give her your numbers, even if you call her. When she does get her visa, give her $6,000, tickets and instructions.'

He turned to Shazia. She was to be sent back to her family in Lahore and he asked Rana to try to get his sons into Aitchison College, Pakistan's most prestigious private school, whose alumni included the cricketer turned politician Imran Khan. Headley then listed assets he had recently inherited from his mother, Serrill. They were to be passed on to Shazia and their children. There was no mention of his father, Saleem Gilani, who had disowned his wayward son. 'That's all my old friend.'

After hearing about the will, Faiza was furious. She wrote to Headley's US lawyer, John Theis, seeking her rights as his 'legally wedded wife'. Then she brazenly barged into Lashkar's Qadisiya mosque in Lahore. 'I had to wait from 11 a.m. to 7 p.m.,' she wrote, concealing how frightened she must have been entering Lashkar's domain as an uninvited woman. 'I was checked from head to toe. I asked them, "What the hell are you doing?" I said, "I just have a problem about my husband and need to understand what is going on."' When the mosque authorities prevaricated, she began shouting out her husband's name, until *amir* Hafiz Saeed emerged. She complained that Headley routinely assaulted her. She mentioned the pillow talk about espionage and jihad. Thinking that he had already contained the Headley problem, Hafiz Saeed was horrified but he pledged to talk to Faiza's husband.

Headley found out by text message. He felt humiliated and exposed. He changed his email address (impervious2pain@yahoo.com) and hired a lawyer to make his separation with Faiza final. When she received the letter, Faiza called at Headley's home. 'A week ago you were in love with me and missing me,' she shouted at him. 'What happened?' Headley ordered his bodyguard to get her off the premises. As they argued at the gate, she was punched and kicked, before running off tearfully to the women's section of Race Course police station, around the back of the five-star Pearl Continental hotel, pressing assault charges.

Within hours, David Headley was under arrest. He was held in custody and questioned about attempting to kill his wife. Finally, after eight days a senior officer arrived and opened the cell door, ushering Headley out on the orders of 'someone higher up', possibly in the Prime Minister's office. As he put Headley into a taxi, he stooped down and whispered: 'Stay out of the limelight for *all* of our sakes.' Headley went home to Shazia, only to be called to Qadisiya mosque, where *amir* Hafiz Saeed was waiting. 'Shut her up or get rid of her,' he said, referring to Faiza. 'Then, go home and pray for forgiveness.'

Muzaffarabad

High above the House of the Holy Warriors training complex, a circle of tents was pitched in the thin air of the upper camp. Ajmal Kasab and his comrades lay inside, lean after seven months of praying, running and shooting. Their blood ran faster in their veins and they talked among themselves of their 'falcon spirit' being ready to pounce on its prey. They knew their trainers, Qahafa the Bull and Al-Qama, better than their fathers and now they were told by them to go home to make their goodbyes to their families. Ajmal was handed 1,300 rupees (£10) for the journey, with instructions to impress on his mother how *izzat* (honour) would be bestowed for giving her son to a higher cause. In Faridkot, she was delighted to see him, cooking biryani like he was a bridegroom and she was giving him away. When news spread of his arrival, neighbours came to pay their respects, too, noting that Ajmal seemed withdrawn. He wanted to stay at home, he said, and welled up when he left for the bus stop. He arrived back at the House of the Holy Warriors seven days later to discover their group had shrunk once more.

Those left in the dwindling band were told to rename themselves with *kunyah*, or battle aliases, a sign that they had been born again into a new family of the pure. Ajmal could not think of anything original. In the end he chose the most obvious, Abu Mujahid, while Hafiz Arshad became Abdul Rehman 'Bada' (the elder) and Shoaib became Abu Soheb. Naseer Ahmed, the skinny runt, became Abu Umer. They all signed pre-written wills that declared how their breasts shone with purity and how they desired to quench their anger on the battlefield, before celebrating with a film show, sitting in a circle around Al-Qama, watching *fidayeen* attacks in Indian-administered Kashmir. When someone asked if they would be heading over the Line of Control, too, Al-Qama was elliptical in his response.

He was a veteran at preparing *fidayeen* for martyrdom, a task that he often bragged required him to infantilize the would-be commandos, instilling in them a child-like reverence, so that when they had to contemplate their own deaths or the killing of others, they would submit to orders that a freethinking adult would baulk at. He was particularly good on psychology and had spent much time analysing the make-up of each recruit so that when the time came he would match the strongest with the weakest.

By the next morning, the group had got smaller still. Al-Qama revealed that one team had already been assigned, and was en route to Indian-administered Kashmir. Out of an original pool of thirty-two trainees, there were only fifteen left, and in August they returned to the warm campus of Muridke, outside Lahore. In the stagnating Lashkar swimming pool, down the far end of the camp, they practised treading water for hours and recovered objects thrown into the viscous water.

The group shrank again when two recruits ran away. Not everyone wanted to become a martyr. Al-Qama told *chacha* he needed a date for Operation Bombay. The longer it took to launch, the more time there was for the boys to brood.

Ajmal conceded to the others that he was terrified, and wished he had stayed home with his mother. Abdul Rehman 'Chhota' (little) was suffering more than any of them. Once known as Mohammed Altaf, he came from the brick kilns of a village so impoverished it had only a number, 511, located thirty miles from Vehari, the Punjab's City of Cotton. Breaking the rules, Chhota called home a dozen times, and was overheard asking a family member to pay Lashkar to free him.

The outfit could not lose another recruit and Abu Shoaib was ordered to mentor the desperate Chhota. Although he was the youngest at only eighteen, Shoaib, with his unruly black curls, dense eyebrows and stubby jaw, had emerged as a resilient fighter. After a martyrdom lecture, Al-Qama had asked if anyone was scared. Shoaib had raised his hand. 'What is there to be scared of when the only thing to look forward to in this life is death,' he told the class.

Al-Qama gathered them all together, waited for quiet and asked them to close their eyes 'There is nothing more a brother can give than his life for jihad,' he told them. 'And his reward will be infinite.'

September 2008 – Karachi

Early in the month, an apprehensive Ajmal Kasab and twelve others were put on a train for Karachi, with no idea where they were to be deployed. The group included Ajmal's sidekicks Umer, Abdul Rehman and Shoaib, and were lodged in a place codenamed 'Azizabad'. That was the name of an upmarket district in central Karachi, and Lashkar used it to misdirect snoopers, as their 'Azizabad' was actually in a secret compound in Yousaf Goth, a district in the far north of Karachi, Pakistan's volatile seaside megalopolis. If there is safety in numbers, then here in the City of Lights, among the 21 million legal residents, anything could be hidden.

Azizabad looked like any other family house. But behind its curly iron gates and permanently closed curtains were dorms and a classroom stocked with navigational training manuals, procured by the ISI's double agent, 'Honey Bee'. A map of the Indian coastline was pinned to the wall. For relaxation, there was a small library of jihadi magazines and pamphlets, including the Lashkar primer, *Why are We Waging Jihad?* But after the kinetic camps the boys found it hard to sit around. Since the holy month of Ramadan had also begun, the team were fasting, which only served to increase everyone's fractiousness. When they were not attending training sessions, they mostly slept, idling away the hours until sundown – when they could eat.

An instructor from Muridke, Abu Hamza, joined them. Although only a lowly soldier in the outfit, he was the perfect fit for Operation Bombay. His real name was Syed Zabiuddin Ansari, and he was a

28-year-old Indian by birth, raised in the rural hinterlands of central Maharashtra. He knew Mumbai well. Fluent in Marathi, Hindi and Urdu, he had travelled to Pakistan in his teens, settling in the southern Punjab. Radicalized by watching TV footage of the devastating anti-Muslim riots in Gujarat in 2002, he had joined Lashkar. They placed him back in India in 2006 to amass a weapons stockpile and assist in a series of bomb blasts. His tradecraft had been poor, his cover blown in under a year, with many fellow *mujahideen* slain and jailed, leaving Lashkar with no alternative other than to ex-filtrate him back to Pakistan, via Bangladesh, in a costly operation that had left the outfit's *sura* keen to expel him.

But now, using the name Hamza, he had been given a second chance with a job that even this accident-prone Indian *mujahid* could not foul up. Hamza began to teach Ajmal and the team serviceable Marathi and Hindi so they could talk to a taxi driver and ask for directions. India was a fearful and foreign concept to the boys, so while he was at it Hamza also explained the Hindu caste system, how they ate and prayed. He coached them in its culture, while outside the gates of Azizabad a Lashkar procurement operation was stepped up.

Since April 2008, Lashkar had amassed an Operation Bombay war chest of 2,168,000 rupees (£14,000). The outfit was so used to being sheltered by the ISI that its moneyman did not even bother to use an alias, keeping the funds in his own account at the Allied Bank in Drigh Colony, Karachi.

The moneyman rented safe houses for Lashkar instructors, ten of whom would assist the running of Operation Bombay, and he gave 180,000 rupees (£1,175) to a Lashkar lieutenant and registered boat operator to buy an outboard engine from ARZ Water Sports in Karachi. He purchased sixteen life jackets, an air pump, inflatable dinghies and a boat, the *Al-Hussaini*, a legal carrier, with a Port Clearance Certificate (PCC) BFD-5846 issued by Pakistan Customs. As backup, he bought a second smaller boat, the *Al-Fouz*, paying 80,000 rupees (£522) in cash, and leased a third, the *Al-Atta*. Next he recruited fourteen sailors, signing up a Lashkar sympathizer as *tindal* (coxswain), who was given the codename Hakim-saab. They could rely on Hakim as he had helped them in smuggling operations the previous year.

The boat operator's father, known as 'the 'Hajji', was also put to work scouting for a launch spot, settling on a forty-eight-acre site with five thatched huts and a three-bedroomed brick house in Goth Ali Nawaz Shah, a village beyond the south-eastern fringes of the sprawling city. Less than a mile from a creek that flowed out to the Arabian Sea, it was the perfect spot to learn the basics of sailing and clambering in and out of boats. Here the recruits could prepare for the unpredictable open waters without drowning or being overlooked. The coast guard was reporting unseasonal swells, with massive waves pounding the shores. The newspapers were full of death notices.

Two days after arriving in Karachi, Ajmal and the others visited. Glad to be outside, they happily practised deflating and inflating dinghies, capsizing and righting the boats, stripping down, drying and oiling their weapons after they had been dunked. They unpacked large zinc chests, padded out with pink foam. Inside were detonators, sticky tins of powdered RDX explosive, grenades and cartridges. The first bomb assembly classes began immediately, and afterwards they ventured out into open waters for the first time. For landlocked boys who had lived their lives in the arid scrub, it must have been terrifying.

One hour out from the shore, they glimpsed the *Al-Hussaini*. Hakim-saab, the coxswain, welcomed them on board and familiarized them with marine charts, explaining the basics of navigation. Over the next two days, they learned how to use the boat's GPS system and perfected their cover as a fishing expedition, flinging nets and hauling them in, roasting the fish they caught on a brazier at night, all of them desperate to know when they were sailing and where to.

After three days, Al-Qama turned up. Phase one was over. He announced that he was taking the team back to the dry and cool of the mountains. It took twenty-four hours to reach the House of the Holy Warriors, where *amir* Hafiz Saeed and *chacha* Zaki greeted them with unsettling news. The group that had been living and training together for many months was to be divided. Six of them had been assigned a mission in Kashmir that had just jumped the queue. They all waited anxiously for their names to be called. Ajmal Kasab was not on the list. What had they in mind for him? Lashkar was like a conveyor belt that never gave self-doubt time to seed.

After their colleagues had departed, *chacha* introduced three new men. 'They are *fidayeen* like you,' he explained, understanding how difficult it would be to integrate the new faces. Ajmal discovered that two of the new boys, Fahadullah and Javed, were from villages in his home district of Okara. As they ate, Fahadullah, twenty-four, revealed he was the nephew of Qahafa the Bull. He had two fingers missing from his left hand, which the boys assumed was a battle wound and seemed, in these jittery days, strangely reassuring. In fact it was a birth defect, but the boy had been told by his uncle not to tell anyone, lest they think him unlucky.

Javed was from Gugera, a village north of Okara, the youngest of seven, and had spent his childhood in a *madrassa*. At sixteen he told his parents he intended to join Lashkar. His father, a grain trader, had been furious and tried to marry him off to a fourteen-year-old neighbour. Javed had run away, taking shelter in Lashkar's district HQ at Okara. From there he was smuggled to the Muridke campus, where he disappeared into the training regime, shed his real family and joined another, taking the battle name Abu Ali.

The third new arrival, Ismail Khan, from a North West Frontier Province town of the same name, was the only non-Punjabi in the group. He kept to himself until the thirteenth day of the *Roza* (as the Ramadan fast days are known) – 13 September – when *amir* Hafiz Saeed returned, alongside the Major General.

'The time for jihad has now come,' the *amir* solemnly announced, taking his familiar stance, hands against chest. Ajmal recalled the silence that followed, as if everyone had inhaled. 'You are to attack mainland India.' Ajmal, who had always presumed he was heading for Indian-administered Kashmir, was stunned. Before he could process the information, *chacha* Zaki stepped forward to speak. 'The financial clout of India is created in the powerhouse of Bombay. You are to attack using a sea route.' Ajmal looked around and could see that the others were just as shocked. Lashkar operations rarely strayed into major Indian cities. Behind him, the Major General grinned broadly. He whispered into Zaki's ear before Lashkar's commander continued: 'Are you all ready?' The room stayed silent. Zaki tried again: 'The Major General Sahib wants to see how well-prepared you are.'

He took the quaking boys outside and issued them with AK-47s and rounds. 'Load up and rip up the targets. Fire as many as you want to,' Zaki ordered. The ten let loose, drilling shots into targets until their eyes streamed.

Then they were taken into a part of the camp they had not seen before, entering a room filled with TVs and maps of capital cities from around the world. It was Lashkar's data centre and they were introduced to Abu Zarrar Shah, the outfit's media chief. He had spent the last few months assembling a portable communications network, designed by a team of young, unemployed IT graduates, recruited by Lashkar in Dubai, Karachi and the Gulf States, and codenamed 'the Owls'.

Experimenting with Internet telephony, the Owls had conceived an invisibility cloak to remotely control the gunmen after they landed in Mumbai while shielding Lashkar's involvement. Zarrar's men had rented Internet phone lines and phone numbers from Callphonex, a company in New Jersey. The legitimate service was popular among migrant customers who needed to make cheap calls to family and friends thousands of miles away, using a VoIP system similar to Skype. The gunmen in Mumbai would be able to use local, prepaid Indian SIM cards, to dial leased international numbers in Austria that diverted the calls via Callphonex to Pakistan. It would be difficult for Indian investigators to unravel, as everything beyond the US hub was invisible.

The transaction with Callphonex had been made online, Zarrar passing himself off as a reseller based in India, the money sent as a wire transaction that would at some point trigger suspicion, as it originated in Islamabad. But by then the operation would be under way. 'Zarrar Shah had great knowledge of computers,' Ajmal recalled, dazed by the equipment that he worried was too complicated for all of them to master. Zarrar reassured him that he would have to do nothing other than press the green call button on his Nokia twice, in order to be connected to his Lashkar handlers back in Pakistan.

The Owls had had another simple idea. Zarrar showed Ajmal how he was using Google Earth to zoom into and around a city that none of them had ever visited, travelling through it at street level. Once their individual missions had been allocated, Google Earth would be their guide, companion and tour operator.

Taken back outside, Qahafa the Bull and Al-Qama 'buddied them up' into five teams of two, a classic *fidayeen* formation. Qahafa and Al-Qama had psychologically anatomized the men, working hard to identify types that would complement each other. Team one would be Ajmal Kasab and Ismail, where Ismail was the hard-stepping lead man, capable of carrying impressionable Ajmal, who Lashkar feared could flip or run. Team two was Umar and Akasha, who were similarly balanced. Team three: Shoaib and Umer. Team four: Abdul Rehman 'Bada' and Ali. And team five: Abdul Rehman 'Chhota' and Fahadullah, the nephew of Qahafa.

The attack was planned for the twenty-seventh day of *Roza*, 27 September 2008, which gave them only two weeks. 'You will reach Bombay by hijacking an Indian boat.' The boys were overwhelmed, Ajmal unable to countenance how any of this would be achieved or what his role would be. The Arabian Sea scared them all. The idea of a marine hijacking was terrifying. Hauling an anchor, navigating the undulating currents on their own, landing on a foreign shore, charging into an alien city at night, all of these things weighed on him. Even worse, the proposed date for the attack was also his twenty-first birthday.

Finally, Zaki named the targets, most of which they had never heard of: Chhatrapati Shivaji Terminus, Malabar Hill, the Leopold Café, the Trident–Oberoi hotel, Chabad House and the Taj hotel. Two teams of two each would focus on the last, the most important target.

They were to maim and kill as many people as possible from America, Britain, and Israel 'because these people have severely oppressed Muslims'. They were to keep in mind 'that no Muslim should succumb in the attack'. To create maximum chaos, each attacker would also carry an RDX bomb and plant it at a congested location, making it appear that there were many more *fidayeen* fanning across the city than just ten. The attack was to start at 7.30 p.m., the busiest time of day. Even though it appeared daunting, the nuts and bolts of the mission were simple, said Al-Qama, calling up each team in turn to brief them quietly on their specific target.

Ajmal and Ismail would mow down commuters at CST before heading up into Malabar Hill, where they would cull the rich. Shoaib and Umer would kill tourists with assault rifles and grenades at the Leopold Café, before joining Abdul Rehman 'Bada' and Ali to raid the Taj hotel, which they were to set alight, seizing hostages.

Umar (real name Nasir) and Akasha would lay siege to Chabad House, capturing Jews, executing them on orders. Fahadullah and Abdul Rehman 'Chhota' were to storm the Trident–Oberoi hotel, killing guests and staff, before taking captives.

Each team were shown videos of their target, filmed months ago by David Headley. They studied the complex map he had helped build, overlaid with GPS waypoints, showing how the targets could be accessed from the sea, by taxis and on foot. Those going into the Taj were shown a 3D animation that Zarrar had found on Google Earth, paid for by the hotel as a marketing tool. It enabled them to travel around the south and north wings of the Palace, to spin around the Tower, as well as trotting by the entrances and exits, and along Merriweather Road towards the Leopold Café.

Qahafa took the floor. To blend in, each *fidayeen* would be given fake ID cards with Hindu names, showing them to be students of the Arunodaya Degree College in Hyderabad. They were asked to memorize their new IDs. 'No one will suspect you. Even the police will be misled.'

Crucially, the trainers – Qahafa the Bull, Al-Qama and Hamza, as well as Zarrar Shah – would be with the team all the way. Lashkar was preparing a control room kitted out with phones, computers,

TV screens and detailed maps of Mumbai so the trainers could advise, cajole and steer the operation, minute by minute. The control room would be located in Malir Town, an upmarket military cantonment in Karachi, one of the city's plushest residential enclaves, close to the international airport. The area was patrolled by the security services round the clock – making it the safest place to be, if you were a proxy of the state.

On the fifteenth day of *Roza*, Qahafa the Bull and the Indian *mujahid* Hamza took the team into the hills above the House of the Holy Warriors to let off steam. They were ordered to run and fire, rolling and diving. There was a surfeit of ammunition. 'Do as you please.' They spent the afternoon being taught how to prepare a lunch box bomb, cramming sticky white RDX into tiffin tins layered with pink foam, attaching a fuse and timer of a kind that Al-Qama bragged had been used by the Taliban and Al-Qaeda in 2,800 attacks in Afghanistan and Pakistan. The *fidayeen* capped the evening off with shooting practice. 'Fire until you can shoot no more,' Al-Qama shouted through the confetti of shredded targets.

On the sixteenth day of *Roza*, the barber arrived. He took a cut-throat razor to their *Hadeethi* beards and straggly locks before they were photographed for their student ID cards.

On the seventeenth day of *Roza*, the team returned to Karachi and the Azizabad safe house. An Urdu magazine, *Tayabat*, had been left lying around. Ajmal noticed a brief item about six *fidayeen* who had been martyred in Indian-administered Kashmir. He recognized the names and his stomach flipped. They were his recently departed comrades. He was transfixed by the news, trying to suppress the feeling that they, too, were destined to die. He hid the magazine from the team. It was bad enough that he knew. Why scare them too?

On the nineteenth day of *Roza*, Qahafa distributed ten timers and explained how to prime them, asking each team member to mark one with his name, as if telling school children to label their coats before hanging them in the cloakroom. 'These are for the big bangs,' he said simply. They were taken back to the creek. They sailed out to meet Hakim-saab aboard the *Al-Hussaini*, growing more confident on the water, the captain showing them how to pilot a yellow inflatable speedboat, their landing craft for Mumbai. He taught them how to sink a boat by 'removing its valve' and explained *tul* and *chaurai*, the lines of longitude and latitude. At night they worked on learning their ciphers: names, addresses, colleges. They lay on the deck, staring at the stars.

On the twenty-sixth day of *Roza*, each team member was given a well-packed rucksack containing enough ammunition to launch a sustained terrorist attack and enough food and water to keep them going for more than twenty-four hours. There were a Kalashnikov, eight magazines – 240 rounds – eight hand grenades, one bayonet, one pistol, three pistol magazines, one water bottle, a one-kilo pack of raisins and almonds, headphones, three nine-volt batteries, a battery charger and a tiffin box containing eight kilos of RDX. Supply sacks for the journey were also handed over and contained blankets, rice, flour, oil, pickles, milk powder, matches, detergent, tissue paper, bottles of Mountain Dew, toothpaste, tooth brushes, razors and towels. They were issued with new Western clothes and told to cut out the labels. All of them were handed watches set thirty minutes ahead, to Indian time. Abu Hamza distributed an emergency float of 10,800 Indian rupees (£130) for each buddy pair, a GPS handset, and a black and silver pre-programmed Nokia 1200. Finally the men taped their AK-47 magazines together in combat configuration, allowing a rapid turn-around. 'Sleep well,' Hamza whispered, as he switched off the light.

On 27 September, they set out in two dinghies. The currents swirled around them, the wind whipping in, hauling them on to rocks, sinking the boats and leaving the inexperienced sailors treading water for hours in their life jackets, fearing they would die, until at last they were rescued, disorientated and terrified.

A few nights later, they tried again, another boat having been purchased. A growling storm from nowhere ran them down. They could not break through it. Hundreds of gallons of diesel were wasted and Hakim-saab lost control of the *Al-Hussaini,* steering too close to an Indian trawler that, fearing pirates, fired on them. The crew of seasick Punjabis beat a retreat. Back on dry land, their battle packs and new clothes were taken away and the dejected team were led back to Azizabad. They sat waiting, doing nothing, until Eid arrived on 1 October. Now the trainers tried to rebuild their confidence, throwing a lavish feast, making a biryani from a whole goat. Afterwards, two of the recruits demonstrated how to plant bombs beneath the seat of a moving taxi, without being seen by the unsuspecting driver – while all the others watched and ate sweet *jalabis*.

Then there was nothing. For six dead weeks they sat around. Ajmal counted the days, becoming desperate. They all ate and slept, their frustration and fear mounting – the atmosphere inside the house sliding into paranoia. Finally, on 21 November, the team were woken and packed into a jeep with blacked-out windows that drove to the creek-side base. They got out to find their planners – *chacha* Zaki, Hamza, Zarrar, Qahafa and Al-Qama – waiting in a line. The battle packs, cash, mobiles, satellite phones and GPS machines were redistributed before *chacha* Zaki addressed them all. The weather was fine and a moonless night was coming. This was their window. Brother Ismail was to be made overall leader, while Umer would take charge of the two teams in the Taj. Finally, Zaki told them he was off on *haj*, from where he would pray for success.

'*Amir* Hafiz and all of us have made huge efforts for this mission. Your training must now come to fruition. We have made you capable and skilled warriors. Do your duty and do not bring shame on yourself.' Zaki surveyed the ten frowning faces. He solemnly held out his hands upturned, and prayed like a true *Hadeethi*.

'May Allah take care of you and protect you.'

At 5.00 a.m. on 22 November, the teams were woken for *namaz*. By 6 a.m., they started walking with their packs, reaching the creek.

Ismail was issued with the satellite phone. At 7 a.m., a dinghy drew in, and they clambered aboard. Sea-going currents tugged at them gently for ninety minutes, until they reached a bigger vessel. They boarded and sailed for many hours.

By 9 p.m. that night they glimpsed the familiar silhouette of the *Al-Hussaini*. Aboard, Hakim-saab was waiting and had his crew haul the kitbags and men on to the deck, before he and three others sailed back for Karachi. The ten attackers and a crew of seven set a course south-east across the Arabian Sea, inhaling the smell of fuel and fish that set their stomachs on edge.

The following morning, 23 November, they crossed into Indian waters. From now on, even their cover story would not save them if they came across an Indian navy patrol. Jails in Gujarat were crammed with trespassing Pakistani sailors, some of whom might have been fishermen, none of whom were spared by the courts that condemned them to squalid prisons, where they rotted.

Finally, they spotted an Indian fishing trawler with its elevated wooden prow rising like a Viking warship, its name, MV *Kuber*, painted in black, blue and yellow letters on the wheelhouse. The first test was upon them. As it drew near, a Lashkar brother produced a broken fan belt and waved it in the air as if they were adrift. The two boats came together, and the *fidayeen* leapt on to the Indian vessel, overpowering the crew, wrestling the unsuspecting fishermen on to *Al-Hussaini*, leaving only the Indian *nakhva* (captain), Amarchand Solanki, on board MV *Kuber*. After transferring their kit on to the new vessel, Solanki was dragged into the engine room and tied up.

The *Al-Hussaini* crew slaughtered the rest of the Indian fishing party and threw their bodies over the side, before turning back towards Karachi.

Aboard the MV *Kuber*, the *fidayeen* were finally alone. All of them sat on deck, grim-faced, as for the first time heavy waves reared up and slapped the deck. Brother Ismail knew what to do. He switched on his satellite phone and listened to the static. '*Salaam Alaikum?*' he tried, his voice breaking up as his nerves got the better of him. They all waited, afraid of the phone. Had they been abandoned?

Then a voice: '*Walaikum assalam.*'

They cheered. It was the familiar tone of Abu Hamza, the Indian *mujahid*, replying from the Karachi control room at Malir Town. They had not been abandoned, even if they were pitching and yawing. For the next thirty-two hours they sailed, feeling more optimistic, bearing south-south-east for 309 nautical miles, forcing Solanki to check his boat's course, keeping the control room up to date with their progress. The team took it in turns to stand guard, cook and sleep, writing their duty times in a ruled schoolbook.

At 4 p.m. on 26 November, their confidence ebbed when they spotted the coastline of India. Soon after, recalled Ajmal, 'We started seeing the tall buildings of Bombay.' Stunned, they stood on deck and stared. By 6 p.m., they could see before them all the evidence that a person who had never left Pakistan needed of the riches gleaned from near-stability and partial secularism, a vista of palms, towers and villas, strung with lights, of hotels and offices blazing with neon.

'Make it burn. Set it all alight, my brothers,' Al-Qama had said, as the dinghies left the creek in Karachi. Did he worry that they might waver upon arrival, preferring to abscond, and disappear in successful, mercantile Mumbai? 'What should we do with the Indian captain?' Ajmal asked, snapping everyone out of their reverie, and not wanting to decide on his own.

Ismail got on the phone to Abu Hamza in Karachi control. 'Do whatever you want,' the Indian *mujahid* said, urging them to make the decision. Ajmal looked at Ismail: 'Kill him?' he whispered, shaking. Ismail nodded. Shoaib and Umer held Solanki's legs while Ajmal closed his eyes, scrunching his face up, clutching the man's hair, before cutting his throat, concealing the horror that overcame him.

They had stepped over a threshold. All of them were blooded.

Above deck, the yellow inflatable was prepared. Before lowering it into the sea, they prayed, and changed into their new clothes. Ismail handed out the ID cards and red Hindu threads that Headley had bought at Mumbai's Shree Siddhivinayak Ganapati Mandir, a multi-storey cream-coloured Ganesha temple, popular with Bolly-wood stars.

The few signs that pointed to Pakistan as their homeland had been shorn and they had been turned into faceless martyrs in a conscious process of attenuation that saw their willpower and self-image whittled away, until they felt grateful for being sent to their deaths. Looking at the others, their hair slicked down with almond oil, Ajmal recalled being briefly unable to tell them apart. They could be anyone among one billion people, he thought. They were no one.

Above the roar of the Yamaha engine, Brother Ismail held a GPS aloft, like the boat's figurehead, guiding them to the darkened huts of Badhwar Park and the fishermen's colony that David Headley had earmarked as the perfect landing spot.

'Let's not bring disgrace upon us all,' Ismail shouted before the engines were cut, and the boat glided between the fishing boats, nudging up to the shore.

Ahead Ajmal could hear muffled voices, and inhaled the smell of frying fish and fenugreek that made their stomachs growl. They allowed their eyes to grow accustomed to the gloaming, their ears attuning to the foreign accents. A TV was blaring, tuned in to the India–England cricket match. In the shacks ahead, a boisterous crowd of drinkers had gathered, their silhouettes weaving and swaying.

As he leapt ashore, Ajmal recalled *chacha* Zaki's parting blessing: 'May Allah make true everything you wish for in your heart.' He raced up the slip and into the city, heart pumping, tears in his eyes.

An hour later, David Headley received an SMS. With M1 (Shazia) ensconced in Chicago, he was back with M2 (Faiza) in a rented apartment in Lahore. 'Turn on your TV.' The sender was Sajid Mir. A second text bleeped soon after, from M1 herself. Shazia was watching television, too, and she congratulated her husband on 'the graduation'.

5

Lambs and Chickens

Wednesday, 26 November 2008, 11.30 p.m. – the Taj

A legion of camera crews from all over the subcontinent swirled around the Taj, reporters, anchors and their producers pooling in the lanes around its perimeter, their kitbags spilling and cables coiling. 'The city that never sleeps has been brought to its knees this Wednesday night by unprecedented multiple terror attack, bringing areas from the south to the north of the metropolis under its grip,' a *CNN–IBN* reporter bellowed, in the manner of Dashiell Hammett. Everyone was shouting to be heard, illuminating the night sky with their floodlights, leaching into each other's sightlines.

From his eyrie in the Rendezvous Room at the top of the Tower, the Marine captain, Ravi Dharnidharka, looked down over the scene in dismay. Why had no one locked down the perimeter? It all seemed out of control. The only thing that was missing was the most important thing of all: where were the blinking lights from the rescue vehicles? Bob Nicholls, an old hand in Mumbai who had had many dealings with the security establishment, feared that the response, when it came, would be too little, too late. 'We're going to have to look after ourselves,' he warned.

Down below, on the third floor of the Palace, Will and Kelly sat holding one another, listening out for the sounds of commandos clattering in to save them. 'That's what happens, right?' Will asked.

One and a half miles away, Commissioner Gafoor sat outside the Trident–Oberoi in his staff car, playing it by the book, which required him to lead from a secure position out in the field. But he and his front-line forces remained invisible to the besieged citizens of a terrified city and its guests. The specialist Quick Response Teams had finally made it downtown, only to be assigned to marshal the press, although they were so outnumbered that they hung back, listless and demoralized. Small units of police and soldiers aimlessly circled the hotel, like pedalos in a park, following Gafoor's instruction not to take on the gunmen inside the besieged buildings. They were to stand down until the National Security Guard (NSG), India's elite counter-terrorism force, arrived – Rakesh Maria had called for it almost immediately. 'Let the correct agency handle it,' the Commissioner argued, paralysing the whole emergency response network.

What no one in Mumbai realized was that the NSG was still penned in its barracks near Delhi, a three-hour flight away, and could only be mobilized when the Maharashtra government requested help. Yet state officials were still not ready to admit they were overwhelmed. The MARCOS, India's equivalent of the UK's Special Boat Service or the US Navy SEALs, were more accessible, with some men stationed down the road in Colaba. They could literally have jogged to the Taj. But they also required Maharashtra to make a formal call to the Western Naval Command. There, officers already had reservations, making it clear in high-level secret discussions that the MARCOS were 'the wrong dog for the fight'. Trained in anti-piracy actions, these Marines were happy on a Halo drop into a heaving sea, strapped into their 30kg kit, each with a crossbow across his back to silently knock out sentries on a ship's deck. But a five-star hotel was unknown territory.

It was more than two hours since the gunmen had entered the Taj, and so far only six policemen had followed them in, led by Vishwas Patil, the Deputy Commissioner of Police of Zone 1.

Inside, Patil, Rajvardhan – the chief of SB2 – and their small team were still flummoxed by the hotel's complex layout, while the gunmen seemed to have a far superior understanding of it and were using it to their advantage, playing hit-and-run among the 567 guest rooms. Recently the Black Suits had come up with an idea to narrow the odds, suggesting that the hotel's CCTV room, on the Palace's second floor, could afford a bird's-eye view.

Patil consulted Rajvardhan, who, in the last half-hour, had locked down the hotel's exits, immobilizing its lifts, and evacuated hundreds of guests hiding in ground floor shops and restaurants. He was ready for the hunt but warned they would need a guide to get up there. The Black Suit Puru Petwal, who had helped evacuate the Tower lobby, volunteered.

Petwal and the police party gingerly crossed into the Palace lobby, and almost immediately an ear-splitting blast knocked them off their feet. The gunmen were at the top of the Grand Staircase, hurling down grenades. Rolling clear, Petwal suggested an alternative route, leading the shaken team up a fire exit. Rajvardhan was cursing. Petwal was armed only with his mobile phone. No one had body armour or helmets. The police team of constables and inspectors had about fifty rounds between them. The two DCPs only had side arms, which were practically useless unless there was close-quarters fighting. They faced men with a full complement of firepower.

'The only person you can reliably kill with a high-power 9mm is yourself,' Rajvardhan whispered to his batch-mate, recalling the old training mantra about drawing your pistol, as they loped along the second floor of the south wing, passing the Taj Data Centre.

Inside, Florence Martis was agitated. Faustine had finally got through to her at 10 p.m. and had tried to break it to her gently. 'Don't get scared,' he said, 'but gunmen are inside the building. You should hide.' Faustine tried to steady his daughter: 'The Data Centre is not on the hotel map. No outsider can know it's there. I will come for you. Do you hear?'

But Florence *was* scared. She felt like a shaken bottle of cola. She frantically looked around: desks along three walls, half a dozen chairs, a small number of terminals and a printer, a couple of ancient upright fans. There was a small stationery room, where they hung their jackets, and the server room. She entered the latter, and her phone rang. 'Hello?' It was Precilla, her mother. 'Where *are* you?' she asked. 'Mum, I'm trapped in my office.' Florence felt tears welling, imagining being curled up on the sofa in her mother's arms. But right now she needed inspiration and not consolation.

Florence scrabbled for a calming thought, settling on Faustine on a Sunday, the only time all of them were together. He was steaming *idli* (savoury rice cakes), with mutton stewing on the back ring. Later, they would go to Mass at St Lawrence's, where they always sat on the same bench. She imagined walking in with her father to greet the congregation.

She turned off the lights, locked the door and sat in the dark, praying for her father to come. Suddenly all the phones started ringing. Was it the gunmen, hunting for hostages? She left the server room and went into the storeroom, hiding behind the coats. But it felt too claustrophobic.

There was smashing and splintering. She covered her ears. Someone close by was breaking down a door. Was she imagining this or was it real? Shots rang out below, possibly beside the pool. The smashing stopped and she could hear talking. The voices were in an unfamiliar language. Then there was screaming, gunshots and footsteps.

'Dear Lord,' she prayed, 'please save me. We have always prayed to you.'

One floor above the Data Centre, to the left of the Grand Staircase, and in room 316, Will and Kelly also heard desperate cries and then gunshots. It felt as if the bullets were drilling through the walls. Will got on his hands and knees, hunting for his mobile phone. He recovered it from a pile of clothes beside the bed. Hands trembling, he punched in his father's number. It was early evening back in England, and Nigel Pike was at home. After Will's mother had died from cancer five years previously, Will and his siblings had rallied round their father, bringing them closer together.

'Dad, we're in a situation,' Will whispered. 'The hotel is being attacked. It might be terrorists. We need help.' Nigel could hardly hear his son but caught the gist of it. 'Sit tight and keep your phones switched on,' he said, trying to keep the horror out of his voice. A dad was supposed to solve problems and yet he felt engulfed by this one. 'I'll make some calls.' He put down the phone and lit a cigarette. Will and Kelly were almost 4,500 miles away. What could he do to help?

Back in the Taj, someone knocked on a nearby door. Will and Kelly lay still in the dark, blood rushing to their heads. 'Answer? Don't answer?' Footsteps moved along the corridor. They could hear knocking at another door. Kelly lay down on the carpet, covering her ears, her heart thumping so loud she was sure Will could hear it. Will got up and crept over to the door to peek through the spyhole. 'Let's call reception,' whispered Kelly. 'They'll know what to do.' The call connected to the hotel's automated answering system. 'Fuck.' A dawning realization hit them both. No one was down there. 'Leave a message,' said Kelly, clutching at straws. 'Tell them we are stuck.' Dear Hotel, we are prisoners on the third floor. It felt ridiculous and, anyhow, Will did not understand the menu choices. He could not work out if he was still stoned or was addled by fear.

'We need to keep busy,' he said, as he began tearing the room apart, scouring it for hiding places. Kelly joined in, searching for vents in the ceiling, or cavities in the walls, both of them thinking how it was done in films. What tricks were they missing? It sounded stupid, but what would MacGyver do? He had loved the ingenious TV secret agent whose show he had watched obsessively as a child, transfixed by how McGyver had deployed his scientific know-how and his Swiss army penknife to get out of any fix. 'What about the cleaning cupboard?' he suggested, remembering an unmarked door he had spotted on their dash back from the staircase. 'Too exposed,' Kelly said, ruling it out. At least in this room they could try and get the windows open – if it came to that.

Will was sweating, every creak and distant footfall pounding in his head. Something was scratching around in the ceiling. They listened intently. There was some kind of scuffle going on up above them, feet drumming, furniture scraping and raised voices. Did they hear gunshots?

Up on the fourth floor, Rajiv Saraswati, an Indian businessman, had opened his door a chink, thinking that the police had arrived. Seeing a gunman, Saraswati tried to shut it, only for his assailant to let off a burst of rounds, catching Saraswati in the hand and body. Crying out, he shoulder-charged his door, summoning the strength from somewhere deep inside to force it shut before crumpling dead on the floor.

DCPs Patil and Rajvardhan had reached the CCTV room on the second floor of the Palace, but were struggling to get to grips with the system: half a dozen sub-screens on a monitor, which flicked between different cameras on different floors every few seconds, none of which were clearly marked. 'What a mess,' Patil cursed. The Black Suit Petwal took over, competently scrolling back and forth, while Patil's radio operator radioed Rakesh Maria, the Crime Branch chief: 'Tell Region Sir that we have sealed some points, operation is on inside.' There was no response. Patil grabbed the handset: 'Send help. With weapons, helmets and body jackets.' Control relayed the information across the grid: 'Zone 1 Sir is in the Taj.'

Rewinding the evening's CCTV recordings, Petwal found something. Patil and Rajvardhan crowded around to watch footage of two gunmen, one dressed in red, the other in olive yellow, entering the Tower lobby at 21.44. They positioned themselves either side of reception, and pulled out rifles. As guests began scattering, many of them falling, one of the gunmen threw a grenade, and the screen flared and popped. Petwal searched and pulled up more footage: catching the same two strolling along to the Northcote entrance, AK-47s cocked, the red one having turned his baseball cap back to front, ready to work.

Rajvardhan rattled off a quick assessment. Two operational gunmen meant they were working in pairs, which told him that there were at least four and possibly six or eight. If one team were out roving, others were acting as cut-outs, and no doubt stationed at the top of the Grand Staircase, taking control of the high ground, to choke off the main entrance and exit to the upper floors. One of them looks so fragile that if I gave him a slap he'll snap, Rajvardhan thought. But he studied how he held his AK-47. It was notoriously difficult to shoot a semi-automatic weapon with one hand – unless you were a Bollywood action hero. And yet this gunman wound the weapon's strap tightly around his forearm, pulling its wooden stock into the crook of his elbow and down on to his bicep, the way that the Special Forces were trained to.

The Black Suit found them again. In the Palace lobby at 21.55: the gunmen in red and yellow were joined by a third gunman, all in black, and a fourth dressed in a grey long-sleeved T-shirt. The black and the grey men were the two who had shot up the Leopold, crashing into the Taj through the Northcote entrance, surprising the waiter from Aquarius, Adil Irani. Petwal wound on, finding all four gunmen climbing the Grand Staircase to the first floor. One spun round and shot up Faustine Martis's Sea Lounge, while the others headed towards the Crystal Room, where the newlyweds Amit and Varsha Thadani were supposed to have made their grand entrance.

A sequence flashed up of Patil engaging the gunmen on the stairs. The DCP grimaced. If only he had had a rifle he would have ended it there and then. Petwal spooled on until 22.27, when the cameras caught the yellow gunman once more. Now he was on the fifth floor of the Palace, ringing the doorbell of room 551. They watched as the unwitting guest answered and was shot, his killer calmly stepping over the body to enter his room. The Black Suit rang through to Kudiyadi, the security chief, to check the guest list. It was Chaitlall Gunness, CEO of the State Bank of Mauritius. Someone would have to inform his family. Thirteen minutes later, the yellow gunman came out followed by the red gunman, who began knocking on neighbouring doors. They seized another guest and dragged him back into 551.

The police could not hang around. If the gunmen were not

stopped, they would continue to pick off guests, turning this assault into a prolonged kidnapping crisis, perhaps the worst of its kind in recent history.

The next frames showed all four gunmen entering room 551 at 22.48. Fast-forwarding the tape, Petwal turned to the others. 'I am a hundred per cent sure there are only four terrorists, and they are in that room together,' he urged. 'We have to move on them now.' Patil hesitated. Commissioner Gafoor had told everyone to wait for the NSG or MARCOS. Already they had pushed the boundary by giving chase without authorization.

Patil got on the radio. If they were going to storm the room, they needed backup. The Control Room agreed but the team sent struggled with the internal layout of the Taj. 'Assault Team 3 to South Control: We need location of Zone 1 Sir.' Patil's radio man tried to assist: 'Zone 1 Sir is on the *second floor* of Taj.' The labyrinthine hotel was confusing everyone. 'Assault Team 3 to Control: new Taj or old Taj?'

For ten minutes there was a flurry of muddled messages, before Assault Team 3 vanished. Patil was getting frustrated, and Control sent in a second unit, Assault Team 6: 'If you have bulletproof jackets, report to Zone 1 Sir on the second floor.'

Up in the CCTV room, the cameras showed that the four gunmen were still inside 551. But with every passing minute, the police were squandering the opportunity. Exasperated, Patil grabbed the handset: 'There are three, four terrorists inside Taj . . . We need help now.' Control confirmed it had assigned two teams of men and weapons: 'We have Assault 3 and 6 with weapons and bulletproof jackets.' But no one had arrived. Was it cowardice or a cock-up? 'We are still unassisted,' Patil radioed again. Then, Assault Team 6 came on to the network and revealed it was still lost: 'New or *old* Taj?'

Petwal called everyone over. 'It's finished,' he said, pointing to the screens. The four gunmen had just exited 551 and walked off camera. For the next forty minutes the police scoured the cameras. At 23.23, Petwal found them again. 'Sixth floor of the Palace,' he shouted. The gunmen were knocking on the door of the last room before the fire escape, at the pool end of the south wing, 632. 'Who is in that room?' Patil demanded. He recalled that Karambir Kang had told him that his wife and children were trapped on the sixth floor. 'Get the General Manager on the phone,' the DCP ordered his radio operator. Despite their differences, Patil felt for Karambir.

The General Manager was standing outside by the Gateway, which he had turned into an improvised control point for hotel staff, along with the Taj's group security chief and the hotel's shaken owner, Ratan Tata. He did not react when Patil told him the news, but calmly described his apartment's exact location on the sixth floor, the sea-facing southern corner at the opposite and of the corridor from 632. When he got off the phone he was agitated. He had told Neeti to sit tight and wait for the security forces to come, fully believing they would. Now the gunmen were up there and there still was no rescue party. Karambir's universe was caving in. For almost two decades his world-view had been informed by the gusto with which the private sector solved problems, especially the pragmatic Tata group. He had lost sight of the old India and its anaemic, foot-dragging public sector, in whose hands the lives of his wife and two young sons now rested.

The Taj's group security chief asked to speak to Petwal. If the police acted now they could trap the gunmen on the sixth. 'Tell DCP [Patil] to make two teams: one to go from the north and the other from the south,' he instructed. 'Our boys will escort the teams.' Even if the police inside the hotel did not have the firepower to kill the terrorists, they could pin them down in that room.

Patil agreed. Having lost the gunmen on the fifth, he was not going to let them get away again. But he still needed backup and he had to seek permission. Patil got back on the radio, urging Assault Team 6 to make their way inside: 'The terrorists are in room number 631 [sic] of the sixth floor of the old building. I am near the CCTV. I have three, four policemen with me. Please, you have to cover the sixth floor. You have to cover lifts of both sides. Control the staircase. You will get them automatically.'

Finally, Commissioner Gafoor called in and Patil presented a fait accompli: 'Sir, there are three terrorists in 632 and two in the lobby. In all there are five [sic] terrorists. I have people with me. I need help immediately.'

Commissioner Gafoor said: 'Understood.' But amid the chaos of the multiple attacks and bomb blasts, he had not heard Patil or chose not to listen to him, as he hung up, without issuing any new orders. Incredulous, and egged on by Rajvardhan, Patil radioed Control. The backup must come now: 'I am watching the CCTV camera. The lobby is safe.' He radioed again, five minutes later: 'The terrorists are *still* in room number 630 or 632. Convey what I am telling you to assault [team].' In desperation, he tried Rakesh Maria, too, on the private officers' network: 'Terrorists are in room number 631 [sic]. I have three, four people with me. DCP Rajvardhan is also here.' Could they have the green light now? Maria was overwhelmed, but encouraging: 'Well done [Patil]. I am sending assault teams to you. Army columns are also coming. They will surround the hotel.'

Patil and Rajvardhan waited. No one showed. Five minutes later one of the gunmen emerged from room 632, walked over to the CCTV camera and tried to smash it with a chair. Through the broken lens Patil could just make out two other gunmen piling up carpets and linen in the corridor, which they set on fire, filling the sixth floor with coils of smoke. The hotel was burning, the flames making the cameras flare, the smoke clouding them. The CCTV room was almost blind.

In room 632, a sharp double knock had jolted K. R. Ramamoorthy from his slumber. The banking executive from Tamil Nadu, whose friends called him Ram, sat up, his mouth parched. He went over to the window. It was pitch black, the waning moon having slipped away around 11.15 p.m. Down below nothing moved. Half an hour before, the 69-year-old had fallen asleep, waiting for bad news to pass.

Retired from a career transforming mediocre banks into international success stories, Ram had flown in yesterday to fulfil his non-executive duties at a finance company board meeting. He also had family commitments, and had wanted to catch up with an old colleague from the Reserve Bank of India. Earlier, he had eaten in Masala Kraft and strolled around the Gateway, as was his habit, watching the pony traps carry honeymooners around the bay. He had been disturbed by scurrying figures on the fifth floor of the hotel on his way back up, before being advised by the Taj operator to go to his room as some kind of crisis was under way.

A woman working for the board he served on had called around 10.30 p.m.: 'Sir, are you safe?' For the first time, he had begun to think he might not be. As he got off the line, he heard shots. He had lain down on the bed, restlessly snoozing. And now, someone was knocking on his door.

A bright voice called out in English: 'Room service.' For a minute, Ram thought of asking for some water. He told himself off and closed his eyes. He had to make the room appear empty in case gunmen were on the prowl. But he was no good at trickery. A modest person, he was a banker whose goal had been to make the institution memorable rather than the man. 'All my life I struggled not to be seen,' he told colleagues, explaining that he despised conspicuous consumption, with the Taj perhaps his only perk. 'Banking is opium: other people's money. It makes you drunk,' he warned. 'I was never fooled by the allure of debt or the promise of credit.' He disliked the trappings of status and never had a car pick him up from the airport when a taxi would do. 'We do not want to be above anyone else or to be seen to be,' he had told one of his teams, extolling the virtues of modesty.

Fifteen minutes later there was another knock. 'Shoe polish?' the voice called. Ram now knew someone *was* targeting his room. '*Nahi chahiye* [I don't want]', he blurted out. *Why have I done that?*, he cursed. A bullet punctured the door. He ran into the bathroom and crouched on the floor. More shots sounded out and two gunmen barged in, spotting straight away he was in the bathroom. He was weak, they heaved, and the door smashed backwards, leaving him sprawled under the sink.

Two young men shoved an AK-47 under his chin, so close up that he could smell their sweat. He felt faint. They were only twenty-four or twenty-five years old, younger than his son. The taller one wore a red cap with something written on it, a red T-shirt and looked like a gym trainer, fit and muscular. The other was shorter and thinner. Ram did not know why, but he began to well up. 'Please don't kill me,' he said. The men remained silent. As he tried to make eye contact, they signalled: 'Pull your shirt off.'

Terrified, Ram froze and they smashed a gun butt into his head, and then again, down on to his collarbone. He stared at them slack-jawed. The pain was agonizing. 'I have blood pressure,' he cried out, thinking even as he said it that this was the banker's curse. 'Strip,' one of them shouted, ripping at Ram's *kurta* (smock) and hauling him into the bedroom, tying his hands together with a plastic bag. They pulled down his trousers and ripped off his holy Brahminical chord, which they used to bind his legs. He was naked and hobbled. Humiliated, he closed his eyes. The larger man came over and smashed his gun into the banker's back. Ram felt his bones breaking. What did they want? Could they not simply ask for something? His body screamed, his heart racing. *Are they going to beat me to death in my bedroom, such a pointless, pitiful end to everything?*, he thought, crying out loudly now, coughing and wheezing, which only brought the gun butt down harder. He tried pleading for his life. The taller one kicked him and hissed in his ear: '*Choop raho* [shut up].'

Ram heard something land on the bed, a zip and then a metallic clanking and a click. A mobile phone rang and one of the gunmen answered, talking in Urdu. Ram got the gist. They were speaking to someone called *Wasi Bhai* (Brother Wasi). 'We have a lamb here,' said a gunman, sounding smug. Ram tried to calm himself. 'Come on, Ram,' he exhorted, recalling the face of his dearest mother, who had always prayed for him. *Will her prayers help me now?*, he wondered. If this was it, he wanted 'a quick end without pain'. But the door opened and two more gunmen entered, amid a swirl of acrid smoke.

11.45 p.m. – Colaba

A ten-minute drive away, Deven Bharti, the Crime Branch deputy, was waiting, eyes half closed, in an unmarked police car, with his laptop on his knee. With his narrow shoulders and finicky manner, Bharti was difficult to gauge. Often he seemed to be only half listening, when in fact he was recalling faces and constructing a mental timeline. In a force where might was right, Bharti was a subtle digger, a geek who talked nineteen to the dozen when he had got a case down pat. And very ambitious. Right now he was still tracking the phone number – +91 9910 719 424 – that the intelligence agencies had passed down the line, believing the terrorists or their handlers were using it.

In another vehicle a couple of blocks away, the deputy head of the Anti-Terrorist Squad was also waiting for +91 9910 719 424 to ring. Between them they hoped to triangulate the phone and locate a control room from which the attacks were being directed or at least find a gunman. The last call had been too brief for anyone to lock on to, and now they were back to the waiting game.

Shortly before midnight, +91 9910 719 424 came on again. The ATS team worked their way up from the Regent hotel on Colaba Causeway, heading along Shahid Bhagat Singh Marg, while the Crime Branch team began at the President, on Cuffe Parade, heading for Hotel Supreme. The signal was intermittent. Left on to Wodehouse Road, the patrols motored towards Hotel Bluebird and the Celeste, where they lost it. Bharti's men went back over the ground, and into the hotels, demanding guest registers, interrogating the duty managers, sizing up waiters and cross-examining doormen, inhaling the broad strokes of guests' lives: lists of visitors from Pakistan, Central Asia, Bangladesh, the Gulf States.

A few minutes later, Bharti drove north by the petrol pump, swerving around the besieged Chabad House Jewish centre, and then left around the crescent to Hotel Antique. +91 9910 719 424 was active again. The ATS deputy was up at the Shabnam hotel, off Strand Road, two blocks further north. It would make sense for the gunmen's control room to be here, at the heart of the unfolding attacks. Into the lobbies the police teams went once more, quizzing the desk clerks. But the signal fizzled and Bharti parked up.

When the phone came online a third time, the direction finders pointed Bharti towards the New Martin and Fariyas hotels and then on to the smarter Ascot. Finally a message went out to all cars: 'Locked on.' They had it. The number had been captured by three masts and isolated to one grid in Colaba, close to the Taj and the state police headquarters. But they were still a long way from finding their prey. The grid covered a thousand-metres-square area of densely packed apartments and forty hotels, which translated into many hundreds of rooms. They were within reach of the caller, but it would take all night to find him unless they had more clues to work with. As well as physically searching for the phone, the ATS needed to tap the line, in the hope that overheard conversations would guide them in.

Five miles north in Nagpada, an industrial quarter of South Mumbai, inside a Colonial-era villa set back from the highway in a garden of date palms, the ATS technical team were waiting, surrounded by a tangle of USB cables. Their boss, the ATS chief, Hemant Karkare, had called them in earlier, asking them to eavesdrop on +91 9910 719 424, using an Indian-designed interception package, the Shogi GSM monitoring system, which enabled them to divert the calls through a police landline, so they could record and analyse them from their desks.

But there was a problem. The phone company, Bharti Airtel, required written authorization from the ATS chief and the state. The last time anyone had seen Karkare had been on TV half an hour ago, when cameras had filmed him donning his bulletproof vest and helmet, preparing to enter Chhatrapati Shivaji Terminus. The state official authorized to sign was trapped inside the Taj. The ATS technical team had to be patient.

11.50 p.m. – Rang Bhavan Lane

Joint Commissioner (ATS) Hemant Karkare, with his aquiline nose and Kipling moustache, had by now moved on from CST on foot, leaving his driver behind at the station. Hearing that the two gunmen who had mown down dozens of commuters had run towards Mumbai's Cama Hospital, where 370 patients were sitting ducks, he had chased after them alone, reaching Rang Bhavan Lane, a small cut-through that backed on to the hospital. Karkare's radio suggested that the gunmen had killed three residents here already, and had scaled a wall to get inside the hospital, where they had shot dead two staff.

Getting his breath back, Karkare called for backup. Control diverted Ashok Kamte, the Additional Commissioner East. Cool under fire, Kamte, a marksman and weapons expert, had been on his way to assist Patil in the Taj. Control fished around again and came up with the strongman Inspector Vijay Salaskar, a senior figure in Rakesh Maria's Crime Branch. Salaskar was a granite cop who had joined the force in 1983. He was loved or loathed, depending which side of the *nakabandi* you were sitting on. He had claimed more than sixty-five criminal scalps, many of them in opaque circumstances, taking down his first gangster in his first year as a cop. At the start of this year, he had been named in a judicial inquiry probing the shooting of a seventeen-year-old Muslim boy, who police alleged was a felon, although the teenager's criminal record could not be found.

As the policemen gathered at the Cama Hospital's back gate, a bloodied constable emerged from the building. 'Terrorists are on the sixth-floor terrace,' he stammered, explaining that his boss had led six officers up there, two of whom were now dead, while the officer remained trapped inside, badly injured. The police had to get the front covered to stop the gunmen escaping, while Karkare and co. staked out the rear gate. The ATS chief called the Control Room. Even though radio traffic indicated that there were sixty

State Reserve Police Force officers in the area, as well as a Quick Response Team and an Assault Squad, no one was dispatched. Exasperated, he gave up waiting. They had to tackle the front gate themselves. Karkare, Kamte and Inspector Salaskar, together with three constables, jumped into a police jeep heading down Rang Bhavan Lane, even as the gunmen slipped out of the front of the hospital, shooting dead a passing police inspector who challenged them, before circling around to the back of the hospital.

Inspector Salaskar was at the wheel, with Kamte beside him, while Karkare sat in the middle row. In the back were a police driver and three constables, including Salaskar's deputy, Arun Jadhav, a plain-clothed Crime Branch officer. Eleven floors up, residents began calling the Control Room's 100 number to warn that the gunmen and the police jeep were on a collision course.

In the chaos, no one in Control forwarded the messages to Karkare, whose vehicle drove, unsighted, onwards. As it swung round a left-hand dogleg, the crack-shot Kamte glimpsed men with arms and poured fire into the shrubbery. Constable Jadhav saw 'a *lamboo* [tall guy] and a *butka* [short guy]' step out with assault rifles, calmly blasting the jeep, in controlled bursts, as if this were a training exercise, the vehicle rocking and screeching as rounds punched through the door panels.

One constable, injured but still breathing, toppled on top of Jadhav, who, hit in the right elbow and left shoulder, dropped his carbine. A second constable, hit in the chest and neck, slumped over both of them. The firing stopped and Jadhav, who was pinned down and haemorrhaging blood, strained to listen. His boss, the invincible Salaskar, was rasping like a punctured tyre. Kamte and Karkare were grimly silent. *Have we lost them all?*, the constable asked himself, horrified, his eyes filling.

A police vehicle with its lights flashing zoomed up the lane. 'Thanks to the Gods,' Jadhav told himself. But it sped on, although it radioed through what the driver saw: a police jeep shot up and 'three people lying in the lane'. Jadhav heard it on the car radio. *Is something more important than officers down?*, Jadhav asked himself.

Witnesses called 100 to say the gunmen were walking on, towards the Special Branch office, firing at Kamte's parked car and driver, before returning to inspect the police jeep they had ambushed. But no one was sent to investigate.

Inside the jeep, Constable Jadhav, still conscious, heard the doors being opened and the sound of bodies being hauled out. The suspension rocked. Would they also pull out the dead and dying constables on the back seat, discovering him alive at the bottom of the pile? Instead, one gunman climbed into the vehicle, and revved the engine, while the other gunman got into the front passenger seat. The passenger referred to the driver as Brother Ismail and the driver called the passenger Brother Ajmal. Jadhav saw that the passenger 'was tiny, about five feet three', with the build of a camel jockey and fair complexion. It was Ajmal Kasab, the boy from Faridkot.

Ismail put his foot down, and the vehicle slewed this way and that. Jadhav clung on to his colleagues' uniforms, trying to keep the bodies covering him, as the injured man groaned. Suddenly one of their phones rang and Ajmal put his AK-47 over the back of his seat, and, without looking, shot off a burst of fire. Jadhav felt the rounds punch into his colleagues, and the injured men fell silent. Now there was just Jadhav left.

Turning right, the jeep shot out of Rang Bhavan Lane towards Metro Junction. Glimpsing police, Ismail swung the vehicle around, driving towards CST, and into the evacuation of the station's wounded. Ismail threw another U-turn, the jeep heading back up towards Metro Junction, where he peppered the crowd of reporters and police with rounds. Jadhav, weakened by blood loss, prayed that he would not be hit in the crossfire.

'Where are we going?' Ismail shouted across to his partner, needing directions. Ajmal admitted he had left his bag with its maps inside the hospital. Ismail thumped the wheel and Constable Jadhav felt a swerve, as the vehicle headed south. 'One tyre down,' he said to himself, trying to stay conscious and hold in the pain. Somewhere near the Mantralaya government complex, the noise of grinding told him that they were riding on a rim. Finally, the jeep slewed into a concrete road divider in front of the State Bank of Mysore. Ismail and Ajmal flagged down a passing Škoda, pulled out the driver and two passengers, and took off.

Jadhav was alone. He clambered out from beneath the pile of bodies and grabbed a radio: 'Two terrorists have [hijacked] a police Qualis car from the Rang Bhavan Lane.' He bipped the radio again. 'PI Salaskar, ATS Sir and South [sic] Region Sir have been fired at.' The three men were still lying in Rang Bhavan Lane even though Kamte's driver, who had been shot at after his boss was ambushed, called for help three times, his last communication at 00.37.

But, by then, all eyes were drawn back to the Taj, where a juddering, growling explosion ripped through the hotel's Palace wing, rattling the windows, wobbling walls, blasting out doors and dumping clouds of broken glass and plaster on everyone inside.

Karambir Kang was outside the hotel in his shirtsleeves, helping to remove dead and injured guests on luggage trollies, when he felt the baritone blast pass through his body. His eyes shot up to the sixth floor and even before the shockwave had subsided, his phone began ringing, panicked staff calling from all over the hotel. 'There is a wall of fire all the way from the stairwell to the roof,' shouted the hotel's PR director, who was trapped inside the Sea Lounge with a small party of VIP guests. 'What should we do? Run for it or barricade?' 'Barricade,' Karambir shouted, but his thoughts were elsewhere.

Puneet Vatsayan, an old school friend, called from France: 'Is everything all right?' The stoic Karambir, gently eased Puneet off the line, before Partha Chatterjee, a senior Tata executive who had been his boss and travelling companion, flying with him all over the subcontinent, called too. 'Please forget everything. Just pray for my family,' the General Manager insisted. He sensed Neeti and the boys were running out of time.

When Patil called down a little while later, asking Karambir to come up, he declined. The DCP was infuriated as he did not know the police outside were advising the hotel manager that it was too dangerous to go in. Karambir was also over-burdened by a sense of duty. All he could think about was how to round up staff and be the visible, useful figurehead of a crippled hotel. Daring rescue bids would have calmed his fears for his own family, but they could have left the Taj rudderless, risking the lives of hundreds of guests and staff. 'It's important for me to be here,' he said to a colleague.

Taking another call, he was so distracted that it took him a few words to realize it was Neeti. She tried to sound calm for the sake of the boys, whom she clutched on either side of her. 'What was that explosion?' she asked. Smoke was pouring into their apartment and the electricity was shorting. The room's sprinklers had switched on too, dousing them all. 'Probably a small bomb has gone off,' he replied, working hard to hold it together. He recalled what Patil had told them. The gunmen were prowling on the sixth. He warned Neeti not to rush out.

'What should we do?' Neeti asked sobbing. 'You will be safest staying there,' Karambir said gently, suggesting she and Uday should get wet towels to block out the smoke. They should build a barrier across the door and shift to the bathroom, the most secure room in the apartment. And then? The security forces would catch the gunmen soon enough, he assured her. But he no longer believed it.

Thursday, 27 November 2008,
12.40 a.m. – Marine Drive

The normal soundtrack to the city was the growling congestion that turned a thirteen-mile dash from Apollo Bunder to Andheri (and the airport) into a sclerotic, two-hour crawl. However, on this cool, dry, post-monsoon evening, the police and army had locked down all the main thoroughfares, resulting in the kind of profound silence that had not been heard for half a century.

Behind the Taj, in Back Bay, a lone silver Škoda sped up a deserted Marine Drive in the halogen glow, passing the Trident–Oberoi, also under siege, and following the Queen's Necklace, the board-walk of lights, north. 'Škoda car, Škoda car MH-02 JP1276, silver colour, hijacked by terrorists,' an officer radioed, the alert reaching a roadblock opposite the Ideal Café, in Chowpatty, the last major junction before the road wound up into Malabar Hill. Police cocked their weapons as the car appeared, juddering to a halt in front of them. A sub-inspector stepped forward, facing the dazzling head-lights, blowing his whistle. The driver turned on his wipers, spraying the windscreen to obscure the view.

'Switch off the lights, raise your hands and step out.' The car engine revved and the car lurched towards him. At the last minute it swung round, getting stuck on a road divider. Two officers ran to Ajmal's side, while someone shot out the rear window. Ismail told Ajmal to raise his hands and then pulled out a pistol and fired at the advancing police. They returned fire and, to Ajmal's horror, Ismail slumped, shot in the neck.

Ajmal cautiously opened his door. He appeared to stumble before hauling out an assault rifle from between his legs. A policeman grabbed the barrel, pulling and tugging. Ajmal got his finger to the trigger and let off a long burst into the officer's stomach. The police-man lurched back but held on, even as he was dying, the skin of his hands fused to the burning AK.

A mob of khaki uniforms turned on blood-spattered Ajmal, kick-ing, stripping, slapping and beating him, bystanders joining in, too, until someone cried out: 'Stop, stop, we need him alive.' He was pushed into an ambulance, lying on the metal floor, his hands tied together with a handkerchief, Ismail's corpse jiggling beside him. Ajmal's brand-new tennis shoes were left behind in the road.

Calls about the shooting of three legendary police officers in Rang Bhavan Lane were piling up, but the only person to reach the scene was Karkare's wireless operator, who radioed in the catastrophe at 00.47: 'Karkare Sir, East Region Sir [Kamte] and PI Salaskar Sir are injured. We are taking them to the hospital.'

In the Control Room, the tragedy was instantly displaced by other news. Two gunmen had been shot in Chowpatty. 'Where are the bodies?' Maria demanded, calling Chowpatty's Assistant Commissioner. 'One is killed, but one is *alive*,' the officer revealed. Maria was stunned. This was a huge result. Was the tide turning? He called for his staff car, readying to interrogate the prisoner. But before he got out of the door, Commissioner Gafoor rang, telling him to stay put. This was Chowpatty's jurisdiction and its Additional Commissioner would be in charge. Maria was incandescent. The city was burning, and the Taj besieged. The force needed a scalpel to fillet information from the captured gunmen. The Additional Commissioner, who had inched his way up over twenty-five years, was, with all respect, more slow moving. But Gafoor, who was under intense pressure, was insistent and unyielding. This was Chowpatty's show.

Maria bit his lip and quietly dispatched a trusted Crime Branch inspector to shadow the Additional Commissioner and make sure he did not screw it up. There were five questions he needed answering at this critical juncture: how many terrorists were there, who sent them, how had they entered the city, what was their aim and where was the location of their control? 'Open the prisoner's mouth and check for cyanide,' he shouted after his man.

At 00.56, Gafoor came back on the line. Where were Kamte and Karkare? Maria choked. '. . . Sir, Ashok [Kamte] is near the SB office, sir. He is covering the SB office, sir.' But Kamte was not there. He had been down the road, in Rang Bhavan Lane, the victim of a deadly shooting, an incident that had been called in by many eyewitnesses and police patrols from shortly after midnight.

What about the ATS chief, Hemant Karkare? 'Sir . . . Sir, he . . . he . . . he . . . Hemant was . . . sir, at the CST railway station. I will find out the location and tell him to get in touch with you right away, sir.' The Control Room log showed that the ATS chief had called in his decision to leave CST for Cama Hospital at 23.24, more than an hour and a half earlier.

The Commissioner pressed on, unsure of what he was being told: 'I only want to know whether Mr Karkare and Kamte are injured or are they safe?' Maria, normally unflappable, replied: 'Sir, trying to do that, sir. Sir, as for the report . . . that there was firing on East Region [Kamte] vehicle, nobody is injured. As soon as I get through I will get back to you.' There was no mention of the bullet-riddled Qualis in which all three officers had been gunned down. 'You will send a party . . . ?' the Commissioner asked. 'Already done, sir . . . Already done, sir. Additional CP Crime and there are three units of Crime Branch on the job, sir,' Maria said, signing off.

Nine minutes earlier, Karkare's radio operator had called Control to confirm that the fallen officers were in transit to GT Hospital, where all of them were declared dead.

1 a.m. – Nair Hospital

Sandwiched between Mumbai Central railway station and the city's Mahalaxmi racetrack (named after the goddess of luck and prosperity), Nair Hospital lay four miles north of the Taj. Chowpatty's Additional Commissioner Tanaji Ghadge was already waiting, chewing a wodge of paan, a police belt cinching his overfed belly, when Ajmal Kasab was stretchered in.

In a private room of the casualty ward, Ajmal was stripped, cleaned up and placed on a metal bed on top of a green plastic sheet, his torso left bare, a rough wool blanket thrown over his belly. He lay connected to a drip, his right arm and left hand bandaged, both hands blackened with gunpowder.

Ghadge got a camera rolling and focused on the quivering prisoner. Facing the ceiling, eyes closed, Ajmal wailed: 'I have committed a big mistake.' He was terrified. Ghadge leant over, chewing. 'On whose order?' With the simplicity of a country boy, Ajmal replied through parched lips: 'On the orders of *chacha*. The one from Lashkar.' Without being pressed, Ajmal had coughed the one thing no one was supposed to find out – the mastermind behind the attack.

But Ghadge had not noticed. He stumbled over the words 'uncle' and 'lashkar'. 'Lashkar what? Which village is he from?' he asked, confusing the outfit's name with a word meaning 'village defence committee'. He bamboozled Ajmal, too. Soon they were talking at cross-purposes. 'I don't know about his village,' Ajmal said, 'but he has an office.' He was referring to Zaki's headquarters at the House of the Holy Warriors, above Muzaffarabad, another fact that sailed over Ghadge's head.

'Who persuaded you to go there?' Ghadge asked, and the boy winced. 'My father told me, "We are very poor. You will also earn money like the others."'

'Your real father?' Already Ghadge was building his case that the entire family were co-conspirators.

'Real father . . . real father,' the boy replied quietly, seeming to drift back to the tongue-lashings and beatings that had driven him out of Faridkot. 'He said we'll earn money like the others.'

Out of shot, the room was packed with policemen, who whispered urgently. A dozen had descended on Nair Hospital after hearing the news. Meanwhile, Ghadge went back to the beginning. 'OK, what's your name?'

That was easy: 'Ajmal.'

'What's your age?'

'Twenty-one.'

'Where is your *gaon* [village]?'

'Faridkot in *tehsil* [administrative district] Depalpur, district Okara.' Some in the room began to make calls. Here was first proof that the assault had emanated from Pakistan, the fact that Lashkar had worked so hard to mask, using Internet telephony, cutting off all clothing labels, shaving the gunmen's hair, dressing them in Western garb, with bracelets blessed in a Hindu temple tied around their wrists, Indian student ID cards in their trouser pockets.

But Ghadge became wrapped up in recording the suspect's extended bio-data. Directions for Ajmal's maternal uncle's house – the policeman needed them. Questions about his elder brother's wife – name and address? Why had she gone back home after the row with her husband over household expenses – and what was the name of the bank that one passed on the way to their house? He was bogged down in the kitchen sink drama of Ajmal Kasab's family. While, outside in the city, guests and staff were being culled in the ongoing slaughter at the burning Taj, Trident–Oberoi and Chabad House, Ghadge tripped over alien road names, village locations and Punjabi patronymics.

Repeat. Say again. Tell me once more. Even the prisoner grew frustrated, forced into drawing figurative sketches of distant relatives who were illiterate farmers and school kids that he not given a thought to for many years.

He tried to spit it out. 'Look, my father told me we are very poor and then he introduced me to Lashkar men.' He was twisting the story slightly, making his hated father the instigator, when it had been him and his friend, intoxicated by the carnival in Rawalpindi, who had got themselves dragooned into Lashkar. And whether it was the distance between this municipal bed and his cot in Faridkot, or the thought of his tyrannical father and the mother with a brittle laugh whom he would never see again, Ajmal began to cry.

Ghadge trundled on: 'Is your father connected to Lashkar?'

'No, no, no,' Ajmal said, sniffing, righting the record. 'They keep telling people it is jihad. It is a very honourable and daring job. You will earn lot of money and your poverty will be eliminated.'

Ghadge suddenly got on track. 'When did your training start?' Around him, the officers exhaled a collective sigh of relief. In the background, a TV was reporting the deaths of Karkare, Salaskar and Kamte – but all eyes were on the prisoner. 'It was snowing that time,' Ajmal said. 'I was training in Battal village.' Another crucial piece of intelligence slipped from his lips: the Mansehra training camp. Did he hope to save himself, or was it that he had only ever been trained to die?

'Our boss used to tell us that you will go to heaven. I said, "I don't like this . . . and I don't want to stay here." ' His eyes dilated. He had hoped someone would turn up at the outfit's camp to take him away. Instead he had become part of a *fidayeen* outfit. 'We were told, "Keep firing till death",' he said.

Ghadge twigged: 'You are here for jihad?'

'What jihad, sir?' asked Ajmal, crying. The refrain that had been sung in the mountains of Muzaffarabad seemed meaningless in a hospital ward.

'You have killed people like yourself.'

'Yes, God will not forgive me,' replied Ajmal, crestfallen. 'They promised to give big amount of money to my family.'

'Who will give?'

'*Chacha* will give,' Ajmal said.

'Who is *Chacha*?' Ajmal did not fight it. 'His name is *chacha* Zaki. He has a long beard, he is around forty to forty-five years old.' The boy stared at Ghadge. 'He is a jihadi and fought during wars with Russia.' Phones were picked up. The ATS or intelligence services would be able to work out who this *chacha* Zaki was. In a subcontinent without comprehensive DNA databases or identity cards, where complex family names had multiple spellings, and where radicals swapped their birth names for a nom de guerre, long lists were kept of known aliases.

Ajmal recited *chacha*'s words: 'We are Muslims. This is not humanity. They have left you in poverty and are ahead of you.' He looked up at the ceiling and recalled all the other backwater boys who had trained with him. 'They taunt us about poverty. These places are full of poor people, who else will go there?'

'Have they given you money?'

'No. They may have given three lakh rupees [£2,300] to my father.' A small price for a son.

Ghadge summed it up: 'That means your father used you.'

'Yes, sir,' Ajmal replied, lips trembling, as a gloom enveloped him. A pause.

'What was Ismail's role?'

Why hold out? Ajmal gave it all up. 'Ismail was in charge.' Elsewhere in the room, mobiles lit up again with the news that the police had killed the ringleader.

He volunteered two more names. Ali and Abdul Rehman 'Bada'

(the elder), twenty-five, wearing a red shirt, and a red cap with the word 'Yeshu' written on it.

'Yeshu?' Ghadge asked. 'You mean Christ?'

'Yes'

'But you are all Muslims?'

'Yes, but you see, we had to look like *them*.' He spelled it out for the officer.

Red shirt. The call went out. Rajvardhan, in the Taj CCTV room picked it up. Red shirt aka Abdul Rehman 'Bada' was one of the Taj attackers.

The prisoner was flowing. 'There is Umer, Akasha, Fahadullah, another Abdul Rehman, this one 'Chhota' [small]. Then there was Shoaib and Umar.' One month earlier the team had relocated to a safe house in Karachi, where they were paired off into 'buddies' and shown films of their targets in Mumbai. Each pair of buddies had a mobile between them, pre-programmed with numbers to call. There were eight more of them in the city, besides Ajmal and Ismail.

The phone tap was now more important than ever.

There was no time to mourn the ATS chief, Karkare. His deputy, Parambir Singh, had to step up, signing off the ATS intercept request, by which time the intelligence agencies had passed to the technical section two more mobile phone numbers to monitor. Shortly after 1 a.m., +91 9910 719 424, the first of the three, rang, and Inspector Nivruti Kadam, the head of the ATS technical section, sitting in his office in Nagpada, listened in.

'Hello.' The caller was referred to as 'Brother Wasi'. Kadam made a note. Wasi sounded like a nom de guerre. They would check it.

Wasi: 'Man, the media is reporting your room number . . .'

Kadam now knew that Wasi was not a gunman. Wasi was their handler. He was controlling, cajoling and advising the gunmen, and watching the assault on TV. The killers in Mumbai were being remotely directed. Kadam scoured the conversation for clues as to the location of the control – and the gunman, who must be in some hotel room, placing them either in the Trident–Oberoi or the Taj.

ATS needed a shorthand to map the calls. T was for terrorist and C for control or Wasi.

T: 'Yes, there are cameras here.' The gunmen had spotted CCTV cameras.

C: 'Where you can see cameras, fire at them. Keep these things in mind. These things expose you. Where you are? How many guys are there? What condition you all are in?'

Is this their first status update?, Inspector Kadam wondered.

Wasi had a suggestion.

C: 'Why don't you light fires?'

T: 'We have just started lighting the fires.'

C: 'Then we will see the flames of the fire rising here.'

Every action had a reaction. And in this digitally enhanced world of terrorism and counter-terrorism, ATS officers were at their desks listening in to the killers, while their controller in an unknown location coached them, watching for evidence of their actions on rolling satellite news channels.

Wasi jollied the gunmen along.

C: 'Yes, the media is reporting that there is a big operation underway at the Taj. One of your men should keep an eye on the stairs. Methodically, take a hidden, crouching position, wherever there are entry points.'

The ATS had it. This gunman was inside the Taj. Inspector Kadam texted his acting chief.

Wasi had more advice.

C: 'Fetch alcohol, remove the pillows in the rooms, collect all the cloth, set them on fire, methodically. Set fires on two to three floors. Then you sit down and wait.'

Wasi also reasserted the need for discipline.

C: 'Whenever the phone call comes, you must attend it, my friend.'

T: 'OK.'

Wasi explained how things would work.

C: 'Whatever the media is reporting, we will tell you. That way you can work accordingly.'

T: 'OK.'

But Wasi still was not content.

C: 'My brother, you still haven't thrown the grenade. Throw the grenade towards the seaside. There are many people standing there.' Like everyone else, he was watching footage of the crowds milling outside the Taj.

T explained: 'I'm sending the two of them repeatedly, telling them to throw it towards the seaside. They say, "Yes, we will throw it." But they come back without throwing them.'

There was something surreally familial about the scene, like a father talking to an inattentive child. The gunmen were squabbling like kids tired of their duties.

The gunman whispered to someone sitting next to him: 'Brother, they're saying light the fire. Light the fire.'

The line went dead.

Several minutes later, at 01.15, Wasi called again, and Inspector Kadam was listening in.

C: 'Are you lighting the fires or not?' Wasi still could see no evidence on TV.

T: 'We are preparing for the fire. We are gathering clothes.' It sounded like a juvenile excuse.

C: 'My friend, light it quickly. One thing that I wanted to ask you was what did you do with the launch?'

Inspector Kadam stopped writing. A launch? So this was how they had come to Mumbai. Later this evidence would be matched with the eyewitness statements from the fishermen's colony.

T: 'We left it.'

C: 'You didn't open the lock to let the water in?'

T: 'No. We were rushing and made a mistake. We just left it and ran away.'

Wasi, who did not know yet that Ajmal Kasab had been caught, was worried that the launch might expose the roots of the plot.

T: 'The waves were crashing in. We saw a boat. Everyone panicked, shouting, "Navy. Navy." We ran away. Brother Ismail's satellite got left there too.'

Silence.

Kadam noted down 'Ismail', the name of Ajmal's dead partner, and called his boss. They urgently needed to find the launch and that satellite phone.

Every ten minutes the phone rang. Wasi was on the Taj team's back.

At 01.25, another call came in.

C: 'Have the fires been lit yet or not?' From the tone of his voice, he had not yet forgiven the launch and sat-phone fiasco.

T: 'Two men have gone, they haven't returned yet.'

C: 'Have you collected curtains, pillows?' Wasi sounded frustrated, as if he were biting his tongue.

T: 'We have collected everything. We have found a bottle of liquor. We also have hostages with us.'

Kadam texted his boss. It was just as Patil and Rajvardhan had warned. The gunmen had seized hostages. Kadam passed on the nugget and one more: one of the Taj teams had dropped a mobile phone on the ground floor. The cops in the hotel should look out for it.

Wasi wanted more information about the fire.

C: 'Who has gone to do it?'

T: 'Ali and Umer have gone.'

Inspector Kadam underscored: Ali and Umer. Two more names, both of them the same as those Ajmal had given. Kadam noted that Ali had to be the terrorist in yellow, one of the two who had come into the Tower lobby with the crowd charging the front door. Umer was the one in black, one of the men who had attacked Leopold's.

C: 'How many people do you have as hostages?'

T: 'There's only one guy, we're still sitting with him.'

Kadam knew from Patil that this was K. R. Ramamoorthy, the banker, in 632. What were they planning for him?

But Wasi moved on, summarizing the TV news reports, including rumours and conspiracies, seemingly incredulous at how well things were going.

C: 'The whole of Mumbai has been terrorized. More than 260 people have been injured, and some officers have been killed too. Fifty *fidayeens* have entered. Firing is happening at thirteen, fourteen places. By the Grace of Allah, the right atmosphere is building up.' Fear was spreading throughout the city and beyond.

Kadam, who had no idea about the numbers of *fidayeen*, texted his boss: 'Are there really 50 gunmen in the city?'

C: 'The media is also saying that some minister is stuck in the hotel. Set fire to the rooms, so that the minister burns and loses his life.' The TV coverage was proving critical to the assault.

T: 'Here there are five thousand rooms. Don't know where he is.' The gunman sounded sulky.

Wasi had a practical solution.

C: 'That is not a problem. If by the Grace of Allah you set fire to the entire hotel, then he will burn anyhow.'

Inspector Kadam could hear shots being fired. Wasi heard it too.

C: 'What is it? Are they firing?'

T: 'Yes. The work has started downstairs.' Umer and Ali were shooting at something or someone was shooting at them. Kadam wondered if it was the SB2 chief Rajvardhan, firing up from the CCTV room on the second floor. He was always spoiling for a fight.

C: 'OK, my friend, have you covered the stairs?' Wasi was thinking tactically.

T: 'No, we don't. We are here sitting down.'

The ATS wondered why Commissioner Gafoor was standing the men down when they could advance on 632 now.

Inside room 632, Ram was lying with his nose pressed into the carpet, thinking back to what an old woman had once told him at the Ramkrishna Mission in Chennai – that acceptance was the best part of renunciation. At the time he had not been able to understand. But now, terrified and in agony, he appreciated her message. 'Whatever

God has for you, accept it rather than fighting it. To accept it is to accept God.'

He heard a commotion out in the corridor and the splintering of a door. Someone cheered and shouted a report about how they had smashed their way into 639, down the corridor. Soon Ram saw two figures dressed in Taj uniforms shuffling into the room. Both were told to lie face down on the bed. 'Names,' a gunman shouted. 'Adil Irani,' one of the prisoners said. It was the Aquarius waiter, who had fled the carnage on the ground floor and had been hiding in room 639 for three hours.

'Are you a Muslim?' a gunman asked Adil. When he nodded, the gunman let rip. 'You are not a Muslim, you are a blot on jihad. You are a Muslim traitor.' Adil, who was actually a Parsi, closed his eyes and began to pray, as they laid into him with their guns. They paused. 'What do you do?' Adil told the truth: 'I'm only a waiter.' They beat him on the legs and back. 'Come on, now get ready to sacrifice your life for Allah.' He conjured up his son and daughter's faces, and those of his wife and mother.

The gunmen moved on to the other prisoners. 'And you?' They slapped the second man. 'Swapnil Shejwal,' a voice stuttered. 'I'm a butler, sir.'

At the ATS headquarters, the phone rang again and Inspector Kadam listened to a new voice on the line, introducing himself as Abdul Rehman 'Bada'. Inspector Kadam knew that this was the red T-shirt, who had entered the Taj via its Tower lobby using the crowd as cover. 'We have brought two [hostages] along, by the grace of Allah.'

Wasi did not pause: 'Find out where they are from.'

Abdul Rehman shouted at the hostages: 'Where are you from?' Then he addressed Wasi in the control room. 'Don't know what the bugger is saying. He says Parel. What is Parel?'

It was a district of Mumbai.

Abdul Rehman said to Wasi: 'This bastard stays in Bombay. Both of them.' He turned to shout at someone else: 'You are also from here?' He came back on the phone: 'The old man is not talking.' He was referring to the banker Ram, naked on the floor.

In the ATS office they could hear the sounds of scuffling. One of the gunmen was kicking and punching the hostages. It sounded like a rug being aired. Abdul Rehman tried to stop it: 'Umer, listen to me. Listen to me for a minute.' Umer, the terrorist in black with the basin haircut, the gunman who had shot up Leopold's, was thumping Ram and the others. Nothing would make him stop. They groaned and sobbed.

Abdul Rehman screamed at Umer: 'Bloody *khooti* [female donkey] idiot, listen to me. Come here. Listen. Hey, man, listen to me. You don't listen to me.' Umer had worked himself up into a rage, kicking and punching the prisoners. Wasi in the control room tried to intervene: 'Umer?' Umer briefly came on the line: 'Hello, hello, hello?' He was out of breath. Wasi: *'Salaam Alaikum.'*

But the red mist had not cleared. Umer passed the phone back to Abdul Rehman: 'He says the prisoners are from Maharashtra.' Abdul Rehman started shouting at Umer again, while Wasi tried to focus the team. They were at each other's throats and he needed to get some of them out of the room before they killed the hostages or each other. He had an idea. 'Light the fire immediately.' Umer should do it.

Umer would not obey orders. 'Come here,' Abdul Rehman shouted at Umer. 'Our guys don't listen,' he complained to Wasi, who had had enough. 'Make Umer talk to me,' he snarled. Wasi ordered them to give Umer another mobile, so that Wasi could call him directly. They took Adil's phone, Abdul Rehman screaming at Umer: 'Hold this mobile.'

Abdul Rehman tried to programme Irani's phone with Wasi's number but he was all fingers and thumbs: 'What is your number? You tell me.' When Wasi dictated a number, Inspector Kadam took it down, too. He was nonplussed. The number had an Austrian dialling code. He texted his boss. What did that mean? Had they stumbled across a European-backed terror cell?

Umer at last came on the line and Wasi lost his cool. He passed the phone to someone else in the control room. He needed a break. A new voice tried to talk Umer down.

Inspector Kadam created a cipher for the voice: Handler 2.

Handler 2: 'Hello, Umer?'

Umer: 'Yes, this is Umer speaking.' He sounded surly and not ready to submit. He was like a dog that had savaged a sheep, tasting warm blood for the first time.

The handler read out a phone number. 'OK, whose number is this?' Umer asked, spinning out. Handler 2 replied patiently: 'This is *me*. Call me, man. The phone is in my hand.' The handler spoke as if he were talking a jumper off a high ledge.

Umer lost it again and began shouting. He sounded like a man scrabbling up a sand dune and repeatedly sliding back down. Wasi in control grabbed the phone, addressing Abdul Rehman in the red shirt: 'Man, we want to talk to Umer. Tell him there is nothing to worry about.' Wasi decided on another tactic. He said they had good news to share. The other team had killed the ATS chief. What had the Taj team achieved?

There was silence. Umer now took the phone. 'Yes?' he said. 'I am here. He sounded shaky but his curiosity had been pricked. 'Who was killed?'

Wasi said: 'The ATS chief for the whole of Bombay has been killed.'

Umer whooped: 'By the grace of Allah.'

Wasi pressed on: 'A lot of people are injured. They have been killed. Here and there, there is firing. There are people dying everywhere. Everything is on fire. At this time, your target is most important. The maximum media coverage is on the Taj hotel. Brother Qahafa wants to greet you.' It was Qahafa the Bull, the Lashkar trainer, whose nephew, Fahadullah, was in the assault too, presently holed up in the Trident–Oberoi. Inspector Kadam wrote down Qahafa/Handler 2.

Qahafa showed all of his experience in the field, speaking calmly and quietly. 'Brother,' he said. 'Allah should accept your service. The wounds of a lot of people have been healed. The prayer you were taught, don't forget it. Wherever you are sitting, pray thrice. Three times, with full faith, not just half-hearted.'

'OK.' Umer had been stilled by the lion tamer. 'You are facing the sea?' Qahafa asked. He was playing with Google Earth in the control room in Malir Town, and matching it to the TV images had spotted something. 'There is a building on the road at the junction. There are two places there where the police are standing. Go and fire on them. And give the other brothers my greetings. Stay strong. You have touched the world. Heaven, by the grace of Allah, is much better than this.'

Inside room 632, the banker Ram heard voices in the corridor: 'Who have you got?' And then the answer: 'I am from a village, please leave me be.' It was another hostage, Sunil Jadhav, a Taj employee who worked as a bellboy, and who was thrown to the floor, shouting: 'I am not a rich man, sir.' Ram then heard a fourth man pleading. He identified himself as Raju Bagle, from housekeeping. The kidnappers tore strips of sheets and bound both men's hands and ankles.

'My room is now full,' Ram said to himself, as the new prisoners coughed and cried.

At 1.47 a.m. the phone rang again. Inspector Kadam jotted down the time. Qahafa the Bull introduced himself, and Abdul Rehman, the gunman in red, greeted him. The latter seemed back on top of things. He had good news: 'The *mujahideen* have brought back two lambs. By the grace of Allah.'

Inspector Kadam texted his boss: 'Five hostages'. When would the police move on them?

Qahafa had an idea: 'Make one of [the hostages] call and speak to their home.' Then he cheered. 'The dome is on fire!' At last there was footage of the flames.

Another phone rang in the hotel room. Abdul Rehman reported it to Qahafa: 'One of these bastards has got a call. I'll answer the phone?' He found the handset. It was Annie Irani, the waiter's wife, who had been trying Adil's number repeatedly and was now speaking to her husband's abductor. 'Adil is with us,' Abdul Rehman snapped. 'No, he is not OK. He is as wrong as can be.' Qahafa on the other line instructed Abdul Rehman: 'Tell the wife, if you want to save him, then tell the police to stop the operation.' Abdul Rehman told her, adding: 'Otherwise we will kill everyone.'

Someone new walked into the room. 'Speak to Ali,' Abdul Rehman told his handler, passing the phone over.

Inspector Kadam noted down the name. Ali was a name given up by Ajmal Kasab. He was the gunman dressed in yellow. Ali had been out searching for hostages with Umer.

Qahafa greeted him and Ali replied: 'By the grace of Allah we have broken the doors with our legs to light the fire. And we found five *chickens*. We don't roam around this freely at home.' Even the gunmen were amazed by the lack of a counter-attack. 'We are roaming on the third, fourth, fifth floor, waiting for them. Nobody is coming up. Tell those bastards to come up. Someone talk to us, this is no fun.'

Inspector Kadam texted his boss. What were the police waiting for?

Ali had one complaint. He had been struck in the leg by a ricocheting bullet when he gunned down the sniffer dog and its handler near the Palace lobby, and his wound was now bleeding badly. Qahafa passed the phone back to Wasi: 'How is your leg, my brave?' Wasi purred. He rewarded Ali with gentle words. Ali complained: 'It's bleeding and painful.' Wasi had an idea: 'You have to heat some ash and rub it in.'

Then Qahafa returned to business. Who was the naked old man? All the team had gleaned from him was that he was from Bangalore. Qahafar called out: 'Ask the old man who he is.'

Umer could be heard shouting at Ram: 'Name, home, religion and caste.' Umer grabbed the phone: 'He says he's got high blood pressure.' Umer screamed at Ram: 'What do you do?' Inside the room, face down, Ram was thinking fast. A Hindu banker was a prize asset, so what should he say? The only thing he could think of was that he also taught business students. Umer shouted out: 'He says he teaches.'

Qahafa knew that a teacher could not afford to stay in the Taj and told Umer, who confronted Ram: 'A teacher's salary is twenty thousand rupees (£250), here you pay lakhs [hundreds of thousands]. Are you some kind of smuggler? I'll deal with you.' Umer was seeing red again. Ram felt a gun smash down on to his shoulder, his head and his arm. 'I am going to die,' he told himself.

Qahafa could hear a voice screaming: 'Stop, he'll die.' Then Umer's voice: 'Ready now? Where do you teach? Which university? How many traitors have you taught? Killing Muslims. Burning neighbourhoods. I'll deal with you.' Qahafa could hear the screaming again. This time he did not stop Umer, who snarled: 'Father's name?'

Umer came back on the line, calm once more: 'K. R. Rama-moorthy.'

Qahafa paused. Inspector Kadam could hear something click-clacking. Qahafa said: 'One minute, one minute. Dr K. Rama-moorthy? K. R.? Designer. Professor?'

Click-clack.

Qahafa was Googling the name and running it through an image search.

'OK, listen, is he wearing glasses?' He was. 'He is balding at the front?' Umer shouted at Ram: 'Hold your head straight.' Umer replied: 'Yes, yes, he is bald. He's got a face like a dog.' Qahafa had found Ram's online résumé. A top-class hostage. He was pleased.

Now he warned the team that they would have to consider moving, as the fire was roaring. 'Go down soon,' Qahafa said. 'Take [the banker] down. Kill him yourself.' What about the other four? 'Let's put them together and fire at them,' Umer suggested. He turned to Adil and laughed. 'A waiter! The only thing you are waiting for is your death.'

Inspector Kadam heard a strange sound like a lollipop being sucked. He realized it was Qahafa laughing.

Ram tried to retreat into his memories, conjuring the seventh-century Mylapore Temple of Kapaleeshwara in Chennai, where he had once prayed daily to the *devi* (goddess) of the Wish-Yielding Tree and he retraced the way to the central shrine, step by step. But disconcerting noises kept pulling him back to room 632: the fridge door opening, and someone munching a chocolate bar; the plink of a can being pulled and the glug as it was drained; and the heavy, slow breathing of four gunmen, lying side by side on the bed to rest.

6

A Tunnel of Fire

Thursday, 27 November 2008, 1.50 a.m. – Malabar Hill

Savitri Choudhury was at home in Malabar Hill, watching the Taj on television, recalling the hours of disorientation after seeing footage of the Twin Towers fall in 2001. Now her city was ablaze, its most famous landmark was being gutted and her best friend was stranded inside. She had to get working. Broadcasters around the world expected her to be their guide, picking her way through the rumours that were pulling the city apart. But she could not think straight.

The lower floors of the hotel were still brightly lit with silhouetted guests staring out, while the top floor was dark, apart from small pockets of flames here and there. Columns of smoke poured from the roof. Savitri studied the pictures, trying to locate Sabina's room. She counted up to the sixth floor on the sea-facing elevation, thinking of how she had lain on Sabina's bed that afternoon. 'Where is she?' Savitri said to her husband, sitting beside her.

She recalled a lunch with three girlfriends in the early 1990s, at Zen, a Chinese restaurant in Delhi's central Connaught Place, the Empire-era roundabout of restaurants, bookshops and ice cream parlours. Sabina had arrived in sombre black. All the diners had given absent partners the third degree as they tucked into Paneer Ten Pal Style. Sabina had come in for some ribbing about her on-off relationship with Shantanu Saikia, then a much rated (and fancied) rising star at the *Economic Times*. He had been married once before, which in puritanical Delhi made him dangerous; there was also a rumour about his ex-wife having committed suicide.

Over glazed honey apples, Sabina had revealed that Shantanu

was messing her about. 'Dump *him*,' had been the advice. 'He's having his cake and eating it.' Later that night a friend had called to say Sabina was married. 'What the fuck? We finished lunch at 4 p.m. and she was not married then.' Savriti reached a fellow lunch-mate, who filled in the missing five hours.

Savitri had dropped Sabina off at the Khaadi store and Shantanu had been waiting. To woo her back, he had offered to marry her. Fortified by lunch, she hit back at him: 'Sure. But let's do it *right* now.' They had zipped off in his car, but had been ejected from the law courts, which required more planning. They were eventually directed to a less principled priest willing to bless the union without any hoo-hah. And afterwards, as she prepared to ring her parents, rehearsing her 'I have some news' speech, Sabina had cast her eyes down, realizing that she was still dressed in black.

Savitri smiled at the memory, her eyes still transfixed by the TV. How was it that reporters churned around the hotel but no rescue party could be raised? Annoyed and anxious, she called her desk and made a deal with the editors. She would report for ABC Radio, but not the TV. Her face would give it all away.

At the police Anti-Terrorist Squad (ATS) headquarters in Nagpada, the Shogi telephone intercept system was working well, scooping up, in real time, the conversations between the *fidayeen* and their handlers. There were three mobiles in use. One was with the four gunmen in the Taj, the second with the two in the Trident–Oberoi, where dozens had been killed in and around a ground floor restaurant called Tiffin, and the last was with the two gunmen in Chabad House, where an American rabbi, his wife, their two-year-old son and several others were being held hostage. The ATS technical section dispatched regular highlights to the acting ATS chief, and to the intelligence agencies, state bureaucrats and the police command, including Rakesh Maria in the Control Room, near Crawford Market.

The terrorists' identities and the location of their control room remained a mystery. Everyone was struggling to comprehend the hard data too. The gunmen in Mumbai appeared to be dialling Austria, and receiving calls from a number in the US: +1 201 253 1824. A cursory assessment by the US intelligence community suggested that what the ATS had uncovered was not an American or European terror cell but something they had never encountered before: an Internet telephone network, with the gunmen in India dialling a remote hub that re-routed the calls to their handlers, and vice versa. The handlers' control room could be anywhere in the world, even under the noses of the ATS units in Colaba. The Crime Branch's hard-working number two, Deven Bharti, would have to remain in the back of a vehicle, his laptop on his knee, waiting for the next call.

The mobile inside the Taj soon rang again, Deven Bharti's men chasing it down with direction finders and knocking on hotel rooms in Colaba, while Inspector Kadam, with the ATS, listened in.

'*Salaam Alaikum.*' ATS now knew the voice. It was Wasi, the handler, calling the four gunmen holed up in room 632 of the Taj Palace along with five hostages, and he wanted an update. Wasi could see from the TV pictures that flames were leaping from the roof and his men needed to move down.

'*Walaikum assalam*, we've found a room, on the [fifth].' It was the gunman Ali talking, the one dressed in yellow. He had been out scouting for a room where they could shelter from the inferno.

Wasi asked if they had shifted the hostages already. Not yet, replied Ali. Umer was down there getting it ready.

Wasi urged them to get moving: 'Set the rooms above ablaze and come down.' As always, Ali was compliant: 'God willing.' They needed to keep up the momentum and safeguard the prisoners. Wasi told him: 'My friend, do you know what work you have to do? Bring the hostages down with full security. The policemen must be coming up. The policemen shouldn't come close.' They had to keep alert, as surely the authorities would mount a raid soon.

The ATS texted a warning to the police Control Room. Patil and Rajvardhan had to be contacted. The Taj gunmen were heading down and discussing how to take on the police: 'Gunmen spoiling for a fight.'

Ali prepared to check the route down: 'OK, now we'll go. God willing, while coming from there, we will give a surprise. God willing.' As Ali came down the stairs alone, Wasi reminded him of the drill: 'Grenades. Remember. Get ready to throw them.' But Ali was distracted by the opulence of their new surroundings on the fifth floor. 'Just listen to me,' he said to Wasi. 'The entry door is fantastic. Big doors of glass.'

Wasi was wary. Glass would cause them problems. They could be seen through it and cut to pieces if it shattered. But Ali was not listening. He sounded astonished: 'The room is strong. We can't find another room like this. It's big. It's great. There are mirrors, and it's very safe, it has two kitchens. There is a washroom. There is a larder. There are mirrors everywhere.' They would stash their human cargo here and then go after the police.

The ATS texted police control. The intelligence agencies texted Rajvardhan. They had to clear out of the CCTV room now.

Wasi remained concerned. What about the basics: 'Is there water there?' Ali shouted to Umer, the terrorist all in black: 'Is there water here?' Yes, he replied. Wasi said: 'Keep a bucket of water close to you. A towel and water, as the towel will save you. If they throw the gas grenades, then the water and towel will save you.'

Ali was in confident mood as he went back up to fetch the hostages: 'OK. The night is ours, God willing.' Handler Wasi had one more piece of advice. 'You tie everyone up when you bring them down. Tight. Make sure no one is left in the open.' For once, Ali was ahead of him: 'I have tied them in such a way that they can't even lift their heads, thanks be to Allah.' Wasi reiterated the orders, like a schoolteacher. 'You light the fire upstairs.' Set the bombs. And bring the hostages down.

The ATS texted again: bombs. An assault could be minutes away. They felt worried for the men in the CCTV room.

Ali said: 'Pray for us.' He did have one niggling problem, the bullet injury to his leg. 'Because of my leg, I can't do what is in my heart. Walking hurts too much.' Wasi soothed him: 'Don't worry, Allah will help you.' But Ali worried that he was becoming a burden: 'This work was mine alone, but everyone is having to do it together. My leg is not helping me. Pray to Allah that we can make them dance.'

2.30 a.m. – room 632

Up in room 632, a face just inches away from Ram's ear screamed: 'Get to your feet, fat man.' The hostage-banker was bound so tight he was in agony and his wrists and ankles were bleeding. 'Come on, old man, get moving,' shouted the red-shirted gunman, impatiently kicking him in the ribs like a stray dog, before he was distracted by one of his companions calling him out into the corridor.

It was a moment of respite for Ram, who ached all over. As he lay there, trying to zone out, a tune came to his lips. It was the Carnatic songbird Madurai Subbulakshmi, singing the Hanuman *chalisa* (devotional hymn) that he had heard so many times as a child: 'You carry in your hand a lightning bolt along with a victory flag, and wear the sacred thread on your shoulder.'

'Aaargh.' Ram was brought back into the present by one of the gunmen hauling him up by his sacred thread, wrapped around his ankles. He screamed. A gun butt dug into the small of his back. 'Are you listening to us?' The illogicality of being a hostage got to Ram, his captives trussing him in such a way that he could do nothing, and then becoming frustrated by his immobility. The way they beat him until he was overcome by pain and then was expected to give coherent answers. He tasted tears and wondered what had happened in these young men's lives to turn them into such thugs.

In Kuttalam, the village where Ram came from, Muslims had been the local healers, let into everyone's homes, becoming the discreet guardians of the most intimate knowledge. Ram had lived his life free of dogma and the politics of organized religion, shunning sectarianism. Now he struggled to get his head up. Ali, the yellow gunman, was keeping the door open while Abdul Rehman, the red gunman, set the room on fire. What were they doing, burning their own bolthole? Suddenly, the air was sucked out of the space, followed by a deafening *ka-boom*, as a gigantic sound wave hurled everything up into the air. Even the gunmen looked startled as they held on to the vibrating walls. What had they done? They exchanged glances. They had set a second bomb off, this one on the sixth floor, and it had produced a detonation far larger than anyone anticipated. They started shouting: 'Get up, get up, quickly get up.' *How much more can the old building withstand?*, Ram wondered. He knew he was at the end of his tether.

Still naked, he was pushed forward, after the others. Five bruised and bewildered hostages shuffled out of the room and into a smoke-filled corridor, their movements caught by one semi-functioning CCTV camera. Umer, the gunman in black, was standing guard outside the door. Adil, the poolside waiter, was up front. The naked Ram trailed at the rear. 'You, fat man, we *are* going to kill you,' the red gunman screamed, grabbing Ram by the shoulder. 'I will shoot you myself if you stop once more.' Adil feigned breathlessness, slowed up and drew alongside. 'They *will* kill you,' he whispered in English. 'Please, try to keep with us.' Around them, everything burned: a lusty fire ravaging the wallpaper and furniture. Wooden ceiling ribs crackled and split as choking ash swirled around their heads. Soon there would be nothing left but the bare steel bones of the building.

They were led through a service doorway and down a concrete staircase; the coolness of the stairwell feeling like a balm. Then they were pushed back out on to the fifth floor and into a lavish suite with sliding glass doors. Ram could see clothes and possessions scattered around. A guest had fled in a panic. He hoped they had made it out. The five hostages were told to get down on the floor and Ram heard a metallic clack. He turned his head and for a while could not figure it out. The gunmen appeared to be setting grenades around this room too. When the fire reached them, nothing would be left.

*

Three floors down, Florence Martis was in the stationery storeroom when the emergency lights went out. She felt the building shake, a 'whoosh and a dull rumble', the entire hotel seeming to heave and shuffle. Then the Data Centre went dark.

The air-conditioning units wound down with a suck, as silence engulfed the room. Something else was coming through the AC system. She could feel its current. Florence pressed her face close to one of the units and recoiled, retching. Smoke was being blown into the Data Centre. The room was filling up.

She struggled to her feet. Her work phone buzzed. 'It's security, ma'am, where are you?' Was she about to be rescued? 'I am. I don't know,' she stuttered, choking. 'I'm in . . .' Florence began coughing. The smoke filled her lungs. She could not speak.

'Take your time. Where are you?'

'I am . . .' The smoke stung her eyes and addled her brain. She could not get it straight in her own mind and fought to stop herself from fainting, as she felt bile rising in her stomach, her fingers prickled by pins and needles. The line went dead. Then it rang again, this time with a different voice that wrapped itself around her like a blanket. 'Florence, Florence.' It was Faustine. 'Daddy!' she whispered. 'Florence, I am coming for you.' He was saying something about being at the Time Office when she heard a beep and glanced down. The mobile had powered off. She needed to find her personal mobile and a phone charger.

As she hunted about the room, she started back in horror. The Data Centre door had gone. She sat down, quaking. It had been blown down by the blast. Now there was nothing between her and the gunmen. She had to think quickly. Looking around she spotted a desk. She worked herself beneath it. It was a tight fit. She wriggled until she sat flat against the wall, drawing her knees up to her chin. She reached out and grabbed a chair, which she rolled towards her, until it was tucked right under, as if the workstation were empty.

★

Around the corner, the CCTV room had been plunged into darkness too, the blast throwing Patil's team to the floor. Rajvardhan texted a senior Research and Analysis Wing (RAW) agent roaming outside the Taj's perimeter: 'Bomb has gone off on sixth. Hostages on the move.'

Then the fire sprinklers opened up, dousing everyone in warm water, sending the room temperature soaring by ten degrees, the CCTV system fizzing and dying, taking away their sole advantage. Outside the door a roaring could be heard like a waterfall. It made the timber doorframe rattle. A shaken Patil rose and wiped his face. It was 2.45 a.m.

Outside, Karambir Kang stood with his heart in his mouth. He texted Taj security up in the CCTV room, looking for reassurance. The last time anyone had heard from his wife was just after 2 a.m., when she had messaged the switchboard, trying to reach him. Now her phone rang out, unanswered. All the while Karambir fielded calls from staff inside the hotel: 'The building is on fire, the roof is on fire, the dome is on fire.' Should he tell them to stay or try their luck and run? He could not be responsible for so many lives in the balance, but he had to be. When Taj security replied it was with bad news. They were going to have to get out of the CCTV room, which felt like it was melting. Karambir walked away from the crowd, trying his wife again and again.

Inside the CCTV room, the Black Suit Puru Petwal and several other Taj staffers had a plan. They knew of a service lift along the corridor that was easy to reach and would bring them out close to the Northcote exit on the ground floor. But Patil disagreed. He had other ideas. He wanted to head for the Grand Staircase, the most direct route out of the inferno. Rajvardhan said nothing. He was still thinking about the blast. As a reflex reaction, he had opened his mouth as the blast wave passed through them, just as an experienced infantryman dropped his jaw when a round passed over his head, feeling the pull of the air to determine the direction of a sniper. He estimated that eight to ten kilos of what was most likely RDX had just gone up. From his experience in Gadchiroli, he knew that it would take at least that much military-grade explosive to make it feel as if a building of this size were lifting off its foundations.

The use of RDX was telling. A complex melange of white fuming nitric acid and hexamine, it was stable even in extreme heat and was difficult to ignite by accident. All of this made it perfect for the military – as did its potency, which was one and a half times that of commercial TNT. It also made it a good choice for terrorists given the bloodbath and inferno raging all around them. The gunmen's formation in pairs, the hostage taking, their weapons choice, RDX, all mark them out as well trained and motivated, he thought, and backed by a state. They were going to be hard to kill.

Rajvardhan turned to Patil, who continued to argue with Petwal about exit routes. What Patil lacked in tactical sense, he made up for in guts, Rajvardhan thought as his phone vibrated again. It was the state Intelligence Bureau chief. 'Get out now,' he messaged. 'They are talking about blowing the CCTV room, as soon as they've secured the hostages.' Three floors and a fifty-yard walk down the corridor was all that separated the CCTV room from the gunmen on the fifth. That gave them about three or four minutes before they came face to face.

'Everyone out now,' Rajvardhan screamed, throwing open the CCTV room door. More than a dozen of them stumbled out, and into a tunnel of fire, singeing their hair and skin. Patil formed the group into a spear. They needed to move fast and low. 'We *will* head for the Grand Staircase,' Patil insisted to Petwal's alarm. Rajvardhan would give covering fire up into the atrium. Between them, they had one semi-automatic – a Sten gun belonging to an inspector from Colaba police station – but not enough rounds to hold the trigger down.

As they edged forward, the fire was so hot that the sprinkler water transformed into steam. Skeins of soot rose up and then, hitting the buffer of steam, descended in hot wet sheets. Patil was in front, Rajvardhan behind him, followed by Patil's radio operator.

Behind him was Deepak Dhole, a veteran inspector from Colaba police station. Bringing up the rear were three State Reserve Police Force (SRPF) constables. As they turned the corner to face the Grand Staircase, shots rang out: *ack, ack, ack*. Two AK-47s channelled in fire from above them, rounds chiselling sparks out of the marble and digging into the skirting boards. Rajvardhan glimpsed two corpses on the staircase as more rounds poured in, splitting the line. Patil pushed forward, followed by his batch-mate, who sent a burst of rounds up into the atrium. Next came Inspector Dhole and the radio operator. Then Dhole watched in horror as a gigantic ball of flames rolled forward and struck Patil and Rajvardhan, toppling them over. He stared into fire, even as it made his face sting. The ball exploded, leaving behind a puff of soot. The officers were gone. He could not believe it. They were alone. He was alone. No one could have survived the fireball.

Horrified, the inspector looked around. He was now the ranking officer and needed a plan. But Puru Petwal, the Black Suit, wasn't waiting. He saw a heavy, antique wood trunk on the staircase landing, and hurtled towards it, diving inside. 'Not seen and not hurt,' he said to himself. Looking around in shock, Dhole saw that Patil's young radio operator had been shot.

Getting down on his knees, Dhole crawled over. The man's guts were spilling out of a fist-size hole in his stomach. Dhole pressed his hands on the injury, trying to hold everything in, staunching the blood, ripping a strip off his jacket to pad the gaping hole. He clamped an arm around the 21-year-old's waist, hooking his fingers into his belt, propping him up against the wall. A grenade exploded nearby. Dhole's ears rang, his eyes dazzled by the flash. Then he saw one of the SRPF constables falling, sliced by shrapnel. On autopilot, Dhole spun around and laid down fire, until he ran out of bullets. A second SRPF constable went down and lay twitching on the ground, seemingly critical. Dhole worked his way over. The constable had been shot in the chest and was deflating like a snagged balloon. Dhole hauled him across his lap, the constable grinding his teeth, as blood and air streamed out of multiple holes. 'No hope,' Dhole whispered to himself. 'He's bleeding out.'

The firing started up once more. 'We have to leave him behind,' Dhole said, turning to the others, cowed and bleeding behind him. 'To the CCTV room!' He rolled off the fatally wounded constable, got up and ran back the way they had come, dragging Patil's wireless operator as bullets pinged across the atrium. But the CCTV room was now a smoking, door-less cave.

Up on the fifth floor the gunmen had remained in telephone contact with their handler, Wasi, throughout the exchange of fire. Inspector Kadam from the ATS technical section had been listening, horrified.

Ali was breathless and distracted as machine-gun fire rang out. Wasi asked what was going on. 'There is some activity happening,' replied Ali, as literal as ever, 'so we are firing a little.' He dropped the phone, leaving the line open and Wasi calling out for more information: 'What? What's happened?' There was a scuffle of feet and then another voice came on the line. ATS recognized it as Umer, the man who had viciously beaten the hostages: 'Hello, hello.' Wasi shouted: 'What's happened?'

Everyone listening in could hear the chunter of bullets, and the roar of a grenade. Wasi wanted to know *who* was shooting whom. 'Hello?' he shouted into the phone. 'What sorts of sounds are coming?' Umer, who was firing and shouting into the phone at the same time, replied: 'Guns, they are coming. I think someone has come up.' Wasi needed details: 'What's *happening*, Umer?' But the gunman had dropped the phone and run along the corridor to engage the police. Down below, Inspector Dhole had grabbed another weapon and was laying down covering fire. Wasi sounded frustrated by the lack of information.

The ATS and Wasi heard footsteps and more shots. It was Umer pelting back along the corridor to the phone. The gunmen were planning to barricade themselves and the hostages in their new stronghold, the luxurious fifth-floor suite: 'OK, now we keep our door closed?' No, that was the worst possible tactic, urged Wasi.

He issued a warning: 'Make sure that all four of you are not in one room. Got it? Keep that in mind.' Wasi told them to keep up the barrage of fire: 'When you feel like someone has come close and it's a problem for us, then you should shake them up.' Umer understood. 'God willing, we will shake them up,' he cried.

Another voice came on the line. The ATS marked it down as Qahafa the Bull. If anyone understood the mechanics of close-quarters warfare, it was him. '*Salaam Alaikum,*' he said calmly. 'What floor are you on?'

Umer replied, still firing his weapon: 'We are on the floor below the topmost . . .' He stopped mid-sentence. 'One minute. They have fired at Shoaib . . . We'll stop now.' He hung up.

Qahafa called back and spoke calmly: 'Don't cut us off, we are listening.' Now all that could be heard was a roar of continuous fire. Umer returned briefly: 'One minute,' he shouted, and then with a *clonk* dropped the phone on the floor. Qahafa called out, like a coach on the sideline: 'Remember, change your position. Change your position.' Silence. 'OK,' Umer eventually answered. 'Shoaib has fired at those people,' he said panting, but upbeat. Qahafa kept up their spirits: 'Change your position; don't sit together. Throw grenades.' Umer dropped the phone again and Qahafa and the ATS listened to the sound of shoes pounding away down a corridor.

Guns crackled. Grenades grumbled. 'Hello?' Umer was back. Qahafa asked: 'Are they coming from upstairs or downstairs?' Did they still hold the high ground? Were the police pinned down? Umer was out of breath: 'We don't know.' He sounded like he was losing his cool. Qahafa had a solution. The four gunmen should split into two teams. 'Divide the prisoners,' he ordered.

But Umer was distracted. 'One minute, I'll talk to you later,' he cried out. 'Need water.' Qahafa backed off: 'OK, I'll listen; you work.' Then he whispered to Wasi, sitting next to him in Lashkar's Malir Town control room. The police position had been attacked. 'Shoaib fired at them, so they ran off.' They needed to press home their advantage. Qahafa shouted into the phone: 'Divide into two teams; divide the hostages.'

But all he could hear was Umer grunting and screaming. He hoped he was not falling to pieces. 'Umer, Umer, pray, brother, make less sound. Umer, stop the noise.' Qahafa tried another tack: 'Umer, Umer, throw the grenade.' No response. 'Umer, Umer, firing is on, my friend, firing.' Had they been overrun? He shouted into the phone, using the one ploy that always worked. 'There are twenty thousand rupees for you,' he said, 'if you take them out.'

But Umer was gone, although the phone line remained open. The ATS and Qahafa could hear new voices talking: men whispering in English and Marathi. 'Open it, man,' a voice said. 'Untie it quickly.' The ATS wondered who else was still there. 'Release his hands first.' In Nagpada they speculated that these must be the hostages trying to escape. Where was Umer? Another new voice: 'That's it. Now open the window.' Had the police made it up from the third floor? 'Smash the glass.'

Qahafa whispered to Wasi, next to him: 'I think this is someone else.' What had happened to the four gunmen? 'It's the army talking, the mobile has fallen; someone is breaking the door,' said Qahafa, confused. 'Umer?' he called. Silence. The line filled with the cascading sound of a window exploding.

'They have been martyred,' Qahafa whispered. 'Praise be to Allah.'

Down on the second floor, on the landing of the Grand Staircase, the Black Suit Petwal was still inside the great wooden box and could hardly breathe. He waited, counting, until a break in the firing. Then he flipped open the heavy lid, leapt out and bolted for a pantry, where, seeing a fire hose, he turned it on and squirted a circle around himself, creating a wet buffer.

Further along the corridor, close to the CCTV room, Inspector Dhole, who could smell his clothes and skin burning, spied a row of fire extinguishers, as incoming rounds and grenades continued to pummel his position. His hands and arms stung as shrapnel sliced into them. Everyone in the column had been cut and burned, and they were three men down. On a UN mission to Cyprus the inspector had undergone intensive training in fire-fighting. He recalled that the instructor had been a Pakistani army officer. 'Now I'm fire-fighting to save myself from the Pakis,' he told himself, running for an extinguisher, pulling the pin, and focusing the jet all around his men. The skin on his arms blistered. His face felt like it had been flayed and when he brushed his head with his hand, hair came away. He eyed up the next fire extinguisher. 'Let's go,' he shouted, spurring the others on.

Dousing and running, as the fire licked all around them, he reached a doorway and kicked it in, the column falling behind him into the cool pitch black. 'God's grace,' he said to himself. 'We have seen death and escaped.' He pushed through another door and before him a fire crew loomed, gesturing for them to run. Ecstatic, he realized that that they had reached an exit. Inspector Dhole lapped up the fresh air, falling to his knees. A paramedic ran over, accompanied by an officer he knew well from Colaba station. 'Name and rank?' the policeman asked. 'Dhole. Inspector,' he muttered, confused that this man was treating him like a stranger. What was up with the dimwit? He ran his fingertips over his face, finding great blisters. The fire had disfigured him. He motioned for the cop to come nearer. 'I have terrible news,' he said, his voice cracking. 'We have lost men. Patil Sir and Rajvardhan Sir are among the dead.'

Upstairs on the fifth floor, in room 520, five hostages bound hand and foot lay in the dark, with smoke pouring in through the door left open by the departing gunmen. The banker Ram wriggled and twisted, struggling to release the tight bindings digging into his bleeding ankles and wrists. Adil Irani, who was beside him, whispered: 'Sir, they've gone. We need to get out.' The two men could barely see each other through the gloomy smoke-choked room. The three on the far side of the bed were whimpering: 'We're going to burn to death.'

Ram rolled over. With every muscle straining he struggled up and pulled one hand free. 'Find something to cut us loose,' urged Adil as Ram hobbled over to the dresser, his fingers feeling for the central drawer. Pulling it open, he felt inside, scrabbling over the prayer books, a folder of writing paper and a slim envelope of cotton wool. No scissors. He groaned. Feeling around on top of the dresser, his fingertips brushed something metallic. A blunt fruit knife. Better than nothing. He seized it and attempted to saw at Adil's bonds.

At the ATS headquarters, and in the Lashkar control room in Malir Town, Karachi, eavesdroppers were still trying to make sense of what they were hearing, as the mobile phone dropped on the floor by Umer continued to transmit. A man could be heard struggling: 'No, it's not cutting. It's not cutting with the knife.' In Karachi, Qahafa the Bull wondered aloud if he had been too quick to conclude his gunmen were martyred. 'Umer?' he called out, hopefully.

Ram dropped the knife and went back to the drawer, finding a sewing kit with tiny scissors. He stumbled around the room, freeing everyone, until all five sat rubbing their wrists and ankles, wheezing in the toxic fug. Outside the open glass doors, fire flowed like lava. They were still trapped. The butler Swapnil reached over and slid them shut, using wet towels to seal the gap. Their lungs burned. How would they get out? Adil spoke first. 'I know where we are. The windows, it's the only way.'

The young waiter pitched a heavy waste bin against the glass, smashing a single pane before the entire frame gave way in an explosion of glass. As smoke was sucked out, fresh air gushed in and they greedily gulped it down. Ram dared to hope for the first time, and watched the waiter climb out and call over from the ledge. A few stars shone in the sky, but otherwise it was pitch black, the hotel's tiled roof mottled with inky shadows.

The ATS and Karachi control both picked up Adil's shout: 'Help, help.'

Qahafa muttered: 'Umer?' There was no answer, just the same voice crying out: 'Help, help.'

Beckoning the other hostages over, Adil pointed down. They were in the top inside corner of the south wing, facing the pool. Beneath them was the sloping gabled roof of the floor below and, three floors down, a concrete terrace that ran across the top of the Crystal Room. 'We can climb down there,' Adil said. Ram looked horrified. 'Come on, sir,' Adil urged. He squinted, catching something moving down below. He heard footsteps and saw a figure scurry across the terrace. Was it a gunman? Studying the silhouette, he was sure it was Puru Petwal. After escaping from the CCTV room, the Black Suit had made it out of the second-floor fire-trap unharmed. Emboldened, Adil waved and called out, trying to get Petwal's attention. 'Help, help.' He then realized Petwal was not alone. Five housekeepers were with him. They were waving up. Adil looked down and saw that they were signalling to someone else.

At the ATS and in Karachi control they heard a voice brief the others in the room: 'What are they saying? It's the Taj guys.' Adil leant right out, and spotted a female guest below him, hanging from a drainpipe. He could hear her sobbing. She was frozen and trembling. Petwal shouted: 'Please, ma'am, keep going. Don't lose your nerve.' Everyone below watched as she inched down. Then she stopped again and shook her head.

Edging out on to the gable, Adil at last saw the full scene. A male guest lay below on the terrace, with his legs splayed at an unnatural angle. Like many others stuck inside the stricken hotel for six hours without any sign of a rescue, he had decided to take his chances. But he had fallen, smashing on to the concrete. He looked like he might be dead. Petwal and others ran over with blankets and duvets. 'Jump,' they shouted up to the woman. From above, Adil watched her let go of the pipe, and tumble through the air, and into the folds of bed linen, before being carried off the terrace, alive.

Petwal came back and for the first time spotted Adil sitting on the gable. He signalled: 'Wait', and ran inside, returning with a coil of fire hose. He motioned for Adil to pull it up. Shouting back, Adil's voice was picked up by the ATS and Karachi control: 'Wait, man, I'm telling you, you can't come from there.'

Petwal had something else with him, a rope of bedsheets that he tied to one end of the heavy hose, coiling up the loose end before he hurled it up. Once, twice. Adil, who had rammed his legs into the frame of the gable, finally caught the improvised rope and used it to heave up the heavy hose.

ATS and Karachi control picked up the sound of someone inside the room. It was the butler trying to braid his own rope to attach to Petwal's. 'This curtain is thicker than this curtain. Take the pillow.' They attached the rope and the hose to the gable and now they had to slide down, both of them, hand over hand. Offering to go first, Adil pushed off the gable, twisted around to face the building and let the hose take his weight. His last thought before he spun off into an airless world of velvety blackness and lost consciousness was of being glad that the others had not seen the tableau of the stricken man below.

At the ATS and in Karachi, they heard someone in room 520 shouting: 'Tie it, tie it, Raju. He is hanging.' Adil had fainted. Ram screamed at Raju Bagle, the housekeeping boy, while Petwal's team held the hose taut, praying Adil would not fall. But the rope was slipping fast through his fingers and he fell, crashing to the ground with a sickening thud. 'Is he dead?' asked a horrified Ram. Because of the angle of the gable, Adil was now out of view. Those left behind in 520 scrabbled around, looking for another exit. Instead, they spotted the abandoned phone.

At the ATS and in Karachi they heard footsteps, and a voice. Raju Bagle: 'I think your mobile is here.' Ram: 'No, no, it's yours.' Then came a dawning realization that the handset didn't belong to any of them. Ram: 'Whose is it then?' A pause. '*Arre* [Hey], it might be a bomb or something, don't touch it, throw it away.' A thud.

In Karachi, Qahafa the Bull finally disconnected the line.

Down on the terrace, Adil came to, staring into Petwal's face: 'Are you OK?' Shooting pains gripped his chest. His ribs felt broken and his feet were bleeding. But he was alive. 'You fainted, man,' he heard Petwal say, giving him a bearhug. Behind, he could see the house-keeping boys gathering up the body of the other fallen guest, a 39-year-old German TV producer, Ralph Burkei, who would later die from his wounds. His wife, Claudia, who was at home in Munich, had missed his last call, in which he had said he was going to try to climb out of the hotel. She would not learn of his death for several hours more.

Summoning all his strength, Adil got up and limped into the sight of those hostages still in 520, waving up to them, clutching his ribs. 'Come down, you have to try,' he called. Swapnil, the butler, sitting on the gable end, shifted his weight awkwardly, hesitated and then began rappelling down, without making a sound. Next came Raju Bagle, the housekeeping boy. Ram was left with Sunil Jadhav, the bellboy. They looked at each other. Who would go next? What lay ahead of them was a Special Forces obstacle course. Sunil signalled he would rather take his chances than stay and he hauled himself on to the ledge, twisting himself around, and sliding off.

Ram was alone, listening to the crackling fire behind him. His mind felt like a pack of shuffling cards. He sat on the ledge, his legs dangling. His collarbone ached, and his back and hip were badly bruised. Even though he wanted to live more than anything in the world, his body had gone through too much. He could see everyone waving at him. 'Come on, Ram. Please try.' But he had also seen them carrying off the German guest's body. He could not do it. His eyes welled. He felt too broken and old. Ram crawled back into the smoke-logged room, slumping down by the bed. What came to him was an aromatic smell of beeswax and sandalwood, the sound of bells chiming in a buttery hall, and warm feet on cool, pitted flagstones, smoothed by a thousand years of procession and worship. He was back in the Mylapore Temple of Kapaleeshwara, making a wish, as he had done so many times in his life, pleading with the *devi* for his freedom. He chanted. 'Which is it to be?'

Opening his eyes, he saw some pyjamas lying on the floor and remembered his nakedness. Pulling them on, he made up his mind. He picked up the wet towels from the floor, wrapping them around his face and shoulders, slid open the glass doors and stumbled out into the flames. He wanted to live.

7.

Deep Night

Thursday, 27 November 2008, 3 a.m.

One mile north of the Taj, Amit Peshave, the manager of the Shamiana coffee shop, paced the corridors of Bombay Hospital, his neatly parted hair awry, his black suit encrusted with dirt and his white work shirt flapping. He looked like he had been sucked up and spat out by a tornado. The hospital's windowless corridors were doused in a harsh neon light and it was hard to know if it was day or night in this twilight world of the sick and injured. A smell of rotting blood permeated everything and mournful cries echoed up the stairwell.

In the past five hours, Amit should have died many times over. One of his waiters had been gunned down before him. He had rallied thirty-one diners while under intense fire and witnessed the execution of two guests. Volunteering to search for a missing child, he had also come face to face with a gunman, who shot at him and then threw a grenade. His mind whirled with horror at what had befallen his beloved city.

After escaping from the Taj, Amit had chaperoned an injured British guest to the hospital, running and then walking against a tide of bloodstained and injured people, learning along the way of all the other multiple attacks. As the man was being admitted to hospital, a woman had called his mobile phone from the UK, revealing that her sister (and his wife) was missing, last seen fleeing to the Nalanda bookshop in the Taj lobby. 'Please help us find her,' the sister-in-law implored. Amit had taken down the distraught woman's number, promising to do his best, before texting Chef Hemant

Oberoi, asking to be recalled to the hotel. But the boss insisted he stay put. 'There will be things for you to do there.'

Amit had roamed restlessly outside the ward, looking for a cigarette, until midnight, when he had noticed a dishevelled European woman sitting on the floor, dressed in a bloodstained *shalwar kameez*. As he went over, she had shrunk back, terrified. But he had coaxed a story out of her. She introduced herself as Line Kristin Woldbeck, a Norwegian tourist who had been caught up in the Leopold attack. 'My boyfriend is terribly injured; he has lost a lot of blood. I saw so many bodies.' Amit listened, incredulous. It was the first time he had heard in any detail what had happened at the café.

As they had walked down to the hospital entrance for a cigarette, Amit had spotted a sink. 'Wash your face,' he suggested. 'Yes, my angel,' Line said, smiling for the first time at the thought of this boyish restaurant manager bossing around someone twice his age. He had sensed her relief as she scrubbed off a rusty layer of dry blood caking her hair, neck, face and clothes. He handed her his jacket to dry herself on.

Refreshed, Line opened up about Arne, telling Amit how a bullet had sliced open his face from eyebrow to jawbone, and severed the tops off three fingers. A surgeon was attempting to reattach them. She described her friend Meetu, who had not been so lucky, and bled to death on the café floor. She had had to leave her body behind, as she dragged her boyfriend around the city, looking for a hospital, she explained, tears welling.

Just as Amit and Line came outside for their smoke, gunshots had sounded out. Incredulous, Amit ran back inside as someone screamed: 'GET DOWN!' But where was Line? She had bolted down a narrow alley, becoming trapped. When Amit found her again she was howling at the wall. He hurried her back inside. 'Into the lift, quickly,' he urged, pressing the sixth-floor button. Upstairs, she collapsed on the floor and burst into tears. Calming her down, Amit left her clutching her boyfriend's blood-soaked clothes and listening to the clanking lifts, petrified a gunman was coming up. 'Good luck, Line,' he whispered. 'I have to go.'

Down below, Amit had returned to his injured British guest and caught the news from hospital porters that the most recent gunshots had come from Rang Bhavan Lane, where an ambush had killed three senior police officers: Hemant Karkare, Ashok Kamte and Inspector Salaskar. If *these* guys can die, Amit thought, what chance is there for the rest of us? Spooked, he desperately wanted to return to his colleagues at the Taj. He texted his chef, Boris Rego: 'How's things?' Rego was busy helping out in Chambers. He tried the Golden Dragon chef, Hemant Talim: 'You OK?' Talim was preoccupied, too. Everyone seemed to be working at full tilt to secure the guests. 'Just wait,' he was told.

Back inside the hotel, Sunil Kudiyadi, the Taj's security chief, sent a text message to Karambir Kang and Chef Oberoi, who were working out whom to evacuate next. There were still five significant pockets of people trapped. The first was in the Zodiac and Starboard Bar; diners and guests who fled the lobby at the start of the evening.

The second was in the function rooms on the first floor of the Palace, the Gateway and Prince's, where the powerful Hindustan Unilever board had been dining. The hotel's 23-year-old Assistant Banqueting Manager, Mallika Jagad, who was chaperoning thirty-seven trapped guests and twenty-eight staff in the Prince's Room, had ruled out an escape down the Grand Staircase. But waiters had started fashioning ropes from curtains and tablecloths to escape through the sea-facing windows, should the fire reach them.

The third group was the 150 diners and Korean conference delegates shuttered away on the top floor of the Tower. The biggest group of all was in Chambers, on the hotel's first floor: 250 refugees included tycoons, business leaders, MPs, and a high court judge, as well as the journalist Bhisham Mansukhani, his mother and her friends, the yacht owner Andreas Liveras and his cruise director, Remesh Cheruvoth, Mike and Anjali Pollack and their dining companions.

Disparate guests were trapped inside rooms from the second to the sixth floors of the Palace, among them Amit and Varsha Thadani in 253, and Will Pike and Kelly Doyle in 316. These were the hardest to protect – as Karambir Kang knew, fretting about his own family. And they were the most exposed. Alone and listening to everything: they heard the gunmen pacing the corridors, kicking doors, shooting into some of the rooms, and lighting fires. Some could also make out the excruciating sounds of those gunned down trying to run for it, including a 71-year-old Australian businessman on the third floor, who tried to flee with his wife. He was shot dead, his wife left injured and in agony. Her screams for help were audible to Will and Kelly, and sent a chill down their spines.

They had been stuck in their room for more than five hours now and were struggling to hold it together. After the second bomb, the electricity had gone off, so they were without air conditioning, light or power to charge their mobiles. As 3 a.m., the deepest part of the night, approached, the room grew darker until the light was lost altogether. Only the occasional vehicle headlamp flickering a trail across the wall gave them a fleeting moment of reconnection with the world outside.

Will was at the windows, searching for signs of a rescue. 'It's completely deserted out there,' he whispered to Kelly. All he could see was the Arabian Sea. That afternoon it had looked cool and inviting, but now that the moon had gone it was a brooding slick. Deep terror was turning to hopelessness.

He shuffled back beside Kelly, shivering despite the heat. Time moved in its own special way in the middle of the night and the noises, distant booms and cracks, seemed to linger for an age.

Out of the blue, Will scrambled to his feet. 'Gin and tonic?' he asked, summoning the last dregs of positivity. He made a limp joke about not needing to worry about racking up an eye-watering mini-bar bill, as he clowned about with straws and stirrers. 'Thanks, Will,' she whispered, as she took a sip. They *were* going to get through this.

He tried to conjure up their blissful months together, but before long he spiralled back down again. Here they were, still in their flip-flops, having run out of fags, on the tipping point of disaster. The absurdity and horror of being trapped together, the chaos they had left in their wake in London, and not knowing what any of it meant, made no sense at all.

It was a struggle to recall that just twenty-four hours earlier they had been contemplating the plaited bamboo ceiling of their boutique cottage at Ciaran's resort in Palolem Beach, anticipating a night of luxury at the Taj. They drained their glasses. Now what could they do? What, he thought, was the etiquette of personal space in a life-altering crisis? Were there social rules to conform to – even now? On a mundane level, he needed a crap. But flushing the toilet could alert the gunmen. He went anyhow and they lived with the shit, piling paper on top of it.

The explosions started up again, rattling their windows. Smoke was getting through the towel barrier and still no one was ringing. There were no updates. No prognosis. Just Will and Kelly, two empty glasses and the turd in the loo. He texted his father. With his phone battery running low, he was rationing these morale-boosting exchanges. 'What's going on, Dad?' Nigel, who was glued to the TV back at home, three phones on his knee, was still trying to get information from the Foreign Office in London. 'Sit tight, they *will* come for you soon.' Kelly called her mother, weeping into the phone.

Explosions rolled down the corridor like a massed band. Glass splintered somewhere on the third floor and wood snapped. It sounded as if a boot had been planted through a partition wall and was now being twisted and flexed. At least the woman crying out along the corridor had stopped. Kelly picked up a fruit knife and handed it to Will. It was small and blunt.

They moved to the bathroom, sliding into the bath, facing one another. If the Goan holiday had brought them closer, what would surviving this do? It was a defining moment. 'Why are we in the bath?' she whispered. 'There isn't any logic to it.' Will smiled. 'At least we are together,' he said. Kelly grimaced. The line sounded hackneyed. 'OK, if the worst happens then we'll die together,' he added. She closed her eyes, trying not to cry. She wasn't planning on that.

The telephone rang. After such a long silence it sounded like a fire alarm. Will scrambled out of the bath, thrilled to receive a call. 'Hello!' It was a woman's voice, calm and reassuring. 'Hello? Mr Doyle? Mr Doyle?' When they checked in, this mistake had made him hoot. Now he just wanted to know what they were doing to get them out. 'Stay in the room, Mr Doyle, the situation is under control. The police are here.' She rang off.

Will was stunned. Was that it? More worryingly was this a ploy? The caller had said she was ringing from the switchboard, but for all they knew a gun might have been held to her head. Whoever it was now knew room 316 was occupied and would be sending up their henchmen. Kelly tried to reassure him. But Will was working himself up. As if to make his case, gunfire pattered down the corridor, with a huge shell smacking into the marble floor and walls adjacent to their room. Kelly and Will slipped back into the tub.

A single shot was followed by a shrill scream. A door was kicked open. Then another shot. Along the corridor they were executing people. 'We're going to die,' Will whispered, surprised that he had said it out loud. Neither of them wanted to seem weak. He leapt up. 'GET BEHIND THE DOOR!' They both squeezed behind the bathroom door, Kelly crouching, Will still gripping the fruit knife. 'What the fuck am I going to do with this?' She looked into his eyes: 'He's going to come in and you're going to stab him in the neck.' Will stared at her doubtfully. Then he reached for his whirring phone. 'Will,' his father texted, 'get out of the building now. They have set it on fire.'

They left the bathroom and crept over to the window. Kelly knew what he was thinking. 'We're sixty feet up,' she said, her heart racing. There was no one coming to help them, he replied. 'Everything is burning.' He started pulling the sheets from the bed. 'Kelly, help me.' The windows were their only choice. They tied together whatever they could, while she found some scissors in the desk drawer. 'Look, we can use these to cut up strips. Let's pull down the curtains too. Get the towels.'

They cut and knotted lengths together, braiding a lengthy escape cord. Will stepped back and paid out the coil. 'It's not strong enough,' warned Kelly. 'Let's give it a try,' he replied. They pulled a tug-of-war across the bed. The rope held so they dragged it to the windows. Will grabbed the marble coffee table and hurled it, but it bounced, smacking him in the face. 'What the fuck.' Bruised, he threw it again. This time the inner pane cracked and the third time, the outer glass exploded too, allowing the cool night air to flow into the sweltering room.

Will felt a twinge. He looked down and saw he had cut his arm open; blood was dripping on the carpet. He pressed on with the task, knocking out the remaining shards. He leant out, feeling the wind on his face, as Kelly looked at the gaping frame with horror. Will stared up and saw flames flaring off the roof. He looked down and there was no task force of rescuers, only journalists filming from the Gateway. 'Kelly, we have to give it a try.' He would go first. She began crying, pleading with him not to. The whole thing seemed so haphazard. But Will was already anchoring the rope to the desk. Testing it, he tried to peer over the bulbous parapet of their balcony. 'I can't see the ground,' he shouted. He turned and gave her a kiss. 'I love you,' he mouthed, as he slowly allowed the hand-made rope to take his weight, feeling its resistance, edging to the lip of the balcony and dropping down. Kelly tried to steady him as a tiny flicker of hope sparked inside her. She could see them leaving India with a tale to tell and a story that seemed to have cemented their headlong rush into a relationship.

The rope went limp. Kelly tugged at it and it rushed up to meet her. 'Will!' She hauled up the great, bulky rope in folds, with the disappointment of a fisherman reeling in a broken line. 'Will!' She poked her head out of the broken window, but could not see down to the ground. Looking sideways, she spotted a woman at the window of an adjacent room. Kelly started tying the rope around her own waist, and was about to lower herself over the parapet, when the woman waved to her, in an exaggerated mayday.

She mouthed some words, as shouts might attract the killers. Kelly studied her lips and got some of it: 'Don't. Climb. Down.' Kelly frowned. The neighbour waved and continued mouthing. 'I can see him. Your boyfriend is dead.'

One floor down, in 253, the newlywed Amit glanced at his watch and noted, with exasperation, that it was 3.15 a.m. and they were still stranded. When the last big blast had gone off, it had blown their door off its hinges, and he had found himself staring into the corridor, mumbling 'This is our 9/11', while Varsha ran around behind him, screaming, 'Shut the door.' At more than 80kg, Amit could bring some force to the equation and, after he had come to his senses, he had shoulder-charged the broken door and slid a set of drawers in front of it, while Vasha took a floor lamp, ramming it up against the handle.

Now he heard a mobile phone ringing out in the corridor. He recognized the tone, a Nokia, as he had one just like it. For some reason he counted . . . eight, nine, ten . . . before a massive detonation rang out. They had to get out now. Presuming that the mobile had set off a bomb, he wondered where the next one was planted. None of their improvised measures were going to last long. Amit ran over to the windows and could see that people were climbing out further along the building, trying to escape. Filmed by the TV crews, these pictures, with their haunting echoes of 9/11, were being broadcast around the world.

Tired and hungry, Amit was no longer sure he could think his way out of this, but jumping was not an option. A mercantile entrepreneur, normally brimming with ideas, he needed to figure something out. Crawling over to their broken door he peered through again, seeing only a deep red haze and what looked like bodies lying on the carpet. 'Get back,' Varsha hissed. As he turned to reply, both of them heard the *fwap* as a round bored through the door at hip height, narrowly missing him.

He joined Varsha on the other side of the bed. They could hear footsteps and voices right outside their broken door. 'I think they are going room to room and killing guests,' Varsha whispered. They stared at each other. Partying with all their friends on Sunday, married on Tuesday, would they be dead by Thursday? Why had they not stuck to the plan and got married in Goa? Amit berated himself.

He crawled towards the minibar, Varsha watching in the gloom, as he grabbed several beers and a half-bottle of wine. She was about to point out this was hardly the time to get loaded, when he spotted her expression and explained that he was going to throw the bottles at whoever came through that door, going for the tender, breakable bits. 'Look, I know how to shoot a gun, so if I can take a weapon off them, I'm going to blast our way out of this fucking hotel.' Although Varsha had known Amit for many years before they got married, she felt that she understood him better now, and she believed him.

Voices started up again. They ducked down, listening to a language they could not understand. 'It's *not* Urdu,' Amit whispered. 'Do you think its Pashto?' He hoped these men were not from the Af–Pak border. To him, that conjured up a frightening picture of Pathan tribal mercenaries.

His phone buzzed. It was his brother, well intentioned, asking if he was OK. He had already called about half a dozen times, as had so many other people. Amit snapped, whispering fiercely: 'Look, shut the fuck up, and get off the phone, there's people outside the door and we cannot risk talking.' It sounded harsh but his heightened senses heard the vibration of the phone as an avalanche.

His phone buzzed again. 'Who is this?' It was *The New York Times*. 'Get off the fucking line,' he rasped, incredulous that they had got his number. 'What you going to do, come and *save* me? We need a fucking helicopter, have you got one of those?' He turned off the phone. 'They think I am going to say where we are, you know, broadcast which room we're in. Idiots. Everyone should stay off their phones,' he said to no one in particular. 'There should be a news blackout. Why isn't there a blackout?'

Tap, tap, tap. They looked at each other. Don't breathe. It was next door. *Tap. Tap. Tap*. Someone was rapping on 254. Amit crawled into the bathroom, which had a shared wall, and signalled for Varsha to follow. They listened to a crack and the sound of a boot against a lock, then a security chain splintering off the flimsy frame as the gunmen broke in to the room next door.

Amit recalled seeing its female occupant earlier in the evening. They had come up together in the lift and exchanged pleasantries. Now Varsha clung on to Amit as – *pap, pap, pap* – small-arms fire broke out and angry voices barged into the room. They heard a bed scrape and the TV smash. Since the standard rooms on this floor were identical, they could place every footstep. The bedside cabinets were thrown about and the marble coffee table knocked over. The voices argued, pacing towards the windows and then the bathroom, outside which stood a tall wardrobe. Then they heard a guttural scream; a woman had been found hiding inside.

'Aaaargh,' she cried. 'Get off me. Leave me alone.' She was so close they could hear her breathing. *Phsk. Phsk*. Rounds came flying through their shared plaster wall, just above their heads. He motioned for Varsha to lie flat. The woman was shouting and being dragged out into the corridor. 'Help me,' she cried. 'Somebody please help!' Varsha buried her head in her arms, trying to block it out. Amit mumbled under his breath that he was going to rip them apart when they came for them. But he did not move.

After a minute, it sounded as if the shouting woman was being bundled back into her room. *Ack, ack, ack*. Several shots and then yells in that strange language. Then the sound of boots walking away. Listening to the terrible silence, gripping Varsha's hand, Amit said: 'They didn't just shoot her a couple of times, they emptied a magazine into her.'

The woman was not dead. 'Help me, someone. Please help.' She sounded weak, as if she was fighting for her life. What should they do? If they went out they, too, would be shot. Amit and Varsha locked eyes and stayed put, trying not to listen as the whimpering became ever fainter.

3.30 a.m.

Directly below them, on the first floor, DCP Vishwas Patil was slumped in the shadows of the Crystal Room, reliving his escape from the ambush and the fire. Starving, thirsty and covered in soot and scratches, he had no idea that outside the hotel the police were mourning his demise – and that of Rajvardhan.

They had escaped by hurling themselves down as the fireball had exploded, taking refuge inside the Crystal Room, where Patil was now nervously checking and rechecking his Glock. Beside him, Rajvardhan cut a tablecloth into strips to bind his ankle, ripped and twisted when he rolled to avoid the flaming cartwheel. He knew he had broken a bone but was trying not to think about it. For hours, grenades and AK-47 rounds had rung out all around them. Singed and soaked, they had listened to hellish screams, incapable of doing anything about it. Now there was just blackness and the throaty roar of the fire.

'How many times do you have to look in the magazine to know that we only have five rounds between us?' Rajvardhan snapped. He knew that Patil did not deserve his scorn but he was angry, tired and in agony. Here they lay, the slender resources of the police matched against a well-stocked and superbly trained private terror network. Rajvardhan felt as if he had every right to be armed as well as those he faced, and wanted to be secure in the knowledge that backup was on its way. Right now he could believe in nothing. They both knew they were alone, blocked in by the inferno and the heavily armed gunmen who were still somewhere out there. Rajvardhan's last sight of Inspector Dhole and the others from the CCTV room was of them retreating, flames closing around them, as bullets rained down. 'Why *did* Dhole go backwards? You never go backwards. Didn't he know that?'

Rajvardhan took in his new surroundings, glimpsing the remains of a wedding celebration. Both men needed food and he chomped into a half-eaten apple, while Patil cruised among the abandoned banquet dishes, picking up someone else's half-drunk Coke.

How ragged this grand salon looked, Patil thought, as he grabbed a slice of cake. People who came here probably earned in a day what he accrued in several months. A forest of pink flowers lay trampled at the far end, of a kind he had never seen before. Platters of elaborate salads spilled on to the floor and had been crushed into a mush. There was a broken sponge cake that resembled an exploded volcano and he made out the two names entwined in hearts on a shot-up plaque beside the door. 'Amit and Varsha Thadani.' Had they made it out alive? 'Come on, let's go,' he said, rising from the sodden carpet. 'Attack is the best form of defence.' Rajvardhan shook his head. He, too, wanted to hunt down the gunmen, but the odds spoke against this plan. He was wounded, this place was a labyrinth, they were outgunned, and he had no more energy.

Reluctantly he hobbled to his feet, and they edged into the murky corridor. In the gloom they pressed their backs against the smooth, cool marble wall, sliding towards the Grand Staircase. 'You go ahead,' whispered Rajvardhan, 'I'll cover the rear.' Patil inched on and then raised a fist: 'Stop.' He held up two fingers and pointed: 'Armed. Straight ahead.' Rajvardhan caught sight of two dark shadows, scurrying downwards with their weapons. 'I think I can do it,' Patil whispered. 'If I get a clean head shot.' Rajvardhan pulled Patil closer. 'I believe you. But what about the others watching their backs?' He pointed up to the blazing dome. 'Let's say you get off a couple of shots. Your pistol's accuracy beyond fifty feet is massively reduced. Chances are you will wing them.' By contrast the AK's curled magazines carried thirty rounds, and a flat, Russian-style clip could pack up to a hundred. 'If they've taped their mags together, you can double that count. Do you get it?' Patil sagged. The best they could hope for was to retreat and get out alive.

They edged towards a service corridor and Rajvardhan glimpsed another figure and stopped. Staring through the smoke, waiting for it to clear, he saw the silhouette of a Western woman. She was creeping towards the staircase, her clothes blackened and burned, trying to escape. She presented another problem. Without his uniform, he probably looked like a terrorist to her, and any screams would alert the real gunmen. As he weighed it up, she sensed his presence and turned, staring into his eyes. Rajvardhan had no choice but to motion 'calm' with his palms held up. He mouthed: 'Friendly.' Her eyes widened, and she bolted like a spooked deer, leaving Rajvardhan thankful that at least she had fled silently.

Limping heavily, he entered the service corridor. Ahead, Patil prayed it would be unguarded. When they reached the outer kitchens, their boots stuck to drying blood. Climbing down a service staircase, they found a passageway that led towards the lobby. After three hours inside, Patil could smell the familiar scent of his beloved city.

He ran on ahead, with both hands raised: 'Police, police.' A small throng of officers scurried forward, as he shouted: 'DCP Zone 1 approaching.' They looked perplexed and then they cheered, rushing over to greet the dead men. 'You are a ghost,' one of them said, patting Patil, who pointed to Rajvardhan. 'This man needs medical attention.' Someone called an ambulance as the Joint Commissioner Law and Order and Deven Bharti, the Crime Branch number two, rushed over, delighted. After four frustrating hours with the mobile direction finder, Bharti had been deployed to man the police command post in the Taj lobby.

The Joint Commissioner, who at the start of the attacks had been ordered to run the Taj operation while his street-savvy colleague Maria languished in the Control Room, asked for a debrief. Whatever they knew would be crucial for the Intelligence Branch and Research and Analysis Wing, and for the Special Forces, should they ever arrive.

Rajvardhan looked stunned. He had expected to find the lobby bristling with Quick Response Teams, armed with their AK-47s and 9mm pistols, dressed in bulletproof vests and lightweight helmets, but only a few officers were milling about. There was no rescue operation in play? The JC shrugged. 'Police Commissioner Gafoor ordered the QRTs to seal the perimeter.' For the slim-built man who kept his own counsel, this was as good as a slagging off.

'Where are the Striking Mobiles?' Rajvardhan asked. Many had failed to report, as the ancient self-loading rifles they carried had no rounds in them. Could anyone blame them? The JC pushed on. This was not the time to conduct a post-mortem, although there were many things he could not fathom, mistakes and errors of judgement that resounded across the city, with stories emerging of no-shows from experienced officers who, as soon as the bullets started flying, were somehow not where they were supposed to be. All hinged now on the National Security Guard. It was the right force for the job. But it had still not arrived in the city and there was not even a clear timetable for its deployment.

The JC made himself a wager: there would be no inquiry worth its salt, when all of this was over. This was not the UK or the US, where a powerful commission would bear down on every institution. The establishment would thwart any such investigation. No one would put their head above the parapet and afterwards the old, inefficient, corrupt regime would continue to rule the roost.

Right now, the JC needed a detailed picture: strategy, terrorist numbers and materiel. He called over a navy commando, one of the MARCOS. Two teams had just arrived. Rajvardhan was nonplussed. Patil looked incredulous. For all these hours they had been made to hold their ground while the Special Forces gathered their might. Now, with the NSG still a no-show, there were fewer than twenty MARCOS in the building from an outfit with a fighting strength of 1,000. Those who had come did not even have Kevlar vests or helmets. And it wasn't as if they had had any distance to travel. These units had come from Colaba, less than a mile to the south.

Patil prepared to follow the MARCOS in. They would need a guide and he was the logical choice since they had no idea what they faced or how to find it. Rajvardhan, too, pledged to come back, after he got his leg seen to. Patil's phone buzzed – Commissioner Gafoor: 'You are not to go up. Repeat. Not to go up.' Gafoor was afraid of a friendly-fire incident. 'The MARCOS go up on their

own. The DCP will stay down and make sure the Taj is contained.'
Patil was directed to supervise the perimeter cordons.

Incredulous and frustrated, he took himself outside, dazzled by
the lights and camera crews and hubbub, while the MARCOS
headed up through the smoke and into the dark, hoping to re-
activate the CCTV room. There were still no hotel blueprints
available and so they had no inkling of where they were going.
Somehow they made it to the first-floor landing unchallenged. They
clambered up to the second floor too. And they jogged past the
smashed, unmarked door to the Taj Data Centre that no one knew
existed.

Crouched in her homemade bunker, squeezed beneath a desk,
Florence Martis comforted herself with the thought that it was
so dark and smoky no one could see in through the broken door.
'I'll deal with daybreak when it comes,' she told herself as the
silence became one degree heavier and she began humming her
favourite *filmi* tune. 'You surely would know. You are the one I'm
crazy about.'

Her father Faustine had promised to find her and she did not
doubt him. He was a bloodhound and had never let her down.
She recalled how, during her terrifying school board exams, when she
had been too scared to eat he had turned up on his scooter with rice
and chicken. Her mobile rang, shaking her back into the present.

'Hello. Who is there?' she asked tentatively. A man's voice
answered. 'Hello, Florence, my name is Roshan.'

Roshan. She did not know a Roshan. She presumed it must be
a Taj technician calling from another part of the world since
the Data Centre dealt with the Taj globally. Did he not know that
the hotel was besieged? 'Roshan, now's not a good time,' she
whispered.

'Listen, don't put the phone down.' He sounded determined, she
thought. 'Just tell me, are you stuck in the Data Centre? No one can
work out where you are. Faustine says you are missing. I used to
work in the Data Centre too. I know every inch of it.' He had heard

about Florence through a friend who knew Faustine, and he wanted to do whatever he could to help father and daughter.

Florence perked up. 'Oh, thank God. Thank you, Roshan. I am fine, but please get me out of here. The door has gone and I am choking.' She did not really understand who he was, but she liked the tone of his voice. 'Look, Roshan, if they kill me . . . I mean, they want to.' Her mouth was dry and her empty belly grumbled. She could think in sentences but only half of it came out of her mouth.

'Keep calm, Florence,' Roshan said. 'I will stay on the line until someone finds you. Florence. Are you still there?' She cradled the phone as the song came back into her head, and she began to sing to Roshan: '*Hey Shona, Hey Shona* [O sweet one, O sweet one]'.

Outside the hotel, the TV cameras caught Karambir Kang unawares. Unshaven and haunted, he stood with Ratan Tata, whose grandfather had built the hotel. Chairman of the Tata group, the conglomerate that owned it, Tata had been at home when the attacks had begun and was advised to stay there while the police worked out what was going on. Instead, he had come straight down and waited half a night, barely sleeping, incredulous, as flames wreathed the family's jewel. 'I *cannot* believe the hotel is burning down,' Tata said to whoever was in earshot. 'It is just not possible.' Karambir Kang stared into the inferno too. His eyes were red. And in that brief second, as he craned his neck, the cameras trained on him, his misgivings were on show. A giant man looked as if he were made of straw.

The centre of the blaze seemed to be the exact point where his family's apartment was located. The TV was reporting that a firestorm had engulfed the top floors, consuming everything in its path. The gunmen had hauled guests from their rooms, keeping them prisoner elsewhere in the Taj, the TV anchors said, bludgeoning some in full view of the CCTV cameras, sending a message to police that they were impotent.

Earlier, Neeti had done what her husband advised her: locking herself and the boys in the bathroom of their apartment and blocking any cracks with wet towels. With Uday huddled up beside her, she had cradled Samar, stroking his hair. It was hard to believe that only a few hours previously, the boy had been talking on the phone to his grandfather in Bahrain. 'Samar, I'm coming to Bombay soon. Will you let me sleep in your bedroom with you?' Of course, Samar had replied, happily.

A Taj executive came over and put his arms around the General Manager's broad shoulders. 'All we can do is just hope and pray that Neeti and the boys have been taken hostage and are not in the suite.' Only the southern side of the sixth floor was burning, he pointed out. If they had made it to the other end of the building there was a real chance they would be found alive.

Karambir took a few moments to walk down to the seafront, where a soft, salty breeze blew in. Looking out to the horizon, he called his parents 3,000 miles away in Bahrain, where they were visiting his sister Amrit. 'I don't think they've made it,' he told his father, his voice cracking. If Neeti were alive she would have found a way to stay in touch. Nothing had been heard from her for an hour. 'Be a brave Sikh,' his father told him. 'You are an army general's son,' he continued, recalling how his boy had been an enormous baby at eleven pounds, someone who had grown up on his father's war stories in a succession of army compounds. The infant Karambir had loved nothing better than to be driven around in the army staff car and his father had wanted him to become a soldier too. What could he tell his son now? He handed the phone to Karambir's mother. 'I can't save them,' he told her. 'Then go and save the others,' she replied gently. 'You are a brave boy.' Both of them were weighed down by loss.

Eventually, Karambir spoke again. 'I will be the last man here,' he pledged. He thought back to the family's rushed breakfast routine that morning, their last shared moment. The hotel which had consumed so much of his life had now taken them from him for ever.

He rang off and turned back to face the stricken hotel, the flames reflecting in his eyes. He saw incredulous and terrified faces in the crowd that was watching as well. Karambir Kang had to find the strength to carry on.

Up in her Malabar Hill apartment, Savitri Choudhury studied the chilling Taj pictures too. Nothing had been heard from Sabina for several hours now. There was something she needed to do. She called Shantanu: 'I am watching Sabina's room go up in flames. She can't get out of there. You know that, right?' Shantanu was still in Delhi, unable to fly until dawn. 'Please,' she said. 'Make your peace. Call her and say goodbye.'

Up in the Rendezvous Room, the diners from Souk and the Korean conference delegates were anxiously watching the Palace burning far below them, when a message came up from the Taj's security chief, Sunil Kudiyadi. 'The MARCOS have gone into the Palace wing. It's time for you to get out.' Across the eastern horizon, the first hint of dawn was turning the sky oyster grey.

Bob Nicholls, the private security chief, gathered his team of ex-commandos and Ravi Dharnidharka, the US Marine captain. Defending the Rendezvous Room had been straightforward: boxed into a citadel, with the lifts jammed and the fire exits sealed. But descending more than twenty floors with a large crowd of agitated diners, with kitchen implements as their only weapons, was perilous.

'In the Marines we like to say, "Don't take a knife to a gunfight",' Ravi said, as much to himself as anyone else. Earlier, when they had passed through the kitchens, he had not gone looking for weapons like the others, worrying about the false hope kitchen knives brought. Most of the diners were already on tenterhooks. Some were falling to pieces. Then there were his relatives, whom he had a duty to protect while maintaining a safe distance. The Korean trade delegation, with their faltering English and complete incomprehension about how the subcontinent worked, were strung out.

Ravi had still not told anyone he was a US Marine, as ideal a hostage as the gunmen could hope to find. He also privately worried that Nicholls's team seemed a little gung-ho. That might have been a pilot's prejudice; his eye filtered through the Harrier's cockpit, calculating the odds within fractions of a second from thousands of feet up. A commando was a different kind of warrior, smelling whatever he was about to overwhelm, getting as close to it as the rules of engagement permitted.

There was one thing they agreed on: Ravi and Bob's team could see why India's Western Naval Command had been reluctant to send in the MARCOS. The marine commandos would have no experience of urban warfare. The Taj would be as alien to them as a foreign land. Now they were in, they would do well to even find the terrorists in this pitch-black, smoke-filled labyrinth. 'The wrong team is facing down embedded terrorists who have controlled the hotel for many hours,' said Ravi. Bob agreed: 'They will be lucky not to kill each other.'

In the crow's nest, it was decision time. Kudiyadi had advised them that the MARCOS had no plans to come up the Tower, and at best would act as a decoy in the Palace wing. Bob's team could use this diversion to slip through. Ravi liked the idea, having believed all along that their best hope was 'not having to fight'. Bob relayed the message to his men. 'A coordinated, slow-mo evac,' he told the crew, warning that 150 civilians would need careful managing. 'What about the police?' someone asked. Couldn't they help? Bob shook his head and switched on the PA. 'If we are going to get out, we have to do it ourselves,' he announced. The room was silent. Stepping outside without armed backup was a terrifying proposition to the civilians.

'No rescue is near,' Bob stressed, relaying a warning from Kudiyadi: 'All power will be cut once a certain number of floors are ablaze, so we will become trapped above the fire line.' Ravi suspected that their chance of getting out if the fire spread into the Tower 'was about zero'. The diners agreed to evacuate and Bob rang Kudiyadi on the staff radio: 'Come up if you can.'

They would send down the civilians, ten at a time, with a minute in between, women and children up front. 'We will *all* get down,' Bob reassured them. Ravi looked at the cousins and uncles he had not seen since he was eighteen years old. How did they come to be here on *this* night? You could not calculate the odds. Getting up the courage to excavate his past had been a leap. Finding the time in between America's wars to travel to India had been a struggle. They had only ended up at Souk at the last minute, while other family members had plumped for Tiffin in the Oberoi's lobby. In the last hour, he had been hearing terrible stories of how it had been shot to pieces by gunmen.

Bob addressed everyone: 'We don't know where these gunmen are, so we have to be silent.' If Bob was getting his information from cable news, they should presume the terrorists were doing the same, so no phone calls. 'Shoes off.' Everyone should be ready to jog or run in silence. 'All loose change out of your pockets.'

Privately, Ravi had listened hard to the soundtrack of what was happening below and completed an aural inventory: a mixed cache of AK-47s, small arms, probably 7.65mm or 9mm, grenades and, most worryingly, some kind of high explosive. This showed just how hybrid this Mumbai raid really was. To Ravi's way of thinking it combined the random terror of an Islamist outfit that sought to cull civilians ruthlessly, the kind of slaughter whipped up in Fallujah by Al-Qaeda in Mesopotamia, with the skills deployed by amphibious commandos like the US Marines. 'All we have to do is *evade* the enemy,' Ravi reiterated.

He felt a tap on his shoulder. A smartly dressed man was worried his elderly mother would not make it down the fire escape. 'Leave me behind, please,' Rama Parekh, aged eighty-four, implored. Ravi shook his head. 'We're not leaving anyone.' He suggested a chair. 'We will take turns to carry you.'

The barricades were dismantled piece by piece: furniture, cushions and sections of the Rendezvous stage. As Ravi lifted down the last upended table he heard movement outside in the stairwell. 'Holy shit,' he said under his breath, turning round to Bob, who stood holding a meat cleaver. It could be one of the gunmen for all they knew. Gingerly, Ravi opened the door and saw two frazzled and sweaty security men in black suits, armed with radios. 'Sunil!' shouted Bob, rushing forward to greet the security chief, Kudiyadi.

As they entered, they brought the smell of fire and gunpowder with them. Horrified guests stepped back.

The doors swung open, allowing the beaters to go ahead, scouting the porthole windows on each landing. These looked into every corridor and were potential kill zones. The forward units would try to provide a continuous assessment of risk, fed back through the convoy of diners, the first detachment of which was about to be dispatched down the stairwell. The commandos crept down, the fire escape walls sticky to the touch as the daytime humidity gave way to a cold, dry night air. They were within a foot of the landing and then in full view of the dimly lit corridor ahead. They clambered down the next flight. Nothing moved. The Tower was like a ghost ship, with the hotel management having contacted most of the guests, warning them not to come out until they were called by name.

'If something is moving,' Bob said, 'presume it's not friendly.'

The first scout came back, drenched but happy. 'Nothing to report.' Bob counted off the first pod of ten diners, Ravi making sure his family was among them. As they crept down a bitter smell filled their nostrils. Soon a flexible column was snaking down and almost immediately someone's mobile phone rang out. Bob turned around to hush them and saw the Koreans were loaded down with their shoes and conference goody bags. How the hell were they going to keep this procession under control?

A clatter of rounds echoed up from below and the line sharply concertinaed. Had the advance party encountered somebody? 'The shots are away from us in a corridor,' reassured Bob, relaying the whispered information back. 'Please keep moving.' Ravi, at the rear, had had to abandon the chair. He could not swing it round the sharp angles of the fire escape and instead hitched Rama Parekh over his shoulder like a coal-sack. She clung on, silent. She's a toughie, he thought as he descended.

After what seemed like hours, Bob reached the single digits and then the fifth floor, which reeked of burning carpets. With every step they were getting closer to the gunmen and here the fire escape abruptly ended as the modern Tower met the top of the original

Palace wing. 'Where do we go now?' He assumed that the fire exit would coil around the Tower to the ground floor, but the scouts ahead reported that it crossed an open corridor. The column of terrified civilians would have to run the gauntlet along a floor that had not been cleared: a perfect sniper's trap.

They readied the crowd in the stairwell. 'We have to go.' Bob urged those around him to remain silent, wondering what other obstacles lay head. How, for example, were they going to signal their presence to the Indian security forces to avoid a blue-on-blue slaughter? Kudiyadi had been in constant touch with the police, but had the message got through? Bob felt queasy. 'We are going to have to break into the open with hands raised, and then gallop.'

Everyone cleared the 50-metre-long corridor without incident and edged down another few flights, until they came up against a fire door. Was this it? It seemed too soon. They had to open the door to prevent a crush. But then, which direction to run in? Bob was no longer sure of their orientation. Ravi shuffled up the line and with a final heave threw back the exit to see two army *jawans* (constables) sitting on the pavement, smoking and with their rifles in the air. As they looked up in surprise, Bob grimaced. They were out, at the back of the Tower, facing Bombay Yacht Club.

'Run,' he shouted, releasing the first guests. One, two, three, four, they hustled into the night air: 'Don't stop. Head for the Gateway.' Finally, they were all outside. Fearing the column might be pursued someone jammed the fire door shut, doing a solid job, forcing a piece of wood into the handle. No one would be getting through that any time soon.

As Ravi ran, Rama Parekh still hanging on to his back, he was astonished to see crowds freely milling around in front of the hotel, well within AK-47 range. Police lay in the road, and squatted behind barricades, while soldiers idled around as if the main action were over. Where were the commanding officers and the cordons? From the hush of the Tower and a well-organized descent, he was now buffeted by bedlam. A camera crew hustled over, trying to grab an interview.

Ravi listened out for the *pith, pith* of the first rounds kicking up dirt, his battlefield sense driving him on against the human current until he finally felt far enough away to put Rama down. He wondered if he had broken her ribs, but she thanked him warmly. 'Ravi.' He heard his name being called: 'Ravi. Ravi.' It was some other relatives, who had been waiting outside for hours. They reached for him, hugging him, hustling him towards a car, confirming the terrible news that two cousins and an uncle had been killed in the Trident–Oberoi's Tiffin restaurant.

Before Ravi could take it in, he glimpsed Bob being carried along by a great paper chase of reporters, waving their pads and cameras. There was one last thing he needed to do. 'Bob,' he shouted, waving at him. They looked at each other incredulously and felt a mixture of elation at the triumphant evacuation and trepidation at the potential for calamity that still existed at the perimeter and the dangers to be faced by Sunil Kudiyadi, who had already gone back inside. 'Look, I couldn't tell you up there,' Ravi said. 'I'm a US Marine pilot.' He proffered his hand. 'I flew sorties in Iraq. Just so you know, I had to protect my family and myself, and that's the only reason . . .' Bob hushed him. He did not need to say anything. Ravi felt himself pulled inside the car, with one passenger shouting directions: Titan Towers, in Breach Candy. He could see Bob waving.

Bob smiled. All night, he had been trying to figure out which kind of military Ravi was. 'Pilot,' he said to himself, as he grabbed his commandos and headed off to the Brabourne Stadium, where the cricket tournament was supposed to have taken place. Now they were out of the hotel they had nowhere to stay. They would contemplate the night in the hush of the empty bleachers.

8

The Shadow of Death

Thursday, 27 November 2008, 3.40 a.m.

Outside the hotel a cheer went up as news of the successful Tower evacuation reached Taj staffers. Until now everything around them served as a reminder of how they had lost control of the hotel. Although the Tata group's emergency administration point had shifted from the Gateway to the safer environs of the President hotel on Cuffe Parade, Karambir Kang remained outside too, seeing, smelling and listening to it all. The Souk story was a fillip, and ranging distractedly up and down Apollo Bunder he received several more pieces of encouraging news.

The fire brigade had just entered Best Marg, the tree-lined lane alongside the south wing of the Palace, and extricated a handful of guests from the city end of the sixth floor. Not everyone had died up there. There was also news of Sabina Saikia, the food critic, who had been staying just a few feet away from where Neeti, Uday and Samar were trapped on the sea-facing side. She was reported to be sending texts or making calls, which suggested she was still alive.

Her friend Ambreen Khan had received several texts while she sheltered to the north of the hotel, at a friend's apartment off Pedder Road. At first she had stared at them in disbelief. She had checked the number and sender's ID. She thought she was hallucinating but they were definitely from Sabina's phone. 'Incredible!' Ambreen studied the TV pictures of the blazing Taj and re-read one text. 'You once told me about a dream you had,' her friend had written. 'I am the most popular girl in town. We are by the sea and I am lying on a charpoy. On one side of me is Shantanu and you are on the other.'

Ambreen sometimes felt like the invisible partner in their marriage, a conduit to their children, passing on messages from a distracted mother. 'Shantanu is asking everyone to visit one by one.' There was a long pause before another text. 'My stomach is hurting, and my mobile phone is the only light, but I am thinking about this dream. In it you rolled over on the charpoy to face me and you said: "You will die."'

Ambreen gasped. Was this really happening?

In the lobby, Sunil Kudiyadi regrouped with his Black Suits. Exasperating news had come that the big guns of the National Security Guard (NSG) had only just left Delhi, meaning it would be many hours more before they reached the hotel. Buoyed by the Souk triumph, the Black Suits decided to go it alone one more time, attempting a second evacuation, this time bolstered by the MARCOS. Kudiyadi texted Chef Oberoi. 'Please come down to the lobby if you can. It is clear. Gunmen are on upper floors.'

King of a business predicated on infinitesimal tolerances, where the distance between the knife and a dinner plate is measured by a half-bent thumb, Oberoi noticed as he rode the service lift down to the ground floor that his usually pristine chef's whites were bloodied. He rubbed at the stains, trying to suppress a mounting feeling of dread at what he might see on his first foray outside the kitchens since 9 p.m. the previous evening.

Taking a deep breath, he slid back the lift gate and emerged through a service door that, when closed, appeared to be a marble panel. Checking to see if the corridor was clear, he crept out into the darkened lobby, a waft of burnt wood hitting him as he clocked blood tracks by the entrance to the Harbour Bar. When he reached the police command post next to Shamiana, Karambir Kang and Kudiyadi were waiting. As they shook hands, Karambir quietly revealed his family were probably dead. Oberoi was horrified. The General Manager had said nothing during their frequent phone and text exchanges and so he had presumed that Neeti and the boys were safe. He could only guess at the pain Karambir was feeling, but this was not the time to dwell on it. They had to weigh up a plan. Joined by the Joint Commissioner of Police and a MARCOS commander, they sifted through their options.

The MARCOS wanted to leave the NSG to clear and lock down the Tower. It was a complex operation that they were not trained for and they had the wrong equipment and insufficient men. So where to focus their energies? The guests locked into the Zodiac and the Starboard Bar on the ground floor were safe enough for now, having barricaded themselves in. Those trapped in the function rooms on the first floor with the Banqueting Manager, Mallika Jagad, were a more urgent case, but she was reporting that their corridor still rang with grenade explosions. How was a 23-year-old keeping control of these veteran executives? 'Alcohol,' she responded dryly. 'I've a great single malt that is helping to incentivize them.'

That left the Chambers. Invisible to the world, but easily accessed through the service corridors, the hotel's private club was the obvious choice for evacuation, especially as among those stranded there were politicians and assorted tycoons with powerful voices. 'OK,' said Karambir, 'let's do the Chambers.' Preparing to assist, the JC called through to the police Control Room, requesting backup. Commissioner Gafoor, still stationed in his car outside the Trident hotel, flatly refused. 'You have the MARCOS. Stand down until the NSG arrive.' Only Kudiyadi's Black Suits would go into the fray – armed with their radios and supported by a small unit of marine commandos.

Chef Oberoi headed back through the invisible marble door, adjacent to the Harbour Bar, tying it shut it behind him with a napkin – the broken lock was one of those items on a long snagging list that never got seen to. Taking the old service lift, he stepped out into his domain that still smelled reassuringly of lye and candied fruit. He worried that such a large number of people could not be taken out through the main lobby as the gunmen were still roaming the sea-facing Palace corridors. He and his staff would shepherd the Chambers group through the hotel's backstage areas and out via the Time Office on Merriweather Road. Now all he needed was volunteers from the Kitchen Brigade.

In Merriweather Road, Sea Lounge's head waiter, Faustine Martis, was trying as hard as he could to get back into the hotel. Catching wind of the successful Tower evacuation, he buttonholed a reporter for the *Hindustan Times*: 'Who's out and where?' The reporter said: 'A hundred and fifty or so from the Tower so far.' But no one from the Palace. Faustine looked forlorn and rushed towards the Taj's staff entrance. 'They are planning something new, too,' the journalist shouted after him. But he didn't hear.

A Black Suit caught hold of Faustine trying to enter. 'You're going the wrong way,' he told him, gently turning him around. It was the fourth time they had knocked him back and on each occasion he had given the same desperate story: 'My daughter's inside on the second floor.' The Black Suit asked him to be patient: 'Please, sir. We will get to everyone.' But Faustine wasn't waiting: 'She'll be dead by then,' he shouted. 'The room is already filled with smoke. The door's gone too.' He was tearful and determined.

When a small column of police appeared shortly before 4 a.m., Faustine tagged along, and as they reached the glass security box, he darted down the one-porter-wide stairway. He had done it. Now he intended to exploit his knowledge of the cellars, the locker rooms and vaults to reach the first-floor kitchens. From there he could use the service lifts to head for the Data Centre. Somewhere near there his daughter was waiting for him.

4 a.m. – the Chambers

Inside the Chambers library, the New York financier Mike Pollack was agitated. The longer he, Anjali and their dining companions remained in the dark, the more pessimistic he became. Pollack admired the Taj staff for getting them this far, especially Chef Oberoi's unshakeably positive number two, Vijay Banja, a jovial character with a mop of unruly hair who had helped them escape from Wasabi. But it was obvious to Mike that the Chambers was only a respite. He was a fan of Mumbai, a season-ticket holder. But the security forces had to get themselves into gear.

All around him mobile phone screens glowed in the darkness. Some of the conversations made him feel like his teeth were getting drilled, including that of an Indian MP, who seemed to be giving a live TV interview. 'We are in a special part of the hotel on the first floor called the Chambers. There are more than 200 important people: business leaders and foreigners.'

Pollack whispered to Anjali: 'Can you believe it? This fucking idiot MP is blabbing our exact location to CNN or something.' Friends in the US began texting to say that the Indian MP's interview was already being reported. A siege had just become something far more deadly. All of his fears came to a head and, impulsive as always, he called Anjali's cousin, who was the legal guardian of their two boys. 'Things are looking bad. Please take care of them if we don't get out.'

Anjali pulled Chef Banja to one side. It is my job to take care of you. Was there a plan? 'Don't worry,' he reassured her, taking her hand. 'I'll die before I let anything happen to you.'

If hell is other people, then the journalist Bhisham Mansukhani was plumbing its depths too. Ensconced in the Lavender Room, along the corridor from Mike and Anjali, he was observing a hostile confrontation: a guest castigating a waiter for failing to provide the right charger for his mobile phone. What a prick, Bhisham thought, before recognizing the angry man as Gunjan Narang, someone whom he and the newlywed Amit Thadani had been at school with. Even then Gunjan had been a bully. After the buzz of arriving in the exclusive Chambers had subsided, Bhisham was beginning to feel nervous. He had been in the Taj for almost six hours, forced to listen to the intimate and fatuous, eavesdropping as some guests lambasted their contacts in the upper echelons. One man was heard trying to raise a helicopter from the Indian Air Force that he suggested could hover over the Chambers terrace.

Bhisham kept telling himself that the only unexpected boon was that he had avoided another big fat Indian wedding. Only Thadani could have talked him into coming to one of those, a request from a childhood friend that had forced him to renege on his personal oath never to do the assembly of ceremonies, feasts and parties that most posh weddings had become. He prodded Amit on his Black-Berry. Nothing had been heard from him or Varsha for hours. Bhisham tried his friend in the Press Club: 'Is it true that they are going room to room shooting?' Another friend, a writer at *The Times of India*, texted back better news: 'Fire brigade dousing fire.' Maybe Amit and Varsha were safe after all.

His train of thought was interrupted by a sensational whisper: Souk had been evacuated with *no* casualties. He felt a glimmer of hope and began texting friends once more. '4.10 a.m.: Waiting for evacuation.'

In the Chambers library, close to where Mike's party was sitting, the yacht owner Andreas Liveras noted a flurry of activity, shaking his head. For the last couple of hours he had remained on his chaise longue, keeping in regular touch with Nick Edmiston out on the *Alysia*, assuring him everything was under control. 'Remesh,' he said solemnly, speaking to his trusted aide, who sat on the floor beside him, '*we* are staying put. Running is a fool's mission.' He laughed. 'These people can't even help themselves.'

It wasn't that Andreas was cruel. Remesh told everyone that he couldn't wish for a better boss. But strangers found his directness obnoxious. He had always known what he wanted and worked on other people's indecision. These days, if you were not straight out of the starting blocks, Andreas talked over you, the legacy of having struggled to build his fortune from nothing, one cake at a time, the catering millions augmented by those derived from the yacht-chartering game. If anything, Andreas was too full of life to be dragged down by other people's poor judgements and ineffective choices.

What he had in mind now was an armed escort. 'We will wait for people with guns,' he told Remesh, fielding calls from his four worried children in London. 'Mr L., they are planning to take foreigners,'

Remesh warned between calls. 'You tell them you are Syrian.' With his Cypriot complexion, Andreas could get away with it. But his mind was elsewhere. He had had an idea. He would get his story out, kicking the British government into heaping pressure on the Indians, precipitating a speedy rescue mission. Maybe the SAS would be mobilized. The best way of starting this particular fight would be to call the BBC, he judged.

Within minutes of having explained his predicament to the newsroom in London, where it had just turned midnight, he was patched through to the reporter Matt Frei, who conducted a live interview on the rolling BBC News 24. 'I came to have a curry in the Taj Mahal hotel, which is the best restaurant here,' Andreas explained, as the BBC showed footage of dead tourists being taken out of the Taj on luggage trollies, including the Canadian couple shot by the pool.

The besieged hotel was the top story in the world right now, and Frei was delighted to have an eyewitness inside. 'And then what happened?' he prompted. Andreas continued: 'As soon as we sat down at the table we heard machine-gun fire outside in the corridors. We [got] under the table. [Waiters] switched all the lights off. The machine guns kept going. Then they took us [out] into the kitchen and from there, into a basement, to come up into a salon. There are two or three salons here and there must be more than a thousand people here.' The number he plucked from the air was large enough to attract attention, a typically bravura performance.

Frei tried to get the facts straight: 'Andreas, where are you?' The interviewee paused, irritable: 'I am in a *salon* in *the* hotel. We are locked in here. No one tells us anything. People are frightened. The last bomb exploded forty-five minutes ago. The hotel is shaking every time a bomb goes off. We are looking at each other and everyone jumps, living on their nerves.' The bulletin coming to an end, Frei interjected: 'We have to leave it there. Andreas, good luck.' The BBC signed off. Had he done enough to grab Whitehall by the collar?

Moments later, they heard a rumpus, shouting and barging coming from the Chambers foyer. Liveras closed his eyes, sitting back on the chaise longue. Whatever was happening, he was having no part of it. Bhisham texted a friend: 'People in hall.' An evacuation was starting. He was going to take his chance. He roused his mother and her friends.

A Taj security officer walked between them, issuing instructions. 'Turn off your phones. Take your change out of your pockets.' The evacuation was happening right away. 'We are going to get you all out. Please be ready.' Bhisham and his mother moved towards the kitchen exit, along an unlit corridor. 'Form an orderly line.' After all the inaction he now felt eager but drained. Ahead, he heard raised voices and people jostling and pushing. 'Can you see those foreigners jumping the queue?' someone shouted, as a group of Europeans forced their way ahead. Bhisham spotted the school bully Gunjan again, who was now with his family.

'Everyone hold steady. You'll all get out,' the Taj Black Suits urged, trying to keep things fluid and affable. But the mood was darker than in the Tower, where diners had elected leaders and scouts to escort them. 'Everyone will make it, if you form a line. Turn your phones off. Absolute quiet.' There were a hundred more guests here than in Souk, and they were narrating their own exits: calling, texting and Tweeting.

Down at the front, through the open door, Bhisham could just about make out Chef Hemant Oberoi, who held his hands up for silence. Next to him was Chef Banja, who had kept up everyone's spirits. Before them stood the white-jacketed *chefs de partie*, with their grey neckerchiefs, the most senior and accomplished in the kitchens, and their sous-chefs. Also present were the blue-, grey- and brown-uniformed apprentices, the *plongeurs* or dishwashers, and the *marmitons*, the young kitchen boys who scrubbed out the deep casserole dishes.

Chef Oberoi marshalled his Kitchen Brigade, explaining that in a few minutes they would begin escorting guests through the kitchen, down the stairs by his cabin and out of the Time Office staff exit. He needed volunteers to form a human chain around the evacuating guests in case of any unforeseen disaster.

Nitin Minocha, the Golden Dragon's senior sous-chef, who wore a neatly clipped soldier's moustache and had a pair of chopsticks perennially in his top pocket, stepped forward. He had already shown tonight that he could keep his head, having locked down his restaurant and concealed diners, before evacuating them to Wasabi, and then out of the firing line into Chambers. Chef Banja joked that tonight Minocha would become 'a soldier in whites', aided by Hemant Talim, his sous-chef, who also volunteered. Effervescent Talim, who was Amit Peshave's friend and former room-mate, had worked at the Taj since 2002 but was still so youthful that in the kitchen he was known as 'the Chicken'. As a result of working on the wok station he had developed a formidable forearm and was the hotel's premier arm wrestler.

Oberoi clapped Talim on the shoulders just as Thomas Varghese, a Syrian Christian, who was head waiter in Wasabi, raised his hand. Varghese, master of the night shift, was a favourite in the kitchens as he defended the Taj staff in the employee union and he could manage his restaurant almost single-handedly: eleven teppanyaki seats, nine sushi places, and twenty free-standing tables.

Chef Oberoi called out for Boris Rego, the quick-witted sous-chef from Shamiana. Amit Peshave's 'Indefatigable Rego' had escaped when the gunman had shot up the coffee shop earlier in the evening and fled through the kitchens to the first-floor service area. For the past three hours he had been helping muster guests in Chambers. Now he stepped forward, as did Kaizad Kamdin, a 6 foot 4 inch Parsi who worked in the banqueting halls and was known universally as Brother Kaiz, and Zaheen Mateen, a lithe, hot-tempered Rajasthani who worked in Zodiac Grill.

As the chefs formed a protective line, the first thirty guests were called forward into the darkened kitchens, with the Indian politicians putting themselves at the front. Everyone was asked to remain calm. 'There are coaches waiting for you at the other end,' Chef Banja urged. The Anti-Terrorist Squad had turned up too, but only to escort the MPs. 'They'll take you to the President, where the hotel's General Manager is waiting.' Everyone nodded, but almost immediately the line snagged. A pantry-man came running up. Shouting could be heard from inside the Chambers. There was a tussle blocking the free flow of guests in the murky corridor and angry words could be heard floating out. Oberoi stepped up: 'I'll go in.' The Executive Chef would straighten things out. 'Keep everyone calm. Keep together. Keep moving,' he shouted over his shoulder to Banja, Minocha, Talim, Varghese, Kamdin and Mateen.

Ack, ack, ack. With his back to the Wasabi corridor and the service lift, Chef Minocha was standing adjacent to Oberoi's cabin, hands linked with Kaizad Kamdin and Hemant Talim, urging guests along, when he heard what sounded like a mason knocking out tiles. 'What?' Exasperated he turned to see Chef Banja to his right, looking similarly perplexed, red rosettes suddenly blooming on his whites, before his knees gave way and he sagged to the floor. A fine spray of blood filled Minocha's nostrils as he also fell, the realization finally dawning on him that the gunmen had just found their way into the kitchens and were firing into their backs.

Ack, ack, ack. The Brigade broke apart, the human tunnel disintegrating, staff and guests bolting for their lives.

As emergency lights flickered and dipped, Minocha saw the floor around him transforming into a crimson rink. Instinctively he crawled away from the firing, ankles and shoes flashing past his sight line, as still upright guests and staff ran, screaming like gulls. 'Head for the Time Office,' he urged himself, as he thought he saw a crowd retreating into the Chambers, while others plunged downwards, heading for the pitch-black cellars.

To Minocha's left, Thomas Varghese was running with his arms outstretched like a scarecrow. What was he doing? Minocha realized he was not escaping like the others, but shepherding strays away from the gunmen. Deliberately, Varghese ran into the line of fire, trying to narrow down the angle of the shooter, before staggering and falling. As he sank to the floor, Minocha watched an engineer who worked in the hotel's plant room come out of nowhere and rush forward to take Varghese's place. One of the Taj's legions of invisibles, Rajan Kamble blocked the gunman's path for a few, vital seconds before taking a round in his back.

Minocha tried shutting his eyes. When he opened them nothing had changed. He snatched a look towards Oberoi's cabin, and saw the Executive Chef had come out of Chambers and was standing on tiptoe, watching with a horrified expression as chefs' pleated hats flopped down out of sight, like seals dropping into ice holes. Minocha felt himself floating away into unconsciousness, carried along in a sea of bloodstained chef's whites. He wondered what had happened to the simple plan.

Inside the chefs' canteen, where Oberoi was taking cover, the ceramic tile with his kitchen prayer on it was flecked with blood: 'So bless my little kitchen, Lord,/And those who enter in,/And may they find naught but joy and peace,/And happiness therein.' Standing beside it, Chef Oberoi wracked his brains. *How the hell did they know we are all in here?* He was terrified by the thought that the gunmen had found their way in via the secret marble door on the ground floor, with its make-do napkin fastener. He was brought out of his soul-searching by screaming rounds that smashed into stainless steel cabinets and washstands.

Edging out of the doorway, Oberoi spotted Banja, his friend and foil since 1986, lying prone and bloodied just a few metres to his right. He couldn't reach him and felt sick. Was this how it would end? He had overheard Banja pledging to Anjali Pollack and others that he would rather die than let them suffer and he prayed that Banja was just concussed. Everything had a fix. You learned that at the Taj, where the tectonic plates of service frequently ran slightly out of kilter, overheating and colliding, only to be eased back into position with the helpful jolt of someone's elbow.

Just then a gunman locked eyes with Oberoi and let off a furious volley. Blind panic washed over the Executive Chef and looking around for a way out he glimpsed two assistant managers heading down towards the cellars and a third figure madly waving at *him*.

It was his Food and Beverage Manager: 'RUN.' He was pointing to the stairs. A group of staff and guests pulled the dazed Oberoi towards them, all of them descending into an unlit warren of cabins, lockers and storage rooms. He tried to drag himself away. 'I need to get to Banja,' he cried. Someone stopped him: 'Sir, please don't go back, it's too late.'

Up above, Chef Minocha had come to his senses. Lying in a pool of blood, he knew he had to get up or die. But although he sent the command to his limbs, nothing happened. He looked down and saw one hand hung limply, the bones in his forearm shattered. With a dispassionate eye, he thought the arm was practically severed and unmendable. All he could think was that he would never work again, forced out of his metier by random firing. 'I'm finished,' he muttered, tears welling up in his eyes.

Ack, ack, ack. The gunmen were back. Using his good arm and legs, Minocha propelled himself crabwise, scuttling between stainless steel workstations, his feet sliding through the sloughed blood. Ahead, he could see Chef Banja, who lay gazing upwards, his curly hair matted with blood. Lying beside him, with his legs at awkward angles, was Zaheen Mateen, the brilliant young Zodiac chef whom everyone feted for his dreamy Kahlúa mousse. He was twitching and blowing saliva bubbles through cracked lips. Mateen had just scored exceptionally in his matriculation exams, ensuring him a place at any of the best graduate schools. Just yesterday, they had all celebrated his future success – but now there was no hope for him.

Minocha glimpsed a figure dashing past, with a stocky frame and thick moustache. Was that Faustine Martis, the Sea Lounge's head waiter? What was he doing? Martis bolted for cover in the meat store, pulling open the heavy door and drawing aside the hessian curtain. Minocha wondered, should he follow? But something pulled him away, back towards the Time Office, and the way out, where he came up against guests running in the opposite direction. They had tried to get out through the Tower fire door, they all screamed hysterically, but it was jammed. 'Someone's blocked the exit from the outside and we are all trapped.'

The crowd parted, one flank heading down into the dark cellars after Chef Oberoi's party, the other carrying Minocha towards the Time Office. Ahead, he could see a bloody Chef Hemant Talim, who was being dragged out by Sunil Kudiyadi. 'Call an ambulance,' the security chief cried out, gently laying Talim down on the pavement. 'Just hold on, you'll be fine, stay with me.' Talim, who had been shot in the stomach, answered weakly: 'Yes, sir.'

Down in the cellars, more than a dozen people were squashed up together in a dark, humid storage space. Chef Oberoi tried to calm the crowd, noticing that in their party were some children who were terrified by the sound of gunfire and heavy boots stamping about. 'I don't want to die. We don't want to die,' two young kitchen porters grizzled, unable to contain themselves, as the footsteps drew nearer. Someone pulled the porters closer, burying their faces. Oberoi wriggled free a hand and brought his BlackBerry up to his face, eyes adjusting to the glowing screen as a cluster of messages downloaded.

Thomas Varghese: 'I'm wounded, sir. Bleeding near the lift.' Frustrated and terrified, feeling responsible, Oberoi passed Varghese's text on to the Taj control at the President. A text from Chef Talim popped up: 'Bleeding heavily, but made it outside. You OK, sir?' *How many dead?*, Oberoi wondered. Many of these chefs had been with him for fifteen years or more. He envisaged the photo on the canteen wall of them all smiling in happier times. Several texts mentioned seeing Kaizad Kamdin, his towering banquet *chef de partie*, lying motionless by the cabin. You could not kill Kamdin! There was no news about Chef Vijay Banja, who was to the best of his knowledge still lying on the tiled floor. Maybe he was alive. What should he tell Banja's wife, or Kamdin's family? He could not write the two chefs off yet.

Nitin Minocha texted: 'Injured. But moving. Are you OK, Chef?' Thank the Gods. Minocha was a hard man to finish off. Oberoi tapped out a reply. 'Great. Get out!!' There was also a message from Chef Rego's father in Goa. He did not want to read it. 'Where is my boy?' Urbano Rego asked. What was the appropriate response? And finally, having contacted Karambir Kang, spelling out the disaster, the Executive Chef came to his family's messages. They were desperate. First: 'Dad get out!' Then: 'TV running a flash: Executive Chef Oberoi dead!' He composed the same message to everyone: 'Alive! Please don't call or reply just yet.'

Oberoi turned his phone off and asked everyone to do the same. Darkness and silence were their only friends. Outside the footsteps drew nearer.

In an adjacent room, Gunjan Narang fiddled with his phone. Narang, who had gone to school with Bhisham and the groom, Amit, had come to the Taj with his family tonight to celebrate his thirty-second birthday in the Golden Dragon. All of them had survived the first onslaught and been led to the Chambers. But now following the stampede and the firing they had become separated, with Gunjan hiding in the store beside his father and a Taj staffer. He prayed for his sister, his wife and her parents, hoping they had made it out. 'We are in the wine cellar,' he texted. 'Where are you?' The Taj staffer beside him could hear footsteps. 'We need a total blackout, sir.' Gunjan ignored him. A text came in from his wife. He punched the air. She and her parents had made it. Where were his mother and sister Jharna? He messaged them again, his screen gleaming as he pressed the send key, and turned to the staffer, for the first time acknowledging him, brimming with anger: 'If you do only *one* bloody thing,' he said, jabbing his finger, 'make sure this doesn't happen again . . .'

Before he finished the sentence, the door was kicked down and live rounds pumped in, shattering hundreds of wine bottles that glugged their contents on to the floor, a fountain of glass showering the staffer, who stifled his tears and prayed as he saw Gunjan and his father slump dead on the floor.

Jharna Narang, hiding in a nearby vault, was chanting. A Buddhist, she believed that enlightenment did not come after death, but was a gift for the living, its secrets encoded somewhere deep inside her. 'I have to believe,' she told herself, blocking out the sounds of destruction by evoking a vision of the lotus flower. 'I have to live . . . my work is not finished yet.' She pushed herself on and inwards, wrapped in the scent and blossom. 'I have a mission to fulfil.' Jharna enveloped herself in a profound silence of her own making and focused on the words of Gautam Buddha: 'We must kill the will to kill.' She should not fear the gunmen or resent them.

Click, clack. The door opened. One, two, three and four rounds pass through her hands and back, spinning her around, shattering her pelvis, sending a searing current throughout her body. 'I cannot die. My work is not finished yet!' she chanted, as the dead weight of another guest slumped over her.

She was conscious of someone flipping bodies and finishing the job. She had to go deeper still, almost to the brink of death. She chanted, relaxing her spasming muscles, her eyes screwed tight, erasing all external signs of life, feeling as if she had drawn a shroud over her skin, so all that could seen from the outside was her punctured, seemingly lifeless body.

Bullets released from a muzzle travel at supersonic speeds, compressing the air before them and creating a shockwave shaped like a bow, a round smooth form striking a conical sound wave that some hear as a whip crack, or even applause. A Wasabi waiter, who had just reached a junction in the corridor, where he had to decide whether to go down into the cellars or on to the Time Office, heard a supersonic snap that stopped him in his tracks. 'Don't go down,' he told himself, dashing for the staff exit.

His phone rang. He muffled it with his palms, fearing it would give away his position, then pressed it to his ear, as he jogged on. 'I'm bleeding,' said the caller. It took a few seconds for him to realize it was his boss, Thomas Varghese. 'I am shot in the leg, lying by the lift in the kitchen. Please send help.'

The panicked waiter stopped running. Should he go back? Rooted to the spot, he listened. All he could hear at the other end of the line was someone walking about, bare feet slapping against the wet kitchen floor, the sounds getting rapidly nearer. 'Sir?' he whispered.

The waiter knew that whatever he could hear, his boss was seeing. There was a metallic click and then *ack, ack, ack*.

The waiter belted for the Time Office, collapsing outside. He dialled his friend Amit Peshave, the Shamiana manager, and cried into the phone: 'Varghese Sir is finished. They have executed him.'

4.45 a.m. – Merriweather Road

By the time Nitin Minocha had dragged himself outside, rooks were cawing, praising the dawn. Street sweepers were already at work, even on this day, after the worst carnage Mumbai had ever seen, building small mounds of fallen leaves, sluicing the road, tamping down the dust. Dazed and in pain, Minocha sat on the pavement, watching them, shivering in the cold morning air, as strangers milled about wearing confused expressions.

So much blood had run through the city tonight that one more injured man was no longer remarkable and he felt as if he were invisible. Minocha staggered to his feet. He was filled with a rage at what he had just seen. He weaved off in search of a policeman, determined to give evidence, provide a witness statement, nailing the killers to the mast. He wanted to help build the case, despite the agony of his shattered forearm.

Along the way, he found a Taj napkin lying in a gutter. He tied it around his arm, using his teeth to pull the knot, so that it became a tourniquet. Minocha could live with the discomfort. He walked with his arm held aloft, attempting to stem the bleeding, until he reached the nearest police post. Bang. Bang. He rapped on the door. 'How could it be locked?' he said to himself in disbelief. Dejected, he slumped down on to the pavement. All night they had waited for assistance. And now where were the cops? At home in bed screwing their mistresses? A passing motorbike stopped, with two men aboard. They looked aghast. 'Hey, man, you look like shit,' the driver said. 'You need to get to a hospital.'

Minocha's chef's whites were scarlet and his arm was mangled. 'Make a call for me,' he implored, pointing with his head to his phone, inside his trouser pocket. He wanted someone to know that he had survived the bloody grinder. The driver found the phone and pressed last-number redial, getting through to Minocha's Uncle Kamal. 'I'm alive, going to the hospital,' Minocha croaked. Kamal had just enough time to tell him about the dismal news reports. Chef Oberoi and many of his kitchen colleagues were thought to have died in the shootout. The motorbike riders took Minocha's phone off him and wedged him between them to make sure he did not fall. 'We need to go now, buddy,' one of them said, fearing that all of the blood had drained out of him.

5 a.m. – the Chambers

Inside the Chambers, staff had worked feverishly to close the doors behind the retreating guests. Four pumped-up gunmen were still out there, circling the club like wild dogs, battering at every entrance and service hatch, rattling locks, smashing glass panes, looking for any way in. Chef Raghu Deora, who worked with Kaizad the giant in the Chambers kitchens and was one of Chef Minocha's closest friends, had volunteered to stay outside, acting as a buffer and a distraction. He was not going to hide from anyone. As he waited, the sound of gunfire revved up like a chainsaw and several people came crashing through the doorway. As they sprawled on the floor he realized they were not gunmen but guests. He had planned his last stand but there was no time to get these people into the locked club. Instead, they would have to remain with him in the danger zone. 'We are all going to survive,' he reassured them, adjusting to the new reality. But he was no longer sure. 'We have to be silent. Take courage.' But Chef Deora was fearful.

Behind the locked Chambers doors, Bhisham and his mother were catching their breath. They had been in the fourth group to leave, and were nearing the kitchen end of the corridor, when the gunmen had burst in from the other side. Now, as he lay on the carpet of the Lavender Room, arms wrapped around himself, trying to control his shaking hands and twitching legs, a Western man appeared in the doorway, carrying a limp body.

It was Mike Pollack shouldering Rajan Kamble, the engineer who had tried to protect the guests. 'He's been hit,' the American financier whispered, gently placing the man on a couch, before heading back out. Mike knew that Anjali was just along the corridor in the library with their dinner companions, Shiv and Reshma Darshit, but he did not intend to join her. He had come to a difficult decision: this was a war. If probability is the likelihood of one or more events happening, divided by the number of possible outcomes, then why double the chances of orphaning their children? From the start he had hated the idea of pooling so many guests in a place like Chambers, transforming it into a potential silo of hostages, and he knew his white skin and accent made him a prime target. Without consulting Anjali, he had decided she had more chance of surviving without him.

'This was never a great idea,' he said to himself, as he set off to find a new bolthole, 'in fact it has turned out to be a fucking terrible idea.' Mike spotted the club toilets and dropped down into a darkened stall, listening to gunfire starting up again in the kitchens. With his head rammed between the bowl and toilet brush holder, he found himself staring into a huge pair of mahogany eyes and his heart leapt into his mouth. Guest or hunter? 'Joe,' a deep voice offered, by way of introduction. 'Mike,' he replied, breathing out. Noting Mike's accent, Joe described himself as 'kind of American'. Nigerian-born, he had a green card. A relieved Pollack fell back into his own world. There was much to be done.

Lying on the floor of the toilet, he texted Anjali, explaining his decision to go it alone. He hoped she had found a good hiding spot with their friends. Next he messaged a colleague in Washington DC who had government connections. Too much time had been wasted already and he asked the friend to arrange for him to get through to the FBI. Within ten minutes he was up and running, exchanging updates and advice with agents. Mike was all set. He lay back in the dark, beside Joe, listening to the harrowing cracks of single shots that sounded as if they were just the other side of the door. With adrenalin coursing through his veins, sound travelled in weird ways, he noted. But the shock was doing wonders for his synapses, which felt as if they were firing in ways they had never done before. For the first time in years all his worries about failure and embarrassment, his pride and expectations fell away. There was nothing to lose. There was no reason now not to follow his heart.

He concentrated on the gunmen and could see them in his head. They were no longer spraying rooms but firing off single shots, as if they were selecting specific targets. Mike could see the hammer cocked, and the trigger squeezed. 'I have total control of my autonomic functions,' he told himself, impressed by the acuity of his hearing and his heightened sense of smell. 'I can readjust to different things instantly.' An image came to him: Alexander the Great riding at the front of his army. You had to feel it to understand it. He also found himself doing something unthinkable. 'Even though I walk through the valley of the shadow of death, I fear no evil, for You are with me.' A man who had often felt as if there were no God found comfort in the words of a psalm.

Anjali Pollack was sitting on the library floor coming to terms with the stark reality as she saw it: Mike was dead. She had last seen him in the corridor waiting for evacuation. In the chaos of the shooting, she had lost him. She was contemplating that there was no way he could have survived that gun battle, when her phone whirred. She cupped it tightly; trying to mask the vibration, when she saw the message from Mike. She was overcome by relief and fury and began sobbing. They were on different paths now, but this was not the time to weigh up the niceties of his solo decision-making processes. She winced as more shots resounded in the kitchens. Some, she was certain, were being fired from within the Chambers. Was Mike the target? She had no idea where he was hiding. 'I have made peace with myself,' she told herself and she began to pray harder than she had ever prayed before. Mostly, she prayed for Mike and the children. 'If anyone has to die, please let it be me,' she urged.

Gradually, she became drawn to the sound of others hiding around her, people who constantly whispered and coughed. Could they not just stay quiet? She cast about, wondering who might inadvertently betray them, her eyes settling on a bronzed, white-haired man sprawled decadently across a chaise longue, tapping on his phone, which shone out like a cat's eye. He had not even bothered to get up during the failed evacuation. And he would not stop texting. It was Andreas Liveras. All around guests, frightened by his endeavours, tried to hush him. 'Be quiet,' an elderly lady urged. He carried on clicking away on his BlackBerry, determined to raise the BBC again. 'Why are we still here, Remesh?' he whispered to his aide. Remesh didn't answer. He had just ducked, having seen two shadows flickering past the library door, one black and one red. *Ack, ack, ack.* Rounds smashed through the door. 'Sir, please stop,' Remesh whispered, touching his boss's knee. *Ack, ack.* Another short burst drilled into the library. 'Oh, my God,' Andreas murmured.

Remesh groaned, feeling a burning sensation bloom across his shoulder. He investigated with his fingertips, and felt blood pooling. He had been shot twice. He slumped a little, clutching his boss's feet, whispering: 'Don't worry, sir, we will make it.' He collapsed on the floor, gritting his teeth. How could this happen? At least Mr L. had finally got the message and quietened down. Remesh lay there, rigid, for what seemed like an age.

Along the corridor in the Lavender Room, Bhisham recoiled from every shot that felt only inches away. He lay on the carpet, his mother sitting beside him on a chair, blocking out the sound, haunted by the sight of his school friend Gunjan Narang diving into cellars from where the most hellish sounds had risen. No one could have got out of that. Sick at having cursed Gunjan earlier, Bhisham felt his mind unravelling.

5.10 a.m. – the Taj kitchens

A reel of rounds pinged off metal surfaces close by. Chef Raghu, who had his back resting against a range, an Indian guest crouched on each side of him, knew instantly that one or more of the killers had found a way in. Seconds later, the gunman was standing in front of them, dressed all in black, but Raghu barely reacted, having already decided on his course of action. He looked into the face. It was not a man but a child. 'Lie down,' the youthful gunman ordered, as the Indian guests began to beg for mercy. Raghu whispered for them to stop, knowing it would make matters worse. They had to avoid making victims of themselves. The guests had no comprehension of the psychology of extremism, but coming from Mumbai, he felt as if he had a doctorate.

'Face down,' the gunman bellowed, before changing his mind. 'Go on your backs. Turn to look at me.' Raghu lay down silently as the guests rolled over on to their backs, offering money, wallets and watches. Raghu wished they would stop. *Ack, ack, ack.* Gunfire bounced around the confined kitchen and Raghu closed his eyes. One sweep and then another: he felt blood splattering his face. Was it his or theirs? 'Raghu is dead,' he said to himself, willing himself to remain motionless as the gunman closed in. Beside him two guests thrashed out their violent death throes.

Sunil Kudiyadi, who had somehow got back in, came running around the corner, stopping in time to see the terrorist in black, sitting between three bodies like a hungry rook, his gun resting on a bloody leg. He turned, spotted Kudiyadi and roared, '*Idhar ao* [come here]', as the security chief pelted for his life in the opposite direction, followed by a plume of rounds.

Bhisham held his breath, blocking his ears. As he prayed for the gunmen to go away, he noticed that the Lavender Room's door was now ajar. 'How the hell?' They needed to shut it but he was so paralysed by fear that nothing could raise him off the floor. He turned to a man next to him and whimpered instructions: 'The door . . . we need to shut it.' If a gunman stepped in they would be the first to die. '*You* shut it,' the man snarled with a look of disgust.

Bhisham took in the twenty or so refugees around him. Some had gone out of their way to make everyone feel safe tonight, acting collectively, making sure everyone had water before turning off the lights, telephones, air conditioning, transforming the private dining room into a dead space. He beat himself up. He needed to do more. When an old lady arrived, supported on a crutch, having crawled solo out of the kitchens, he felt his eyes well up. Then he finally struggled to his feet and, with the help of others, dragged a heavy table and chairs over to the vulnerable doorway.

His mother's friend Dr Tilu Mangeshikar, an anaesthetist at Bombay Hospital, had no time for soul-searching. Her hands were deep inside the abdomen of Rajan Kamble, the injured engineer. A bullet had entered through his back and exploded out of the front, leaving a gaping wound five times bigger. 'You sure got shot,' she said, jollying Kamble along. 'Yes, ma'am,' he whimpered, ramming his fist into his mouth, trying to stifle his crying. Dr Tilu kept him still, worried that his bowel and intestine would flop out. She pushed some fabric inside and held it in place by wrapping a tablecloth around his torso. She felt his pulse. At least his bleeding was under control. 'We'll manage,' she said, as a grenade blast rattled the Lavender's walls. Bhisham fired up his phone and sent a text, anything to distract his mind: 'Evacuation aborted. Shooting in passage. Dnt know if commandos there any-more. Man shot in stomach. Mom with me. Shut lights. Waiting.'

The friend texted back: 'Commandos and navy out there. Should be a matter of time. Dnt worry.'

He sent a message to a friend in Delhi: 'This could be it.' And five minutes later another: 'So what :)'

The friend got back to him, alarmed: 'Can't get thru to you. Fire still on. Ppl jumping off. Are you there?'

Was he here? Bhisham was fast-forwarding through all of the misery that lay ahead of him, his mind a spinning zoetrope of dreadful scenes.

5.15 a.m. – the Data Centre

From the second floor, the Chambers assault sounded like bulls stampeding. Florence Martis listened from her bolthole beneath the desk, imagining the slaughter. With the chair pulled up, phones cradled under her chin, Roshan, the Samaritan who had rung in earlier, remained on the line, calling her name continuously. He had to stop her slipping into unconsciousness as another cloud of smoke was drawn into the room.

A strip of emergency lights flashed on and off, revealing the smashed door. She could see through a tiny window that dawn was breaking and knew she would soon be fully exposed. She concentrated on Roshan's voice: 'Florence, I am still, here for you. Don't forget me.'

She could hear wood snapping and then boots squeaking. Someone was stalking through the room, getting nearer. 'He's searching,' she said to herself, holding her breath, her back pressed against the wall, as a gunman entered. She caught a glimpse of his boots and watched them come towards her. Now she could also see the barrel of a gun. 'R-o-s-h-a-n,' she mouthed into the mobile. 'The gunman is in . . . someone is . . . in the room.'

He wore black trousers. She could smell his sweat and fire. He searched across the desk, his hips just inches from her face, then swivelled around and crunched out, through the busted side door. Florence, her heart pounding, drifted off into a world in which everything looked as if it were stretched out like putty. Another phone trilled in the mid-distance. Was it her father? 'Dad?' What had happened to him? He had told her that he was on his way. But that had been hours ago.

5.16 a.m. – the kitchens

In the bone-cold meat store on the first floor, Faustine Martis was hiding alongside several Taj staffers when his phone began to trill.

Oh, God, he thought, whipping it out with trembling hands, looking aghast at the shiny new handset, a gift from his family. He had no idea how to shut it off.

When it eventually stopped, Faustine stared at the others, apologizing, wondering if the walls were thick enough to have smothered the sound. His fellow staffers watched as Faustine gingerly pulled aside the hessian curtain to peek out of the glass porthole and into the dark kitchens beyond. The frosty glass reflected his own face, and he rubbed at it, before realizing that someone was looking in.

Ack, ack, ack.

9.

Allah Does Not Want You

Thursday, 27 November 2008, 5 a.m.

Amit Peshave was still stuck at Bombay Hospital. An hour ago he had managed to establish that the missing wife of the injured British guest, whom he'd brought to the hospital, had been found alive, but was still trapped in the Taj. Now, he ranged around the white towers of the hospital, where the injured and dead piled up in corridors, desperate to rejoin his marooned friends and colleagues. He texted his boss, Hemant Oberoi.

The Executive Chef was insistent: 'Stay put at the hospital.' He did not reveal why, saying nothing about his own incarceration in the darkened cellars or the Kitchen Brigade massacre. The terseness of the message compounded a feeling of foreboding that had kicked in when Amit received the call an hour before about Thomas Varghese's point-blank death.

He went outside for a smoke, conscious for the first time of dawn breaking. He was just thinking about how a new day brought hope, when sirens screamed and an ambulance pulled up, the doors swinging open even before it came to a stop. Wandering over, he stared at the comatose and bloodied figure on the stretcher and started. 'My God.' It was Hemant Talim, the Golden Dragon chef, his buddy from Abbas Mansions. The last time they'd spoken was several hours previously, when Talim had been in Chambers. An orderly shouted out: 'Liver, kidney and thigh.' Amit stared at the chef. Was he lost already? He whispered into his ear: 'Hemant.'

Amit had an idea. 'Doctor, we need help. This man is dying.' He found an orderly. 'Where are you taking him?' Amit took out a pen and found some paper, noting the ward his friend was being admitted to. This is what he would do for everyone who turned up. Inside a chaotic hospital, with 800 beds, those who lobbied hardest received treatment first.

He waited by the steps, checking every arriving ambulance. Where was Rego Jr, his protégé, who had promised him the pizza of his dreams? Where was Kaizad Kamdin, the Parsi giant from banqueting? Behind the ranges in Chambers and the banqueting halls, he was known as *bawa*, affectionate slang for a Parsi. A weekend hockey player, Kamdin could hold the line tonight, Amit had no doubt. He read back through his texts to check what time he had last heard from Kamdin and other colleagues, when a third ambulance drew up. Amit ran over, heart in mouth. He stared at the body but it was no one he knew. Where was Chef Vijay Banja, Oberoi's generous, loveable deputy? What of Chef Zaheen Mateen, the rising star from Zodiac?

As the dawn spread its slippery light over the city, Amit had found his purpose. Hemant Oberoi, the kitchen God, needed him here to save his colleagues. A motorcycle came by with three men on it. In the middle, he saw a semi-comatose Nitin Minocha, his shattered forearm cradled in his lap and his face as white as the canvas sail on a Mumbai clinker.

'Water,' Minocha croaked, as he was helped down and collapsed. 'Who else?' Amit urged. Minocha simply shook his head and Amit marked his admission in his log.

When Minocha came to, he was lying alone on a bed. Something caught his eye: a black spot on his breast pocket. He pulled out his Golden Dragon chopsticks and saw they had been smashed in two. Minocha was overcome by a feeling of euphoria: a bullet heading for his heart had glanced off them. On his chest was a tender, fist-sized bruise.

5.30 a.m. – the Control Room

At the police Control Room, near Crawford Market, news about the Kitchen Brigade slaughter was filtering through, and Crime Branch's chief, Rakesh Maria, was incredulous. 'Never before have we stood down and waited,' he raged. 'We are being attacked from a position of strategic advantage – and we've not even regrouped.' He had been repeating the same observations to whoever would listen for several hours as a picture of debilitating terror sank force morale.

The Control Room felt like a tense, airless vault, everyone trapped before glowing screens since the assault had begun. Exhausted phone operators lifted their heads momentarily to hear him out before returning to their headsets.

Maria felt claustrophobic and frustrated, emotions he had experienced many times before in this über-political force. It had happened before he got a handle on the serial blasts inquiry of 1993 and again in 2003. But he would never admit to these misgivings publicly. Self-criticism was actively discouraged, the state institutions preferring to create glycerine versions of events that ultimately stifled the truth.

Still, irked by Gafoor's decision to stand down and put all his hopes in the National Security Guard, Maria grappled with the line of command. Why *was* he pinned down in the Control Room doing a job that someone else could have done – and perhaps better? As Joint Commissioner Crime he should have been out there fighting in the streets and in the Taj lobby, rather than stuck, high and dry, liaising with the force across the city. The Commissioner was still in his car parked near the Trident–Oberoi.

Seven hours in and no one had made a go of it. Maria needed to shake things up, so he called the Crime Branch inspector he had sent down to Nair Hospital to shadow the interrogation of the captured gunman, Ajmal Kasab. 'Bring him to Crawford Market,' he ordered. The inspector was nonplussed. Surely the police had got what they needed from the first interrogation, by Additional Commissioner Ghadge? He also passed on a warning that doctors were saying the prisoner's condition had not been stabilized, so they could refuse to release him.

But Maria wanted his turn. He blew up. 'Bullshit,' he shouted. 'I have three good reasons to interrogate the prisoner: Kamte, Kakare and Salaskar,' he raged. 'Bring him here even if you have to put a fucking gun against the doctor's head.' Crime Branch would be handling the criminal inquiry and, he would argue if challenged, it was only right that its chief ask the questions. Maria signed off with a warning: 'Do *not* lay a finger on him and make sure you have sufficient backup when you are in transit. We cannot afford a fuck-up.'

At Nair Hospital, doctors were furious. Ajmal Kasab's patient's notes were marked: 'Discharged *against* medical advice.' The inspector called Maria to warn him but the Crime Branch boss was unrepentant: 'This is no time for the fucking Geneva Conventions,' he shouted.

Half an hour later the disoriented prisoner arrived in the courtyard of police headquarters and Maria called on his way down. 'Take Kasab to the AEC.' This was to be his first ploy, interrogating the prisoner in the Anti-Extortion Cell, Salaskar's domain. The risky manoeuvre of bringing Maria's only prisoner to Crime Branch in a volatile city still under attack was becoming an act of vengeance as much as anything else. 'Now we will see how he feels,' Maria said, running down the stairs and emerging blinking in the courtyard, where for the first time in seven hours he inhaled the chill air, his eyes stinging in the thin light.

A small gathering of heavy, uniformed cops stood stamping their feet outside the AEC, surrounding a diminutive figure wearing borrowed plastic sandals. Maria nodded to his men. 'My heart is telling me I should strangle this guy, here and now,' he hissed, looking at the shivering prisoner, 'but my brain is telling me that he is the only link to this open case.' Ever since Ajmal had been captured, voices all around Maria had proposed the old Mumbai story: one for the boys. He should be allowed to run before being shot. Some wanted to hang him, making it look like suicide.

Tombstone-faced, they all entered Salaskar's world, gawping at the dead inspector's paperwork and effects: suspects' headshots and 'wanted' notices, bamboo *lathi*s and bulletproof vests. Ajmal was put in a plastic chair, a handcuff on his left wrist. If a room could smell of coercion, Salaskar's did. Maria, towering above the prisoner and flanked by the uniformed constables, began talking in Ajmal's mother tongue, Punjabi. It was also the language of Maria's father, who had migrated to Bombay in the 1950s.

Maria asked if Ajmal knew where he was. In his grubby beige and white T-shirt, a wrist and an arm bandaged, he looked a pathetic sight. He really was the most ordinary-looking mass murderer Maria had ever seen. Sallow and greasy, he reminded the cop of the kid manning the deep-fat fryer at the sweet seller's in Zaveri Bazaar.

A good interrogator needed an opener, and Maria was ready: 'You wanted to die and so, just so you know, I am *not* going to kill you.' He pointed to the blunt knuckles standing beside him in Salaskar's room. 'They are not going to kill you either.' He allowed Ajmal to digest the statement.

'These guys,' Maria said, pointing around the room, 'want to do it. But I will not allow it. You have failed in your mission because you are *not* dead. Now the world will come to know how badly you screwed up. You told one of my men that you hoped to be a *shaheed*. Well, my friend, I have news for you. *Allah* does not want you. No one does. The story of your miserable life continues as it always has. No one gives a shit. You are a poor, pitiful failure, even in trying to die.'

Ajmal groaned as Maria struck home. A dust bowl of disappointment was opening up before the prisoner, harking back to his inability to win acceptance, even as a young child when his father could not wait to discard him. While his brothers still out on the streets tonight would strive to accomplish their mission, he could already see that he was to be kept alive until a day of India's choosing, when, he had no doubt, he would be hooded and hanged. One last dismal thought occurred to him, something he would share with a lawyer on a chit that was signed and dated. He saw now that even after his execution no one would claim his corpse. In that moment, Ajmal knew something awful: *I am never going home.*

Maria had many questions. 'How many of you are there in the city? What weaponry have you brought with you? What is your plan? Who is coaching you?' Ajmal had given answers at the hospital to the fat cop whose mouth had brimmed with scarlet paan. Now he was made to go over the same ground. Maria sat back, soaking up that accent, the nasal vowels, the sibilant 's' and rolling 'r', a pendulous sentence construction and phrasing that sounded like a bow saw slicing through a trunk. It was the voice of the eastern Punjab: a vista of landlessness and poverty. Children there were born to sell, and lived to die, in Maria's opinion.

Ajmal detailed the rough location of the fishing vessel MV *Kuber*, explaining that in the panic of thinking an Indian naval vessel was approaching, they had not had time to sink the *Kuber* or throw the corpse of the Indian captain overboard. The coast guard was alerted. He confirmed they had mistakenly left a satellite phone and a GPS handset and described the yellow inflatable dinghy that had brought them to shore. He gave more details of how he was recruited, trained and equipped by Lashkar and then launched from Karachi. That was where the handlers were, too, he revealed. At last, Maria had something new, a priceless nugget, and he sent word to Gafoor and the intelligence people: the whole show was being puppeteered from a control room in Karachi.

The only thing that Maria found difficult to accept was Ajmal's claim that there were just ten of them in the city. How could so few cause so much mayhem? Maria's mind ran through the *modus operandi* – settling on the bomb blasts. He thought about how the timed charges set in moving taxis, detonating all over the city, had projected a larger footprint for the operation. The sobering reality was that one man less than a cricket team had got an entire nation on the run.

Maria was done. The bits and pieces here would be buffed, pacifying any critics. He sent a message to his number two, Deven Bharti, and to the Joint Commissioner Law and Order, both of whom were in the Taj lobby. There were only four terrorists in the hotel, armed with four assault rifles, four pistols and forty kilos of

23. Abdul Rehman 'Bada' (*front*) and Ali caught on CCTV outside the Chambers Club.
Mumbai Crime Branch

24. CCTV screen grabs of Shoaib, Abdul Rehman 'Bada' and Umer trying to get into Chambers in the early hours of 27 November 2008.
Mumbai Crime Branch

25. Ajmal Kasab in the Chhatrapati Shivaji Terminus.
Reuters/*The Times of India*

27. Bhisham Mansukhani (*right*) with Prashant Mangeshikar (*left*) at 11 p.m. on 26 November 2008, shortly after they had been led by hotel staff from the Crystal Room into Chambers. Prashant was the husband of the Bombay Hospital anaesthetist Dr Tilu, who tended to injured staff in Chambers after the failed evacuation in the early hours of the following morning. He survived the attacks.
Tilu Mangeshikar

26. Mobile phone picture taken inside Chambers, showing Bhisham Mansukhani dressed in black and lying on the floor to the right, and his mother, dressed in a black sari, sitting in a chair behind him.
Tilu Mangeshikar

28. The Taj burning.
Reuters / Arko Datta

29. DCP Vishwas Patil was one of only a handful of police officers to enter the Taj on the night of the attacks.
Vasant Prabhu / Indian Express

30. Guests escaping out of windows of the Taj.
AFP / Getty

31. An NSG commando, known as a Black Cat, entering the Taj.
Reuters

32. The Taj's General Manager, Karambir Kang, reacts while sitting in front of the hotel on 27 November 2008. At least 101 people have been killed in attacks by gunmen in Mumbai, including his wife and two sons.
Reuters / Arko Datta

33. Mike Pollack (*third left*) sheltering from bullets moments after he escapes from the Taj.
Reuters

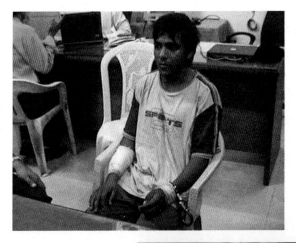

34. Mobile phone picture of Ajmal Kasab being interrogated at the Mumbai Crime Branch, early morning, 27 November 2008.

Mumbai police

35. AK-47 magazines and unused bullets recovered from the Taj hotel.

Mumbai Crime Branch

36. Hasan Gafoor, Mumbai police commissioner at the time of the attacks, giving a press conference.

Reuters

37. The aftermath: looking down from the sixth floor of the Taj.

Sachin Waze

38. Battleground: inside the Harbour Bar after the final battle.

Sachin Waze

39. Arne Strømme and Line Kristin
Woldbeck at Bombay Hospital on
27 November 2008.

Rovert S. Eik, Scanpix, Norway

40. Amit Peshave, former senior
manager at the Shamiana restaurant.

Amit Peshave

41. Will Pike with his
girlfriend, Kelly Doyle,
in Bombay Hospital
shortly after being
operated on for the
first time.

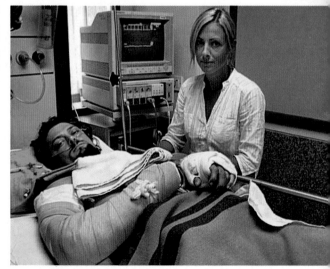

Welcome Home Again.

42. Advertisement placed by the Tata group when the hotel reopened.
Taj Mahal Palace Hotel Collection

43. Memorial for the
dead chefs in the Taj.
Author archive

VIJAY RAO BANJA

KAIZAD KAMDIN   BORIS REGO

HEMANT TALIM   SADANAND PATIL

ZAHEEN MATEEN   GAUTAM GOSAIN

"Never To Be Forgotten"

26-11-2008

44. Mike and Anjali Pollack
on the steps of the Taj just after
they have been evacuated.
Mike Pollack

RDX, an arsenal that was surely depleted. He felt the tide turning, as an egg-wash of sunlight finally spread across the seven islands.

Inside the Taj, Deven Bharti had had a windfall. At 5.40 a.m. a Black Suit had emerged with a mobile phone that had been found near the pool. Bharti examined it and discovered it had only one number stored in its memory – with an international dialling code for Austria.

As Bharti puzzled over the meaning of it, the phone rang.

An incoming number was displayed. It was also an international code, but not for Austria. The prefix was +1 201. Bharti was confused. That was the code for New Jersey, he thought. Bharti recalled that IB was probing the US/Austrian connection to the gunmen in Mumbai. What should he do? He answered the phone.

'*Salaam Alaikum.*' A voice greeted him, asking where he was and what he was doing. The language was Urdu, but Bharti also recognized the accent as from the Punjab. He could not believe his luck. He was certain it was the gunmen's handler. He had to think of something to say, someone to be, something to offer, to prolong the call.

'I'm a waiter, sir, apologies,' Bharti blustered, seeing where the conversation would go. 'I am with one of your men and the phone rang so I answered it.'

'Why didn't *he* answer it?' a suspicious voice replied.

Bharti had to think quickly. 'Your man's injured, sir.' This was proving difficult. 'He cannot talk, sir. He motioned that I should answer.'

The caller hung up. Had Bharti done enough to prick his interest, or was that it? The Crime Branch number two was intrigued and nervous. This entire operation was surreal: men landing by sea, taking a city hostage, calling Austria and being remotely manipulated by handlers who seemed to be in the US. It was unlike anything they had ever imagined. *Is that a problem too?*, Bharti wondered. *Our lack of imagination?* He needed to pack up the phone and get it analysed.

Bharti called Maharashtra's monosyllabic spy chief and an IB liaison officer in New Delhi. The US intelligence community was already assisting, he was advised, having given its opinion that Lashkar was using an Internet call system, which meant all of the numbers were virtual or leased lines, rather than actual locations.

Bharti was impressed. It was cheap to implement and easy to run, only slightly more complicated than Skype. Lashkar was ahead of the game. But for all this planning, it had slipped up. A basic human error threatened to expose the whole group. A gunman, who was supposed to die with his knowledge, had been captured alive.

Gunshots snapped Bharti back to the here and now. Four gunmen were still free to roam inside the Taj killing and maiming. He prayed that the National Security Guard would arrive soon.

5.58 a.m. – fifth floor

Five floors above the police command post, the banker K. R. Rama-moorthy came around in a burning room.

He wasn't sure how long he had lain unconscious, but somehow the fire that raged around had not consumed him. Everything was blackened and steaming as the sprinklers poured down, a poisonous stench and the roaring up above reminding him that at any moment the ceiling might collapse. He had to get going and forget the stabbing pains in his back and neck. He had to stop worrying about his irregular heartbeat and his shortness of breath.

He got on to his knees, and crawled along, feeling his way with his fingertips. Billowing smoke obscured everything and stung his eyes. Occasionally, he lay down flat, like a basking fish, to suck up air. He needed to find a staircase going down. 'Take a break,' he said to himself, scrambling into a corner, gulping. Or was a break the beginning of the end? Up again, he crawled on, his legs feeling cramped, his arms weak, as the fire took its toll on his body fluids, heating him up, and grinding him down.

Finally, Ram recognized the fifth-floor business centre. In normal times this was his second home. But pushing his way in, he strained to see in the half-light and his feet crunched over broken glass. He reached down to touch it and his hand became sticky with blood. He stopped. There was nothing left of the plush chairs and workstations from where he had once sent emails. 'This is hell,' he said, backing out, even more afraid of what lay ahead. Down another blackened, smoke-logged corridor, he crawled, eventually finding some railings running downwards. 'Count the landings,' he said to himself, gasping, until he was certain that he was on the third floor, where the smoke began to clear.

'Light.' He spotted a glare of daylight through the smoke. He crawled towards it, reaching a guest room with its door ajar. *Who is in there?*, he thought, creeping in, praying he had not reached another terrorist control room. There was no one inside. Ram collapsed against a wall and listened. Nobody tells you how loud an inferno is, he thought, as the fire behind him growled, gobbling up all the air. The light was streaming in from the windows. Ram had lost track of time but now realized that it must be day. His hands touched the glass. 'Here I am,' he said, pushing the window open and sucking up the breeze.

He climbed up on to the sill, from where he could see firefighters moving ladders up against the seaward walls of the Taj and pulling guests out of their burning rooms. For the first time in almost seven hours he felt hope. Looking up, he saw a fireman quenching the inferno on the sixth. 'I am here. I am here.' The fireman turned and peered down. He manoeuvred his hydraulic ladder to investigate. Finally, he gestured. A raised thumb: 'Got you!' The banker was overcome. 'I have you,' the fireman roared, swinging down and lifting Ram off the ledge and into the serge folds of his jacket, hugging the old man like he was his father. 'Thank you,' Ram said, trembling. Then he caught sight of something below him. 'There.' Pointing to the second floor, he could see a woman waving wildly behind a closed window. The ladder moved down to her, and the fireman smashed her window with an axe. Shards sprayed over Ram, who hardly noticed. The woman scrambled into the basket, crying. He spotted her mobile phone. 'The phone,' he croaked. 'Please.' Ram's hands shook as he dialled home. When he heard his wife's sleepy voice, he found himself babbling: 'I am safe. I am safe.' He broke down, tears choking. 'It is OK. I am OK.' He could have roared with pain and joy but she seemed nonplussed.

Ram's son came on the line and explained that his mother had gone to bed early and only just woken, so knew nothing of events in Mumbai. Rather than feeling relief, Ram was devastated. How would he ever explain what he had endured, his journey, real and imagined, the terror that had seen him hark back to his ancestral village of Kuttalam, and to a vision of his resourceful mother, a flight to the Wish-Yielding Temple of Mylapore where he had called on the *devi* to help him, memories he sought to shield him from the pain of being beaten and bound. Then he had come round in the jaws of an inferno, his sense of self crushed, his physical self stripped naked, the ordeal forcing him to find a cool, quiet place inside his head that he never knew existed, and from where he nearly did not emerge. 'I need to get away from here,' he muttered, beginning to panic, as the ladder finally touched down.

First Ram wanted to do his duty. He strolled, shivering, to the nearest policeman and introduced himself: K. R. Ramamoorthy – banker, hostage. He explained every moment of his capture and escape, as if in a spreadsheet of detailed evidence. But the exhausted officer showed no interest. 'No one cares,' Ram told himself. He walked on, into the waking city, furious, downhearted and crushed.

A car, its headlights still on, pulled over. Staggering, Ram in his shredded and burnt pyjamas must have looked on the verge of collapse. Did he need a lift? He nodded gratefully and climbed in, the soft seats seeming luxurious after the hours of pain. He sat quite still, and breathed in and out, inhaling the vivid, domesticated smells of vinyl and petrol. 'Please can you take me to Khar Mumbai?' he whispered, referring to the suburb where a nephew lived, Ram once more reliant on the comfort of strangers. 'Indians,' he said to himself, 'are *still* Indians.'

On the second floor of the Palace, Amit and Varsha Thadani were still trapped in 253, watching the teetering hydraulic ladders moving to and fro like swaying giraffes. The inferno bellowed in the corridor outside like a train passing through a tunnel. From the window, they could see guests being plucked and taken down. Some were near enough to call out to, but the newlyweds dithered and waved, keeping their mouths shut for fear of a sniper's bullet. Then Amit picked Varsha up and put her on the window ledge. They seemed to be prioritizing women and children. He waved more furiously and pointed at his wife. A man on the ground talked into a radio and Varsha told Amit to fetch a white towel that she flapped above her head.

A ladder was rising, and she hoped it was for them. Amit held on to Varsha's waist as they watched the ladder flex. It was coming for them. An officer in the basket pointed in their direction. There was no mistake now; a fireman was coming for the Thadanis. He lifted Varsha out, light as a feather, and Amit climbed down, hugging her, both of them giddy. With a swoosh and a judder, they were on the ground in minutes, in the maelstrom of the perimeter, surrounded by journalists: How many dead bodies did you see? Did you witness any executions? What was it like to be threatened by the gunmen? Did you think you would die? How does it feel to be alive? That's how Amit heard it. Low on blood sugar, wanting to tear chunks out of all of them, he suddenly felt an overwhelming love for Varsha and was sick with fear for Bhisham, Gunjan Narang and all his other friends who remained trapped.

He pulled Varsha away, intent on getting as far from the Taj as he could, as quickly as possible. He needed to get home to their Pedder Road apartment. If a policeman stopped him, he would hang around. That would be the only thing that could delay him. Amit was mad now. He wanted to detail everything. He wanted to see the gunmen hang. Over the last nine hours, he had story-boarded everything he had heard, observed, seen and smelled. Neither of them could forget the sound of the woman next door being hauled from her hiding place and killed. But the detectives he approached seemed irritable. 'Indian rules,' he said to himself, thinking how spectacularly bad the subcontinent was at endings.

As they walked away from the remnants of their wedding

reception, Amit glimpsed a figure he recognized. A man who lived by his fecund memory for faces, he struggled to recall the name. So much had happened this evening and his head was pounding. But the big man with a military countenance continued towards them. He appeared spectral as he drew nearer. Grey-faced, unshaven and his eyes ringed with dark lines, he reached out, offering his large hands. 'If there is anything we can do for you, please go to the President hotel, where we will look after you.' The man smiled, and while Amit had no doubt he was genuine, he looked frozen inside. 'Who was that?' Varsha asked, noticing the stranger's striking eyes. 'Karambir Kang,' Amit muttered, incredulous, 'his family live . . . lived on the sixth floor.'

Varsha looked up to the top floor still in flames. 'They can't have made it,' she said, sobbing. Work is all that is keeping him together right now, Amit thought, recalling a story someone had once told him about how the Taj General Manager had got his name. His mother had gone to see a Sikh holyman, who came up with Dusht Daman, the 'destroyer of demons'. That was no name for a child, she had said, settling instead on Karambir, 'a person who does brave deeds'.

Amit called his brother, whom he had rounded on earlier in the evening. They met at the Gateway, and any bad feelings evaporated. 'Glad you could join us,' his brother quipped. 'We were always in charge,' Amit responded, smiling widely for the first time, his trademark laconic manner back in play. 'Take us home,' he said. They needed a shower and a change of clothes. He had to eat. Amit was ravenous.

As they drove off, a commotion started up further along the Taj's front flank. A passer-by had heard groaning and gone to investigate, finding a prone figure. 'It's a foreigner,' he shouted. 'Get an ambulance now.' A crew on standby pulled closer, investigating the young Caucasian man in his twenties, with a patchy beard and floppy hair.

'He is alive,' one of them said, listening to his laboured breathing. 'Can you tell us your name? Your country?' The injured man groaned, his eyes rolling. They tied a brace around his neck, and slid a stretcher beneath him. He cried out as they lifted it and slid him into the back of an ambulance that headed for Bombay Hospital.

In a ground floor examination room, his clothes were cut away, while an A&E doctor investigated his injuries, a nurse on standby with sedatives. 'Pelvis smashed,' the doctor wrote, as the patient let out a wail. On closer inspection, he saw the pelvis had split in two, a break so severe that great force must have been applied to the top or bottom of the bone. 'This guy fell or jumped,' the doctor said, feeling his way around the patient's body and joints.

'Right elbow smashed,' he wrote. Left hand fractured, where he had tried to break his fall. He would need X-rays and an MRI scan. The doctor worried that the spine was also broken, as his legs seemed insensate. The pain was concentrated in the upper body, which meant that the main injury was in the curve of his back. The doctor hoped his diagnosis was wrong, as a T12 fracture meant paralysis. A nurse prepared an injection and the patient's eyes flashed open. Panicking, he tried to flail, before realizing his limbs could barely move. He began shouting at the top of his lungs: 'Kelly, Kelly, Kelly.'

6.50 a.m. – the Chambers

Inside the Taj's private club, sunlight burned around the edges of the blackout curtains. After almost seven hours of darkness, morning seemed like a blessing for Bhisham Mansukhani, lifting his mood, until he saw the evidence of what they had gone through: the flurries of bullet holes in the walls. The journalist wished it were over. He was sick of waiting to die.

A scuffle broke out somewhere. Sweary voices, a pot thrown or a pan dropped and the firing began again. A glass panel shattered. The gunmen were prowling. He looked over to his mother's friend, Dr Tilu, who was still working on Rajan Kamble, the injured engineer. Everyone could smell the infection in the wound now. The patient was slipping. Bhisham seethed at the lacklustre response to this crisis. Why after all these hours was there no rescue party? He stared at Dr Tilu's wan face and that of his peaceful mother and an awful thought came to mind that threw him back into a sickening panic. Daylight had removed their only cover. He wondered, firing up his phone, what had happened to everyone else out there. 'Amit, are you out? Is Varsha OK? Pls respond.' Nothing came back.

He messaged his friend Anahita at 6.52 a.m.: 'There' [sic] heavy firing outside.' Had she heard anything about a rescue on the news?

Bhisham felt as if he were sinking. Friends on the outside sensed it too and rallied round. At 7.23 a.m., another friend, Antoine texted: 'Hang in there, we're all waiting for you.'

Three minutes later, Bhisham replied limply: 'I hope I get out I hope everyone does.'

At 7.38 a.m. Antoine got back to him: 'Im sure u will. The police are almost in control.'

How did he know? The Chambers still vibrated to automatic-weapon fire. Bhisham looked over to his mother, eyes half closed as she prayed. He resented how she twisted the ordinary as proof of the extraordinary, how her goodness made him feel bad. He was irritated by her proselytizing teetotal lifestyle and unwavering vegetarianism, while he could think of nothing better than a glass of ruddy Montepulciano. Their continued presence here, trapped in Chambers, with gunmen firing around them, demonstrated to him that there was no ultimate being. It was all in the roll of the dice. But in her expression he could see the opposite. She thinks that we have all survived so far *because* of her beliefs, Bhisham told himself.

Down the hall in the library, Anjali Pollack was also wondering what daylight would bring. Her children would be awake soon and she was not around to get them up. She texted Mike in his bolt-hole as the *ack, ack, ack* wound up again. How long could this go on for? He replied instantly. He was safe. That was as good a piece of news as she could hope for.

Slumped against a sofa on the other side of the room, Andreas's cruise director, Remesh Cheruvoth, had managed to remain conscious, although his shirt and trousers were drenched in blood. His shoulder and back burned, where two bullets had struck. He needed to make a move, if he could, and he wanted to get Andreas Liveras up too, but the boss had dozed off on the couch. A mobile alarm went off. 'Pah. Pah. Pah.' A wave of shushing and tutting broke across the room, as terrified guests urged for the noise to be silenced. It was Remesh's phone. 'My fault,' he groaned. He looked about him, seeing testy, resentful faces. He wanted to sit up and scream: 'I've been shot and never made a sound.' But making a fuss was not his style.

Naomi, one of the *Alysia*'s spa girls, gently squeezed his arm. 'Remesh,' she whispered. 'Don't talk now,' he replied, wincing. She tugged at his sleeve again. '*Remesh.*' He did not understand. She crawled over to him. 'Mr L.,' she said. He nodded. 'Mr L. is *dead.*' Remesh shook his head. 'Look,' he said, pinching Andrea's leg. But there was no reaction and the flesh felt cold. Remesh ran his hands over his boss's body, praying that she was wrong. He reeled as he saw a bloody clot on Liveras's ashen temple. A single bullet had passed through his head. He had been dead for two hours already and Remesh had even not realized.

Remesh was devastated. They had known one another for almost a decade after first meeting at the Dubai boat show, common love of the sea bringing the calm Keralan and the upstart Cypriot together. He had worked for Mr Liveras for four years, and come to love his irascible boss who gave up every Christmas and Easter to fly down to the Maldives for a special lunch with all of his staff, from the deckhands to the captains. Now, in their greatest hour of need, Remesh felt he had betrayed him. He wriggled his phone free and rang the captain of the *Alysia*. 'Mr L. is dead,' he whispered, crying gently, adding that he and the girls were trapped. Then he called Dion, Liveras's son, whom he knew well, in London. 'Mr Dion,' Remesh urged, barely audible, and now lying down on the floor of Chambers, the only position in which he felt no pain: 'I am so sorry, but your dad has gone. Mr L. has gone. Please believe me, we tried our best.' He said nothing about his own injuries as Dion inhaled. 'Oh God,' he said, 'Remesh, are you OK?' He was floored. 'We have to update our people, and the family. I'll get on to it now.'

Remesh's head swam with grief. Out of the corner of his eye he noticed a small group of guests slipping out into the corridor. What were they thinking? *Ack, ack, ack.* Those still inside the room could smell the woody notes of splintered panelling, as the same guests hurtled back, diving on to their bellies. *Ack, ack, ack.* The firing seemed to be coming from all sides with renewed vigour. Rounds were pouring into the corridor outside. Remesh covered his ears, not sure how much longer he could go on, seeing guests pull out their phones as the library came alive with text messages. One woman piped up: 'Government has launched an operation. NSG is in the city. The Black Cats are coming to the Taj.' A shiver of excitement went around the room.

Remesh fell back, allowing his mind to drift to Calicut, his home town, the city of spices on the Malabar Coast in Kerala, where his wife and six-year-old son were waiting for news. In the panic of last night, he had not even called them. 'Good morning,' he said, ringing now. 'I mustn't be long as I'm stuck in the Taj. But it's nothing to worry about. Got nicked by some broken glass. Can mend it. Pray for me. Love you all.'

Out in the harbour, the guests and crew had begun stirring on the *Alysia* as the sun began to warm the deck. All of them were immediately transfixed by the still-burning Taj. The night had passed but not the danger. For the first time, they could see the extent of the chaos around the grand old hotel: flames coiling and writhing, fire trucks manoeuvring around police cars, camouflaged lorries and khaki jeeps revving. Huge crowds heed and hawed, as firemen plucked guests to safety.

Nick Edmiston stared in the opposite direction, into the sea mist. He had barely slept: all night the navy had been firing flares, anxious to illuminate the dark waters lest more gunmen were sailing in. Every purple and crimson burst had lit up the *Alysia*. What if someone shore-side had taken a pot-shot at them, as the largest, most alien thing in the water? Or would they be boarded? A boat filled with enough fuel to go 5,000 miles would make for a handy escape rig. They had spent a desperate night calculating where to hide and working out what could be utilized as a weapon. All they had found was a small space that would have made a tidy priest hole and housed an emergency generator and an axe. Nick wondered who was capable of wielding it.

Now, staring into the mid-distance, watching small fishing vessels emerge from the horizon, returning with their catch, he had different concerns. They would have left last night without knowing what had happened and were returning to a city that did not exist any more. There could also be gunmen among them for all he knew. Everything looked hostile.

The Estonian captain came over, drawing Nick aside. 'Sir, I have terrible news,' he said. 'Mr Liveras is dead. I'm truly sorry.' Nick blanched, unable to take it in. They had not heard from Andreas for a while but had simply assumed his phone was flat. 'Don't say anything for now,' Nick said, dry-eyed, his logical head taking over. 'Let's get this boat cleared out, and then we can work things out for Andreas.'

A launch pulled up to relay guests ashore. Nick's Indian partner, Ratan Kapoor, had pulled some strings and got his wealthy, entrepreneurial father to call Vijay Mallya, the brewery and airline tycoon, a man with considerable maritime resources. Mallya employed a retired commodore as head of his fleet and this man had requested his serving navy colleagues to grant permission for an evacuation to begin. Some of the 'Ultras' were ferried for thirty minutes across the bay to Alibag. They, too, had been calling their contacts all night, telling their drivers to set off for an agreed rendezvous out of the city. Their diamante belt buckles and patent shoes, their leather trousers and satin gowns, struck a discordant note in the rude daylight. 'They don't want to get snared in Mumbai's chaos,' Ratan explained to Nick. All the guests who had the resources to make it happen had been calculating how to shake loose from their burning city.

Finally the *Alysia* was calm. With the boat powered down, only the Edmistons and their staff remained aboard. Nick found his son Woody. 'Andreas is dead,' he said. His voice sounded confessional. Woody gulped. 'How the hell . . . ?' Irrepressible Andreas had led a charmed life. 'It doesn't seem possible.' Woody looked at his buttoned-up father. Why did he never show any emotion? 'Don't you care?' Woody raged. Nick suddenly let out a roar, his eyes welling up, as all the tensions of the night gushed out.

Watching the Taj burn in daylight on their television screen, a distraught Chef Urbano Rego prayed for his son. He had heard from Boris, the Shamiana chef, sometime in the twilight hours, when he had called to confirm that Boris had, somehow, escaped the kitchen slaughter. Urbano had been euphoric. His 25-year-old son had only joined the Taj in June.

The family had received another call at dawn, an unmistakeable voice whispering into the handset. 'I'm still safe. Don't worry about me.' It was Boris once more. The young chef had slipped the gunmen again. 'I am in the cellar,' he said. 'There might be hundreds of us down here.'

The family gathered on Divar Island, a spit of land in the Mandovi River, in Goa, waited, desperate for the next update. Later, his younger brother Kevin received a call. He listened intently but there was nobody there. Kevin was about to put the phone down when he heard a crackling. He strained and waited. A voice came on the line, thin and vibrating; a ghostly presence: 'Kevin? Dadda?'

Only one person used that word. It was Boris. Speechless, Kevin passed the phone to his father. 'Yes, Baba, I can hear you,' Urbano said, his face crumpling. 'Baba, I *can* hear you. Baba,' he sang into the phone. But all he could hear now was an abysmal silence.

In the Taj, Kelly Doyle had finally got herself noticed and was lowered down to the ground by a fire crew as the sky turned salmon pink. After Will had fallen she had contacted his father by text, trying not to lose control. 'Please keep calm,' Nigel had pleaded, unable to fully understand her disjointed account of some terrible accident. He would alert the Foreign Office, he said, and come to Mumbai immediately, contemplating the nightmare of having to repatriate Will's body. He would bring Kelly's mother too.

Outside the hotel, with no one to console her, Kelly plunged into a chaotic crowd of people wrapped up in their own private tragedies. She could not make herself understood but somehow she would get help.

Without money or any idea where Will's body had been taken, she begged her way across the city, visiting one hospital after another, barefoot and wearing the dress she had worn for a dinner that never happened. The A&E departments felt like warzones and she wandered through them, calling Will's name, contemplating when she would be brave enough to start lifting shrouds in the mortuaries.

Eventually she arrived at the Bombay Hospital, where Amit Peshave was still helping out, tending to his colleagues. Roaming around, she was pointed in the direction of a side room, where an unidentified European man lay in a giant plaster cast. Shock had turned him bright yellow, and the parts of his body that were still visible were covered in blood and dirt. Electrodes were connected to his chest and a plastic pouch fed fluids to his bloodstream, an oxygen cylinder was at his shoulder and he had transparent tubes up his nose and in his arm. She stared at the face and the hairline. 'Will,' she suddenly cried. It was definitely Will. His chest heaved as all around him banks of machines beeped and flashed, monitoring his vital signs. Will was alive. 'Will.' He seemed not to hear her. Euphoric and confused, she tried to grab a nurse as she struggled to find out what was wrong with him. A morphine drip stuck out of his arm. 'Will,' she cried. She studied his face, as his eyelids flickered. He came round and stared up at her, and then at his surroundings, his eyes taking in the mass of wires, tubes and cabling. A machine beside her sounded an alarm as his lids shut fast again.

'He's crashing,' Kelly screamed. She could not lose him again. 'My boyfriend, please help . . .' A surgeon entered and introduced himself as Samir Dalvie, a spinal injuries specialist. 'Please be patient,' he said, pointing to the chaos around them. Will was in shock. He needed emergency surgery on his shattered pelvis but Dalvie was the only consultant who had reached the hospital and he was supervising three operating theatres simultaneously. Kelly nodded, too scared to ask for a prognosis as Will came to again. 'Kelly,' he murmured, 'I love you.' She smiled weakly. 'Please,' he continued, 'get me the fuck out of here.'

10

A Black Cat and a White Flag

Thursday, 27 November 2008, 8 a.m. – Mantralaya,
South Mumbai

The commandos gathered beneath coconut palms in the gardens of Mantralaya, the state's administrative complex at Nariman Point, impatient and anxious. Even here, a mile away from the burning Taj, a smoky aroma filled the air. Twelve hours after the ten Pakistani gunmen had motored ashore in their dinghy, India was finally scrambling the National Security Guard (NSG), with the 51 Special Action Group at its core. They were trained in rescuing hostages and breaking sieges, and their anthracite black uniforms, ski masks and dexterity gave them their nickname: the Black Cats.

Everyone here was on deployment from their army unit, having survived a notorious 780-metre-long obstacle course, christened the Seven/Eight/No by foreign military trainers: a backbreaking succession of crawls, climbs and leaps traversed with a full pack and loaded weapon. Before they could catch their breath, they had to obliterate distant targets and jog through the broiling day and freezing night on route marches that switched altitudes. Dropped into an underground Kill Room that could mirror dozens of South Asian scenarios – markets, tightly packed *chawls*, hospitals and hotels – they were strobed and deafened by klaxons, while trying to hit only bad-guy targets, delivering a double-tap of two bullets, ensuring that whoever went down was definitely dead.

The force was tailor-made for the Mumbai operation. So why, the men wondered, as they checked over their kit in the lush gardens where the overnight dew was steaming, had it taken so long to get them here? Brigadier Govind Sisodia, their Deputy Inspector General (Operations), a small, punchy man, with roving eyes that rapidly took in a crisis, had been asking the same question since the previous evening. He had watched the opening salvos of the Mumbai assault on TV at the force's barracks in Manesar, south-west of Delhi, and informally mobilized the men shortly after 10 p.m. They had been ready to deploy to the technical area of Palam airstrip in under thirty minutes, and yet they had arrived a half-day late for India's worst terrorist outrage, by which time at least 156 people had died with 240 seriously injured. Jyoti Dutt, the Brigadier's boss, was furious about the cack-handed mobilization that he blamed on political incompetence and infighting. But there was no time to dwell on it now.

The Brigadier's head was already swimming after a puzzling series of early-morning briefings that had left him feeling unsure about the mission in Mumbai. The police had told him that the number of gunmen was said to be 'anywhere up to twenty' and the most savage team, locked down inside the Taj, had an unknown quantity of AK-47s, as well as military-grade explosives, grenades and side arms, whereas TV reports had been far more specific, placing the *fidayeen* numbers at ten. No one had much to say on how distant handlers were directing the gunmen, although the NSG had heard that telephone intercepts were being analysed elsewhere.

In Dutt's opinion, the intelligence agencies were being 'positively evasive', skipping over the warnings that ran back to 2006 and offering an assessment so broad that it was useless to a force looking to eke out any small advantage in what they were sure would be close-quarters fighting inside byzantine buildings.

He suspected that the Mumbai authorities were deliberately blurring the picture, obscuring the actual size and capabilities of the invading force, lest they be criticized for failing to engage a small, albeit well-armed and highly motivated *fidayeen* squad. Brigadier Sisodia knew better than to air such views in public. A tight-lipped, invisible soldier, with thirty-three years' service under his belt, he kept his own counsel. He had always been this way and his wife and son mostly inferred what he had been up to from the state of his boots. Since July 2007, when he had been selected for the Black Cats, he had become especially guarded.

He tried to void his mind. The Brigadier's sole focus was his men. Splitting them into three groups that would take on Chabad House, the Trident–Oberoi and the Taj, he told them they would be facing well-trained belligerents, whose aim was to prolong the terror and extract maximum publicity by creating strongholds and executing hostages. There would be no negotiations, the Brigadier warned. 'It is kill or be killed.'

The commandos pressed rounds into the clips of their Heckler & Koch MP5 submachine guns, taping the magazines together, tightened their webbing and pulled down their balaclavas. Boarding his vehicle the Brigadier watched the task force, engines gunning, stream out into the bright morning in municipal buses. Behind came the tactical and weapons specialists, the bomb squad with their dogs, field medics, a communications team that would rig mobile control posts to keep them talking, and intelligence officers instructed to mill around in the crowd near the Taj, giving the commandos peripheral vision.

9.15 a.m. – Apollo Bunder

'Blood, glass, charred wood.' When Brigadier Sisodia finally marched into the Taj, the scale of the destruction struck him. He wondered at the firepower that had carved up the marble floors and blown the crystal chandeliers into smithereens. It was going to be a long, hard slog, he warned, as he established a Black Cat command post beside the police in the Tower lobby, run by a Special Forces colonel and aided by Major Sandeep Unnikrishnan, a sinewy officer whom Sisodia had ordered to lead the Taj units. A product of the National Defence Academy, the elite joint services training college outside Pune, Major Unnikrishnan, a 31-year-old Black Cat instructor, could have chosen to stay behind in Manesar. But he had volunteered.

An exhausted-looking Karambir Kang introduced the Black Cats to the MARCOS commander and to Sunil Kudiyadi, the Taj security chief, who was sitting with a spent huddle of Black Suits. Having run the gauntlet all night unarmed, Kudiyadi's team looked on as he described the harrowing Kitchen Brigade slaughter, as well as the developing crisis in the darkened cellars. Hundreds were still stuck in their rooms in the Tower, too, he warned, and many more remained unaccounted for in the Palace wing, although fire crews had plucked some to safety, at extreme risk to their own lives. Others had been less lucky, caught up in the inferno or picked off by the gunmen, including Karambir's wife and sons, trapped on the sixth floor with Sabina Saikia, the food critic. As condolences were murmured, Karambir raised his hand: 'I will stay here until the very end; otherwise the terrorists will have won.'

The MARCOS commander briefed Sisodia on the Chambers, where his men had engaged in a bruising battle, in which they had been unable to dislodge the gunmen, who had gone to ground in the kitchens. There were still scores of guests trapped inside the club, he advised, all of them shell-shocked after eleven hours.

Brigadier Sisodia asked for the hotel's plans and Karambir handed over a sheet of paper. After all this time, rescuers were still working off a basic drawing that was not to scale and only recorded part of the first two floors. 'Impossible,' the Brigadier snapped. 'We need architectural plans.' Karambir shook his head: 'Sir, we have been searching all night but the man cannot be found.' The Brigadier was uncompromising: 'Obtaining them is *the* priority.'

The MARCOS commander took the Brigadier to one side. 'There are two worlds in this hotel,' he warned, 'the backstage and front of house.' Without the help of hotel staff, the Taj was a treacherous sniper's paradise. At one point his men had pushed through a service door only to pop out, unexpectedly, in another wing, with their backs exposed to the gunmen. The inferno had also left behind miles of unstable corridors that could collapse at any minute.

The Brigadier marched up to the flagging Taj security men and flung them a bundle of flak jackets: 'You're coming with us.'

9.30 a.m. – the Chambers

Bhisham Mansukhani heard a *clang, clang, clang*, and nearly leapt out of his skin. Someone was banging on the barricaded Lavender Room door. 'Open up,' a voice shouted in English. 'Don't move,' someone hissed, as everyone inside inched away. 'Please open the door,' a softer, female voice implored from outside. 'I think it's one of ours,' the club manager whispered, opening it a fraction, to see men in ski masks, brandishing guns, alongside a female staff member. Overjoyed, he threw the door back as a cheer rose up. Black Cats clattered in, hushing everyone with a warning that the gunmen were still close by.

'Walking only,' a commando instructed, as Dr Tilu tried to lift the semi-comatose engineer, Kamble. 'He's dying,' the doctor argued, but the Black Cat was emphatic. As Dr Tilu laid him back down Kamble whispered for someone to contact his wife and two children. 'You'll be able to do it yourself,' Dr Tilu replied, uncertainly. She knew that if they had been freed sooner, his wounds were treatable. But the grinding delays had put Kamble on the danger list.

In the library, Remesh Cheruvoth, the cruise director, was fading too. As the Black Cats moved swiftly through the room, checking for concealed gunmen, someone helped him to his feet. 'Follow us down,' they shouted as Remesh, his shirt blood-soaked, called out weakly: 'I must take Mr Liveras's body.' Bereft, he had carefully laid out his boss on the chaise longue. 'Living only,' the commando snapped, leaving Remesh to undo Andreas's watch, his numb fingers fumbling, finding his wallet too, unclipping his necklace, taking his BlackBerry and Nokia handsets, giving them to one of the *Alysia*'s spa girls. 'Please give them to the captain,' he asked, shuffling away, tearfully, into the hall.

Anjali Pollack, who had been separated from Mike for five hours, came out into the corridor with their dining companions, feeling so euphoric that the Black Cat leading her out seemed 'as handsome as Brad Pitt'. She stopped other guests, asking if they had noticed her 'tall, nearly blond American husband', finally glimpsing soldiers entering the club toilets and returning with a familiar lean silhouette in a crumpled striped shirt. She waved at Mike as the crowd pushed her on, until they reached the Tower lobby, where everyone lurched to a shocked halt. A corpse lay rolled up against the wall. The furniture was shredded by gunfire, the carpets were charred and blotted. Blood was spattered everywhere.

Police stood around, speaking into walkie-talkies while small huddles of masked soldiers oiled their guns. Smoke clung in the morning air like village campfires. As the guests walked towards the exit, broken glass crunched beneath everyone's feet. Someone scooped up a spent cartridge, stowing it in his pocket, but Bhisham did not want any souvenir. He shuffled forward with the others, transfixed by the sunshine streaming through the glass doors.

Finally, he was outside, as cameras clicked and whirred and the warm morning sun was on his face. A police van drew up, and a constable beckoned over Bhisham's aged mother, who was hobbling on bleeding feet, offering to take her to the nearby Azad Maidan police station. Bewildered, Bhisham waved her off, before climbing into a waiting bus. He stared up at the windows of the Taj, wondering if the Thadanis had made it out too.

Mike Pollack caught up with Anjali on the hotel steps. Swinging her around, he whisked out his BlackBerry to snap a picture: Mike grinning broadly, Anjali, caught mid-sob, terror and relief in her eyes.

Ack, ack, ack. Mike spun around, his phone still held aloft, and saw bullets were streaming down from the windows above. People dressed up for the night stood blinking in the day, incredulous. The screaming began as guests dragged one another out of the way. Mike lifted Anjali through the door of an open bus, shouting, 'Lie low,' as Taj staffers formed a human shield around those remaining. Hot bullets and frantic bursts of fire pattered everywhere, as Mike was pulled towards a boundary wall, cowering against it, half kneeling. He heard a click and looked around to see a photographer taking a shot.

Bhisham had his face pressed into the grimy rubber floor of the bus and was crying. 'The whole thing is a crazy film shoot,' he said, broken by the unending terror, as the bus lurched forward, gathering speed, until finally the gunfire was inaudible.

Within an hour he and his mother were home in Breach Candy, turning on the TV news, searching for reports on missing friends, as if it were all a dream. After showering, he pulled the cork from a bottle of red wine he had been given as a gift in Italy earlier that year. This was the right occasion, he said to himself, as he savoured the plummy, rich red fruits and his mother pulled her face into a look of disgust. 'Alcohol *saved* our lives,' Bhisham exploded. 'If I'd not taken us upstairs to the Crystal Room for a drink at 9.30 p.m., you and I would have died in that lobby.'

As the wine softened his mood, he felt a pang of something he could not understand. But it was not for the dead and injured, or even for the grand hotel that was still being pummelled, or for Gunjan Narang, the school bully who he now knew had been slaughtered alongside his family in the cellars, or for others whose fates he still did not know. What he felt was disappointment, or perhaps even sadness. 'I had become so convinced that it was the end for me that I was committed to the idea of my death,' he recalled. Now that he had survived, it was going to take an age to readjust.

Mike Pollack eventually made it back to his in-laws' house, exhilarated. 'Everything that has happened,' he gabbled to Anjali, as they hugged their two sons, 'is literally biblical.' The epic slaughter and disasters of the Old Testament were, to his way of thinking, mythical. But what they had endured inside the Taj was a real, elemental journey. 'Look what humans are capable of when put in harm's way,' he told her, hopping about. 'See what we became? How we all helped each other?'

Mike was already thinking ahead, disenchanted by what he had done with his life so far, playing the high-stakes game at the edge of human possibility. 'These things just fall away in the face of death,' he confessed to Anjali, 'leaving only what is truly important.' He would sell up the hedge fund and channel his money and energies into something more fulfilling.

10 a.m. – the cellars

The dark had a flavour. It tasted like cardboard and smelled of gravy. Enveloped by it, Chef Oberoi listened to the sound of approaching footsteps. He was shattered and dehydrated, his stomach growling. Looking around, everyone seemed to have reached the end. There was a knock on the door. 'Come out.' The small, portly chef stood, quaking in the darkness. 'Please stand,' he signalled to the others – guests and their children, members of his Kitchen Brigade. They would face whatever was out there with dignity.

As Oberoi pushed open the door, torchlight blinded them. Sixteen people, eyes straining, filed out of the door, staring at the masked gunmen before them. 'Follow us,' one of them said in Hindi, and it dawned on Oberoi that they were not *fidayeen* but Indian soldiers. But no one felt elated as they walked silently through the gloom, trying to ignore evidence of the slaughter that had, inexplicably, missed them. Oberoi suspected that he would never be able to forget the sounds of killing as he passed the puddles of congealing blood marking where his colleagues had fallen. After a couple of twists and turns, they were suddenly outside and standing blinking in the warm sunshine, inhaling the smells of a heaving city by the sea.

He caught sight of shell-shocked colleagues huddled together, like the shipwreck survivors, watching the still burning Palace wing, everyone contemplating those who had not made it. Oberoi caught up with their news, and the first report was the hardest to swallow. Chef Banja, his ally and foil, was confirmed dead.

So was Wasabi's head waiter, the iron-man Thomas Varghese. Young Hemant Talim, the Golden Dragon chef, was critical and Chef 'Big Foot' Kamdin had been killed. Oberoi recalled how the Kitchen Brigade joked that he was a giant: '*Kaiz bhai, tereko teri height maar gayi* [Brother Kaiz, your height has killed you].' Zodiac's Chef Mateen was also dead. Oberoi had been waiting for him to hand in his notice, after getting a high score in his matriculation exams that would have secured him a place in any top business school. Where was Chef Boris Rego from Shamiana? Missing. Oberoi winced. Rego's father, Urbano, was a close colleague and a friend, Goa's most famous culinary star. What would he tell him? And what of Chef Raghu, the banqueting chef who had made a stand in the Chambers kitchens? He was also missing. Nitin Minocha, the Golden Dragon senior sous-chef, a Vijay Banja in the making, the hotel's emerging talent, was in hospital, where doctors feared he might lose an arm.

Oberoi needed distractions. He had to work. The chef began to organize visits to hospitals. Ratan Tata had pledged to cover all staff medical bills. Funerals would have to be arranged, underwritten by Tata too. Oberoi borrowed a phone and dialled Chef Banja's wife, Fareeda. He broke the news to her and her eighteen-year-old son, as all around ambulances mustered, ferrying survivors and the dead to hospitals across the heartbroken city.

At Jaslok Hospital, on Pedder Road in Breach Candy, Rajvardhan Sinha, the chief of SB2, arrived. After leaving the Taj with his batch-mate Vishwas Patil, he had hobbled home to find his eight-year-old son getting ready for school. The domestic scene had blindsided him. Up until now Rajvardhan had lived in a bubble of war, prepared to die at any moment. But here normal life was going on. His son was full of questions and Rajvardhan had been careful to stick to the basics. He was caught out when the boy began to cry, running over to hug him, sensing that he had almost lost his father, in a scene of anguish tinged with relief that Rajvardhan imagined was being acted out all over the city. 'The siege is only part of it,' he told his wife, a college lecturer. 'These killers have trespassed on our sense of security.' She had never seen him so worked up before, and knowing that he would not rest until the siege was over, she insisted he get an X-ray.

Two hours later, his ankle heavily strapped, Rajvardhan hobbled back to his office in Rang Bhavan Lane. From there, he called the state's head of intelligence, who confirmed that everything pointed to Pakistan. Rajvardhan was ordered to liaise with foreign intelligence agencies, assuring them that India was on top of things, while probing to see if they had anything that pointed to the direct involvement of the Pakistan military.

Rajvardhan's men had their work cut out, confirming the identities of foreigners who had died in the assault so that their corpses could be repatriated and dealing with the chaos of the paperless living. Many hotel guests and Leopold victims had lost everything, and his men would need to confirm who they were before issuing them with exit permits. He also had the FBI to deal with too. A note on his desk informed him that a parallel criminal inquiry by the Bureau was already underway. He looked out of his window towards the lane where eight hours earlier three senior colleagues had been gunned down: Kamte, Karkare and Salaskar. How had it happened? Soon they would salute them at their funerals.

At Bombay Hospital, Amit Peshave, who had only slept for four hours in two days, was still working. 'Kidneys failed. Four or five bullet wounds. Hip. Buttocks. Hands – twice. Thigh. Groin,' an orderly shouted as a woman from the Taj cellar was pulled out on a trolley, tagged with the name Jharna Narang. Amit recoiled. 'Blood, fluids, clear the way.' The woman's parents and brother, Gunjan, had died, an orderly said, while the gunmen had left her for dead. Amit stared at her blood-spattered face, mesmerized by her murmuring lips that seemed to be chanting.

'Two shots in the torso, one in the leg.' Another ambulance had swung in. As Amit helped with the stretcher, a crimson rivulet of blood poured off the trolley, soaking his shirt and trousers. 'Please, no,' he gasped, almost dropping the body. Despite his parents being doctors, he had grown up with a phobia of blood. As he glanced up at the patient's face, he realized it was Chef Raghu, his friend from Chambers who he thought was dead. Sunil Kudiyadi had reported seeing a gunman sitting on Raghu's corpse, having emptied a magazine into him. Now Amit stared at the gaping, crimson tear in Raghu's whites and a cascade of emotion washed over him. 'Blood and wound packing,' an orderly cried. 'Pull through,' Amit urged, welling up. Raghu's eyes flicked opened and he smiled. 'Hey, boss,' he whispered.

Amit needed to walk. He picked up his soiled black jacket and strolled out into the sunshine, heading towards his dorm in Abbas Mansions. Along the way he bumped into a friend from the Trident–Oberoi hotel. Both of them guessed what the other had been through, so they walked along in silence, sipping a small flask of Honeybee rum. When Amit rounded the corner of the Taj, a soldier stepped out of a gateway, aiming his rifle. 'Stop, or I *will* shoot.' His finger wavered over the trigger. 'Taj staff,' Amit cried in Hindi, feeling ragged and full of hatred for the world. Something about his frantic tone and dishevelled demeanour rang true. 'What the hell are you doing, man?' the soldier asked, lowering his weapon. 'I was inside *there*,' Amit said, pointing to the Taj. 'And now I have to sleep.' The soldier saluted, letting him pass into Abbas Mansions.

Upstairs, Amit threw off his clothes and filled a bucket to shower. When the water finally ran clear, he dried himself off and called his family in Pune, before kneeling: 'Thank you, God,' he prayed, 'for saving my life.' There would, after all, be time for a frame of snooker, for girls and guitar lessons, to take a trip and make his mark. But first he had to sleep.

11 a.m. – the Taj Tower

Inside the Taj, four terrorists continued to pinball around, hurling grenades and shooting up rooms in wild acts that the Black Cats sensed were retribution for the Chambers evacuation. The commandos hoped to contain them in the Palace while they entered the Tower, which promised to be a complex and lengthy operation. There were twenty floors, usually with seventeen rooms on a floor, containing an unspecified number of guests, as well as 140 non-residential rooms – restaurants, kitchens and stores. Only one electronic master key could be found, which would slow down access.

As guests had been told to stay in their rooms in a coordinated ring-round, Kudiyadi feared it was going to be difficult to talk people out. The Black Cats mostly spoke no English and doors locked from the inside would have to be blown open. From experience, Major Unnikrishnan knew that it took an average of five minutes to clear a room, assuming there was no contact. This meant they required an unfeasible thirty-six man-hours to empty the Tower, which would take them to Saturday evening, even before they turned to the six-storey maze of the Palace wing with its 264 guest rooms. Given how late they had come to the city, and how few boots they had on the ground, with only a small transporter plane found for them that could carry just 120 men and their kit, this was untenable. 'Everything needs to be done in double-time,' the Brigadier warned.

Sisodia and Major Unnikrishnan went over the drill. They would start from the top of the Tower, with gravity on their side, the Major advising his men to avoid silhouetting in doorways and windows, reminding them that a blasted door was the area of greatest vulner-ability. Two commandos would stand on opposite sides of the threshold, ready to move, using a manoeuvre known as 'the but-tonhook' that required them to enter, cross and turn back on themselves, dominating the space.

They could not use the same procedure in every room as repeti-tion got men killed. So did talking. Apart from pre-assigned codewords to indicate the presence of guns, hand grenades or other weapons, they would rely on hand signals. Finally, in a building as tall as the Tower, there was the critical issue of resupply. Clearance was resource-thirsty and the NSG were severely limited. They needed to use the charges, grenades and ammunition sparingly.

12 p.m. – the Palace wing

With the Tower operation under way, Major Unnikrishnan came down to the lobby, where police and hotel staff watched the Mahar-ashtra police chief talking on TV. All hostages inside the Taj 'have been rescued', he announced. 'Depends on your definition,' Major Unnikrishnan said, shaking his head, as he turned his attention to the Palace. Before clearance, he wanted to do a sweep, orientating the men, rescuing straggling guests, gathering intelligence on the whereabouts of the gunmen.

He would lead one team into the north wing and up to the still-burning sixth floor, while a second team would do the same in the south wing. As the two teams set off, the Major warned that he would be the first down, drawing a dry laugh from the men gathered around him. They expected nothing less of him, as Unnikrishnan had emerged as a leader back in his training days, when he had been part of Oscar Squadron, known as 'The Olympians', their motto 'Faster, higher, and stronger'. Commissioned in 1999 into the 7 Bihar Regiment, he had been deployed on three tours of Kashmir, and two stints at Siachen, the glacier straddling India and Pakistan that is the highest battlefield in the world. In Manesar, he had dealt with his abilities with modesty and humour, withholding his real profession from social networking sites, where he described his work as 'non-productive human resources'. It was a smart play on the old joke: join the armed forces, meet lots of interesting people – and kill them.

By early evening on 27 November, the Major was first down, but the team in the south wing had become snagged on the fourth floor. They radioed through 'contact' to the colonel on the command post, and sounded out of shape. After spotting several figures scurry into room 472, they had blasted the door, only to find a mattress against it, absorbing the explosion. As they had attempted to enter, they were then caught out by gunmen rushing out with a guest in front of them, deployed as a human shield. Before they could regroup, a grenade had chopped into three of their team, who had to be dragged back down to the lobby by the others.

9 p.m. – the Tower lobby

While Major Unnikrishnan assisted the medics, the north-wing team were debriefed at the command post. On the sixth floor they had broken into Sabina Saikia's suite, finding the lounge destroyed, but the bedroom barely touched. 'There was no one inside,' a commando insisted. Sabina had gone. Next door, they had discovered a disturbing scene, three bodies in the bathroom: a woman and two children. It was Karambir Kang's family, who, as he had feared, had succumbed to the fire.

Someone had to find Sabina's husband, Shantanu Saikia, who had arrived from Delhi at 8 a.m., travelling with Nikhil, her brother. Shantanu, who was already in mourning, was dismayed by the news. He had heard nothing from Sabina since 1.30 a.m. on Thursday morning, when he had made the agonizing decision to say goodbye. Nikhil was also floored. How could his sister have escaped? Until he could get inside and see for himself, he needed to probe every eventuality and headed out into the city to trawl the morgues in case she was one of the unidentified dead.

Outside the Taj, the police sought out Karambir Kang. He silently took in the news about Neeti and the boys, before walking down to the sea to call his mother. He broke down. 'Don't cry now,' she said from thousands of miles away. 'Wait till I come there and cry in my lap.' Karambir could not wait that long. He had to pick himself up right now, for the sake of everyone else who was still waiting for news. They were counting on him, he told himself. He could still make a difference.

Ratan Tata, the Taj's owner, found him. 'Please take time to grieve,' he insisted, fearing that the towering manager would crumble. Karambir shook his head. 'It's important that I don't run away,' he said. 'I come from an army background. You know? There's a certain way you talk and think: discipline, duty and responsibility.' They both gazed up at the burning Taj, Karambir murmuring that if he quit now, so would his staff who had also lost friends and family. Tata understood. Karambir *was* an exemplar. But the fire that had consumed his place of work had also destroyed his family and his home. In truth, as another day came to an end in the besieged city, Karambir Kang had nothing left – not even photographs – and nowhere to go.

*

In the dead of the second night, with the lobby lit by emergency lights, the Taj hotel looked like a sunken hulk being salvaged by divers. Sitting in the long shadows at the Black Cats' command post, Brigadier Sisodia took in updates. The Tower clearance was moving more swiftly than he could have hoped, with most of the rooms already emptied and secured. There had been some misunderstandings, a contretemps with one room of guests eavesdropped talking in Arabic on a mobile phone, who in the highly charged atmosphere were briefly mistaken for an Al-Qaeda cell. Otherwise the Black Cats had worked effectively, winning back an entire day, which meant the focus could soon switch to the Palace, where, twenty-eight hours into the siege, four gunmen continued to roam unhindered.

Elsewhere in the city, the terrorists' stranglehold was easing. Although both the Taj gunmen's phones were out of action, the Anti-Terrorist Squad's technical section were still listening to a handset being used inside the Trident–Oberoi, where thirty-five guests and staff had been killed, and the Black Cats had cornered two gunmen on the eighteenth floor.

One tape – just in – caught a gunman, identified as Fahadullah (Qahafa the Bull's nephew), talking to his handler in Karachi.

Thursday, 27 November 2008, 11.45 p.m. – the Trident–Oberoi hotel, Nariman Point

The recording began with a tirade of gunfire, before a priestly voice came on the line: 'How's it going, Brother Fahadullah?'

A pause. 'Brother Abdul Rehman ["Chhota"] has died,' Fahadullah, the gunman, reported quietly. 'Praise God.' The Oberoi operation *was* unspooling.

'Oh, really?' the handler said almost casually. 'Is he nearby?' He seemed impassive and cold. The ATS thought it sounded like a practised tone, similar to a hospice worker letting a patient go.

'Yes. He's next to me. May God accept his martyrdom. His room is on fire. They are showing it on the TV. I'm sitting in the bathroom.' The ATS imagined the handler searching for those images on satellite TV. Then gunfire drowned out the line. Fahadullah was trapped.

When the shooting paused, the handler got to the point: 'You mustn't let them arrest you, remember that.' News was out that Ajmal Kasab had been caught alive. They could not afford another mistake.

Fahadullah replied: 'God willing. God willing.' Then he rang off.

Minutes later the handler called again: 'Fahadullah, my brother.' There was no answer. 'Can't you just get out there and fight?' He was urging him to sacrifice his life. 'Throw a grenade and try to get out.'

But after more than forty-eight hours of fighting, Fahadullah was exhausted. 'I have run out of grenades.' He sounded pained.

'Be brave, brother. Don't panic. For your mission to end success-fully you must be killed. God is waiting for you in heaven.'

'God willing,' he mumbled. Was he crying? Fahadullah appeared terrified.

The handler chivvied him on. 'May God help you. Fight bravely, and put your phone in your pocket, but leave it on.' When the moment came, Qahafa wanted to be sure. The sound became muf-fled and then a deluge of rounds drowned out everything.

'Fahadullah?' the handler called. 'Fahadullah?'

There was no answer.

Friday, 28 November 2008, 2 a.m. – Taj Palace

Sisodia got the call: the Trident–Oberoi was under Black Cat con-trol. But moments later another call reminded him that the gunmen inside the Taj were as dangerous as ever.

The desperate mother of Florence Martis had contacted the police Control Room in Crawford Market, with news that both her daughter and husband were missing inside the hotel. Florence had been stranded somewhere in the Palace wing since Wednesday night and no one had seen Faustine since he had slipped back inside the hotel in the early hours of Thursday morning. Roshan, a former Data Centre operator, who was keeping the family up to date, had recently rung through with the news that the gunmen had found Florence's hiding place.

Major Unnikrishnan volunteered to extricate the stranded Data Centre worker. He took two six-man teams and climbed the Grand Staircase, passing the bust of the hotel's founder, Jamsetji Tata. As they reached the first-floor landing, coming level with the Sea Lounge, a figure flashed by, an AK-47 braced in one hand, spraying rounds on to the Black Cats' position, tossing a grenade as he tracked out of sight, with spumes of gunfire channelling in on three sides from the rest of the gunman's team. The commandos had walked into a trap and as the blast wave hit them, Unnikrishnan rolled sideways, shrapnel narrowly missing him, but catching a teammate in the legs. It was Sunil Yadav, a man whom the Major had trained and billeted with.

Flattening themselves against the banisters, as the firing intensified, the Black Cats wondered if the Data Centre worker Florence was a lure. Had she been captured and forced to reel them in? With one man exposed and screaming in pain, the Major signalled for the others to concentrate fire on the doorways to the Crystal Room and Ballroom, while he tried to retrieve Yadav.

His fist raised, he prepped the teams. 'Three, two and one.' The Major crashed down on the injured man's webbing and latched on. The men behind grabbed Unnikrishnan's legs, and dragged both men down the stairs. When it was clear that Yadav was out of danger, the Major signalled that he was going to press on, moving into the space created by their split firing positions. On his knees, he released short controlled bursts to the left and the right, before barrelling through the door of the Palm Lounge. Thinking fast, he knew it gave him access to the Ballroom, from where he could work his way around to the Crystal Room, flanking the gunmen, while his men kept up the pressure.

Down below, the Black Cats waited for further instructions. Nothing came. Then the Major's radio clicked. He sounded breathless. 'Don't come,' he rasped. The radio clicked again. 'No comms.'

The others bipped their walkie-talkies to say they understood. 'Do *not* contact,' he whispered.

A nerve-wracking silence followed. What was Unnikrishnan doing? Was he so close to the gunmen that voices on the radio would give away his position? The men resumed firing, pounding the Crystal Room and the banqueting floor doorways, fearing for their leader, as the rear team used the cover to reverse down the staircase with the injured Yadav.

After half an hour, the silence proved too much for them. They signalled to the command post that Major Unnikrishnan might not be coming out and surged up the staircase pumping rounds furiously, forcing the gunmen back in the direction of the Wasabi restaurant. The Black Cats paused. There was no sign of the Major but looking around as the smoke coiled they realized that they had finally taken the landing. They radioed the news down to the command post, where Brigadier Sisodia passed it to the NSG chief, Jyoti Dutt. The Major was missing, but they had forced the gunmen into a corner, boxing them into the Japanese restaurant. The Taj operation finally had some momentum behind it – but at a price.

7 a.m. – the Palm Lounge

As morning light filtered into the Palm Lounge, a Black Cat team moved on the doors, slipping inside, while more men circled around the back. The room was charred beyond recognition, wooden beams glowing and smoking. Plaster had come away from the ceiling. The ash was so deep it felt like they were walking through snow. It took a moment for their eyes to adjust to the stinging smoke, and then they saw the body. From the webbing and weaponry they knew immediately it was Major Unnikrishnan. Rolling him over, his injuries told some of the story. He had pushed through into the Palm Lounge, thinking the fire was coming from behind him, when in fact two more gunmen had lain in wait inside, to his right and left. He had died with his radio in his hand.

They called it in: 'Death confirmed.' Jyoti Dutt asked to talk to the men holding the landing, worried that the Black Cats' aura of invulnerability had been pricked and that the advance would falter. Brigadier Sisodia thought that was the difference between the police and the army. Chief Dutt had come from the former, and worried about the men's ability to shoulder the loss. The Brigadier, seconded from the Sikh Regiment, told him: 'These men will not even register the Major's passing until the hotel is ours.' The commandos needed to move in on the Wasabi right now, he said. They also needed to work out who and where Florence Martis was, as elsewhere in the city hostages were being executed.

8.52 a.m. – Chabad House

At 7 a.m., twenty-two Black Cats had rappelled from an Mi-17 helicopter on to the roof of Chabad House, from where an Indian maid had earlier escaped with the two-year-old son of the rabbi and his wife. As far as the authorities knew, the couple continued to be held hostage inside, alongside four guests, although confusing and shocking intercepts had been recorded of the Karachi handlers ordering their men to kill everyone.

A short while after the rappel, intense gunfire could be heard inside the centre, and at 8.52 a.m. the Anti-Terrorist Squad netted another chunk of conversation that they relayed to the Taj command post, the caller marked as 'BW', for Brother Wasi, one of the handlers stationed in Karachi control. He was talking to Akasha, one half of team two, which was inside Chabad House.

Akasha panted, obviously exhausted. BW put himself in his man's shoes: 'You have run out of water. You're tired. They know it too. They are hoping to arrest you, once you are weak from hunger and thirst.' BW was hoping that Akasha would draw his own conclusions and volunteer to go down fighting.

Akasha understood what he was being told: 'Today is Friday so we should finish it today.' The *jummah* or Day of Assembly, as it is known, was filled with public prayer and it was the perfect time for a sacrifice.

BW suggested Akasha begin his final assault right away: 'Shoot, shoot.' The instruction worked as the line was drowned out by gunfire.

Akasha came back on the line. 'They have opened fire. They have opened fire. Umar, take cover. Take cover! They are firing into our room.' The line broke up and then a weakened voice came back. 'I have been shot. I have been shot. Pray for me.'

Listening in at the precise moment the Chabad siege collapsed, with the unseen handlers listening in too, the ATS were mesmerized.

BW still had to be sure: 'Where are you hit?'

Akasha replied: 'One in my arm. One in my leg.'

BW: 'God protect you. Did you manage to hit any of their guys?'

Akasha was struggling: 'We got one commando. Pray that God will accept my martyrdom.'

A few minutes later the police received confirmation. After thirty-six hours, Akasha and Umar, the Chabad House gunmen, had been killed. There was bad news too. A Black Cat, Gajender Singh, had been killed, as had all the Jewish hostages. Reports suggested they had been sadistically tortured and sexually assaulted, with their genitals mutilated. A phrase rang out from an earlier transcript. 'Remember,' one handler had told a gunman, 'a captive Jew is worth fifty non-Jewish ones.'

9 a.m. – the Taj Data Centre

Inside the Data Centre, Florence Martis, one of the last people trapped inside the Taj, had fallen into a fevered dream. She imagined herself on a boat, sailing out of the harbour, loaded down with fishing nets, ready to cast. Her phone rang and she wondered how the signal reached so far from the shore. 'In dreams you can do anything,' she told herself.

An unfamiliar male voice introduced himself. 'What's your name?' he asked.

'Florence,' she said, as she realized she was no longer dreaming.

There was a pause: 'Where are you? Which floor are you on? Can you describe it?'

It was a Black Cat calling up from the Tower lobby. He heard Florence talking into another handset: 'Roshan?' she said, slurring. 'Are you there?' Florence put her mobile on speakerphone and the commando heard a man's voice. 'Yes, it's Roshan. I'm here.' He was driving to Thane on his scooter and the sounds of a Mumbai commute, car horns, street cries and engines revving, could be heard.

'Roshan,' Florence said. 'Someone is on the office line. He wants to know where I am.' She put the mobile set close to the landline receiver. 'You talk to him,' she said. Roshan, cradling his phone in his neck as he drove, shouted above the traffic: 'Listen, she is in the second-floor Data Centre, above the Sea Lounge and the Gateway Room.' The line seemed to break up and in the background was the cawing of gunfire. 'We'll get her out,' the commando said, before cutting the connection.

At 10 a.m., on Friday, 28 November, two Black Cats entered the Data Centre, calling out Florence's name. Seeing an office chair rattling, they pulled it back to find an emaciated young woman scrunched beneath the desk. She had been there for thirty-six hours. Disoriented and faint, she asked for her father, as the commandos helped her into the corridor, where she noticed that the white marble was now black with soot. 'Careful,' they said, sending her running into the arms of another commando, further along. 'Gunmen are still above us.' Passed from hand to hand, Florence entered the kitchens, staring down at the congealed rivulets of blood. Soon her white plimsolls were smeared too. A present to her from her father on Wednesday morning, they were now crimson and clung to her feet. She did not take her eyes off them until she was carried down into the Tower lobby, where a distant relative discarded them. 'Where's Daddy?' she cried. 'In the hospital,' he replied, choosing his words carefully.

They reached her home by 11 a.m., Florence dipping in and out of consciousness, and unable to recognize her mother, Precilla. 'Where's Daddy,' she asked everyone, refusing to allow the family GP near her, until she heard a voice, whose tone she trusted. Was this Roshan? The Samaritan had ridden over to see Florence's face for the first time. Florence did as Roshan instructed and fell into a deep, sedated sleep, while her sixteen-year-old brother Floyd headed out into Mumbai, with instructions to trawl the city's morgues until he found his father.

Friday, 28 November 2008, 4 p.m. – the Wasabi restaurant

Three transporter-loads of Black Cats from Manesar had now touched down in Mumbai, and more than a hundred commandos were deployed inside the Taj, building a perimeter around Wasabi. As Friday slipped by, they gradually tightened it, pushing in more men. But despite the overwhelming odds, the four *fidayeen* shrugged off the ferocious fire, one pair of gunmen emerging from the ground floor Harbour Bar, taking aim at the commandos, while two more, inside the Wasabi, kept up a constant barrage.

Brigadier Sisodia needed to get eyes inside the north-eastern corner of the building. Outside the hotel, he ordered Black Cat marksmen to climb into the fire service's cherry pickers and take aim at Wasabi's toughened-glass windows with their Israeli sniper rifles. The windows were reflective, making it impossible to see in. 'One shot to pierce them,' Sisodia instructed his marksmen. 'On my signal.' With a staggered crack that reverberated around the docks, high velocity rounds hammered in. Grenade launchers were then jacked up on tripods, aimed at the fracture points and fired in a coordinated burst that created a wall of flames and smoke. With any luck the explosions had also cut the gunmen to pieces, Sisodia murmured, grabbing a pair of binoculars.

When the smoke cleared, he had a perfect view inside the first floor, and could see the gunmen still scurrying around. Three of them took aim at the army outside, while one seemed to be waving a white flag. Or was he luring them in? The Brigadier was astonished.

He ordered a Black Cat team to inch their way through Wasabi's kitchens and hold a firing position at the service entrance to the restaurant, while Deven Bharti, the Crime Branch number two, accompanied a second team that wriggled towards the Harbour Bar entrance, one floor below. On Brigadier Sisodia's order, the two teams opened up, firing in coordinated bursts, cutting up everything inside. Soldiers overheard a gunman crying out: 'No more. For Allah's sake no more.' Outside, binoculars in hand, Sisodia studied the scene. The *fidayeen* were still alive. They retook their positions, firing on the Black Cats and the Gateway. 'What the hell?' Sisodia was stumped. He had never come across such determined fighters before. He walked the length of the Palace wing's ground and first floors, trying to figure it out. He consulted Kudiyadi and Bharti. By the time he had finished taking in views, it was dark and they were losing their footing. Outside, Chief Dutt, also under pressure, advised reporters that the Taj would be liberated by sunrise on Saturday. 'Why can't we call in air support and flatten the entire structure?' the Brigadier said to Bharti, only half joking. They had tried everything else.

Saturday, 29 November 2008, 3 a.m. – the Harbour Bar

Kudiyadi arrived, excited and apologetic. The Taj's security chief had figured it out and was embarrassed not to have come to the answer quicker. They had all overlooked a glaring architectural oddity in this corner of the hotel that any waiter or chef could have told them about: a spiral staircase linking the ground floor Harbour Bar to Wasabi that was protected floor to ceiling by a vast, three-foot-thick impregnable concrete pillar. Every time the gunmen came under attack, they ran for shelter behind it.

'Time for some improvisation,' the Brigadier said to Bharti. If they could not level the pillar they could surely create a weapon with sufficient force to annihilate anything animate cowering behind it. Was it possible? The Brigadier called in the task force's bomb detail. 'What can we cobble together?' The men spent an hour figuring it out. At 4 a.m., they had a plan but were short of components. They needed plastic-coated copper wire, tape, screws and ball bearings too – all of which sounded to Bharti like the components of a classic suicide bomb – but he was happy to take charge of procurement. The Crime Branch number two knew that in a city like Mumbai anything could be found at any time with a little bit of initiative and persuasion. He called in his men. 'We're going shopping.'

In the small side streets around Apollo Bunder, they roused shop-keepers in their pyjamas and forced open steel shutters. By 5 a.m., they were back and the bomb squad sat with wire clippers and pliers, assembling their device. They placed a grenade at its core, around which they positioned sticks of TNT, filling the gaps with plastic explosives. Then they did what terrorists did, pressing in bolts and ball bearings to inflict maximum casualties. They now had the makings of a vicious bang, a blinding flash, and a blast wave loaded with shrapnel. By 6 a.m. they were ready. 'OK,' said Sisodia. 'Now let's build another.'

At 7 a.m., two Black Cat teams wriggled into place, above and below the concrete pillar, their devices rigged on long detonation leashes, ready to be thrown into the Harbour Bar and Wasabi. 'Two blasts, simultaneously,' Sisodia instructed, beginning the countdown. Bharti watched from Wasabi as the pitcher braced himself, a man beside him with a radio counting down in time with the team below. 'Three. Two. One.' Both teams bowled in their IEDs and a blast wave shook the hotel, followed by a howl as the air was sucked in and then forced out, sending great spirals of black smoke and flames shooting into the sky.

A blackened human figure came flying out of the hotel. His legs cycled in mid-air as if he were pelting for freedom, the long black trousers he wore shredded into ragged shorts. He landed with a clatter on a concrete road divider, a dead pigeon falling beside him, where a waiting marksman delivered a shot to his head. A commando ran over, stooping to confirm the kill as Brigadier Sisodia hovered, studying the man's face that was caked in gunpowder and a tar-like residue. His hair was seared, his fists clenched as if in pain. His shirt, blackened by soot and soaked in blood, was fused to his back.

It was Abu Shoaib, the gunman dressed in grey who had attacked the Leopold Café before shooting his way into the Taj. Before landing in Mumbai, Shoaib had been the one who held down the legs of the captured Indian skipper of the MV *Kuber* while his throat was slit. As a young man he had been turned over to Lashkar by his preacher father, the youngest of all the recruits. And before Lashkar, Shoaib had lived in Barapind, a ring of mud-and-brick houses in northern Punjab, that had for as long as anyone could remember lost lives in the cross-border firing, a boy born in a room with a view over the mountains of Kashmir.

Sisodia pulled himself away, as a wave of exhaustion crashed over him. Was this finally over? Fire crews pressed forward to douse the flames flaring out of the corner of the hotel. 'We're going to need the sniffer dogs in there,' Sisodia ordered. Somewhere inside the smouldering bar were the remains of Ali (yellow), Umer (black) and Abdul Rehman 'Bada' (red). While the dog team was called forward, the Black Cats began filtering through the Taj. After almost fifty-eight hours, the gunmen were finally dead but it would take another eight hours to make the hotel safe.

Beside the Gateway, Karambir Kang stood with Chef Oberoi, two men overcome by grief, trying to focus on the future as if it were a life raft, ringed by what was left of their staff, including Amit Peshave and his dorm mates. 'Who has a strong stomach?' Oberoi asked quietly. 'I want it to be *us* that cleans the kitchens. It has to be us.' There was a murmur of agreement.

Vishwas Patil, the Zone 1 DCP, still manning the Taj perimeter, felt relief and irritation as he heard the news that it was over. He was inundated with requests from national and state politicians who all wanted to be escorted to the Taj, posing for photos outside the liberated hotel, looking for a bounce in the opinion polls, men whom he blamed for failing to secure the city in the first place. Patil stared up at the blackened windows, thankful to see that for the first time in three days no one was waving for help. He wondered if he would ever lose the wretched feeling that all this bloodletting had been preventable. The Mumbai way of doing things meant that there would be no searching inquiry to test the force's response, measuring the success of the intelligence agencies and the efficacy of the Black Cats. Patil predicted 'a song and dance show' run by needy retirees from government service, who would sacrifice a few minnows to shore up the whole shaky edifice.

They would not have it all their own way. Not after what the Deputy Commissioner of Police and his colleagues had been through. Patil had already begun to plan a report in his head, outlining what he knew in the five months leading up to the assault on the city, and what his colleagues had known stretching back to 2006. Sketching out his dialogue with the Taj and his higher-ups, Patil began composing the opening sentences as his car drove him back towards his home opposite the Brabourne cricket stadium, where his wife and two children were anxiously waiting. He would send it to the Commissioner on 19 December 2008, the report numbered 23/DI/Zone1/08. And, having learned the Mumbai game, he would simultaneously leak a snapshot of it to a local journalist who had been hounding him for a story – just to make sure that the file did not vanish.

Sitting inside Brabourne was Bob Nicholls. The stadium was the quietest place in town, a refuge in which he had thought through his experiences inside the Taj and also the fate of the Champions League Twenty20. Shane Warne and Kevin Pietersen had already cancelled and the whole shebang needed to be pushed back to allow the city to mourn and re-secure itself. If they were lucky, the tournament might run late next year, but the set-up would have to be razor sharp. Against the odds, this city always bounced back, Bob thought. In his opinion, Mumbai could overcome anything, especially the incompetence of its rulers.

In Titan Towers, Breach Candy, Captain Ravi Dharnidharka was torn between wanting to get back to his girlfriend in San Diego and needing to stay for his Indian family. From an upper floor, he could see multiple funeral processions already wending their way around the lanes below. He had three to attend himself for the relatives who had been killed inside the Trident–Oberoi. But while the residents of this city that he loved looked after themselves, what could they expect from their leaders, who had already begun papering over the cracks, repositioning the catastrophe of the Taj and the sacrifice of guests and staff as India's finest hour?

At Bombay Hospital, Kelly barely took in the news that it was over. She was overwhelmed by the future. A remarkable Indian surgeon had fused some of Will's vertebrae together and placed a cage around his pelvis to keep everything immobile, so that he was ready to be flown back to the UK. But this task was proving the most difficult to organize. Will's father Nigel, who flew in just as the Taj siege was lifted, could not get the attention of overworked British consular officials, who prevaricated over repatriation arrangements and promised but failed to make adequate preparations with hospitals in the UK. Kelly's travel insurance company refused to cover medical bills or anything else, pointing to an exception for acts of terrorism. After they missed their existing return flights, the airline claimed it had no available seats for many weeks, leaving Nigel looking for any carrier prepared to take a stretcher.

Then there was the medical prognosis. It was unknowable, Kelly was told. All she could be sure of, as she looked at her heavily sedated boyfriend, was that the life they had hoped for was gone for ever.

At 10 a.m. on 29 November, Sabina's husband, brother and friend, Savitri Choudhury all stood outside the Taj. The text messages supposedly sent by Sabina early on Thursday morning, combined with the NSG finding an empty suite, suggested that the food critic had escaped the hotel. However, Airtel, the phone company, was currently investigating the phenomenon of 'ghost calls', whereby Sabina's texts could have been displaced to remote towers in the city, and distributed long after they were sent. It was also possible her phone had latched on to a distant mast as the network became inundated with calls on the first night of the attack, giving the impression she was in another location. Nikhil, her brother, had found no answers in the city morgues. 'I have seen bodies that nobody should have to see – burnt, shot, bloated,' he told Savitri. Instead they had pressed family contacts to get them inside the Taj. Even though the hotel remained off-limits, the three were escorted into the lobby, their nostrils stung by the smoke-logged corridors. Black Cats pounded up and down the Grand Staircase, while stretcher-bearers whizzed by carrying disfigured corpses. Savitri stopped. She could not do it and turned around, while Shantanu and Nikhil pushed on.

At the top of the stairs, both men were shocked by the extent of the damage on the still-smouldering sixth floor. The fire had burnt parts of the roof away completely and sunlight was flooding in. 'You are not meant to be here,' a commando bellowed, as they arrived in a tar-black passageway, standing before a charred door. Shantanu paused. Swallowing his pain, he edged into the Sunrise Suite. Sabina's room was divided into three parts: a bedroom, a sitting room with a breakfast nook, and a bathroom. Nikhil could see that the sitting room had been incinerated. 'It was reduced to ash and by ash I mean it was completely gone, there was nothing there except the frame of a chandelier that had fallen to the ground and the metal frame of the dining table that continued to stand, stoical, in the breakfast nook.'

Shantanu and Nikhil walked into the bedroom and were stunned. It had been barely touched, as the commandos reported, although a skein of soot covered everything. The luggage was 'in typical Sabina disarray' but intact. 'It's like even the fire was scared of Sabina, and had crossed over to Karambir's room,' Nikhil later joked grimly.

They sat, forlorn, on the huge bed, where Sabina had jumped for joy, amazed at Karambir Kang's hospitality. Something caught Shantanu's eye and he was drawn to the far side of the divan. He walked round and recoiled. Sabina was there, kneeling on the floor as if praying, her glasses propped up on her head, her forehead resting on the ground. In the early hours of Thursday, 27 November, his irrepressible wife had got down on her knees, resting for an exhausted, sleepy moment, as the oxygen inside the room was devoured by the greedy inferno raging next door. And here, on her own, she had been slowly asphyxiated.

They pulled back the bed cover and a crisp white sheet lay beneath it, as if the housekeeper had just made it. While Shantanu slowly absorbed the scene, Nikhil rushed back downstairs, horrified and crying. 'I want her down in one hour,' he shouted at Taj security. 'I want Sabina with us in *this* hour.' Although they tried to put him off, the fierce will of a mourning brother got the job done, and soon after Sabina Sehgal Saikia came down the Grand Staircase for the last time, wrapped up in a pristine white bedsheet.

Ajmal Kasab talked and talked, spurred on by a promise that at the end of all the questioning he would be able to see his nine comrades, who, according to the authorities, were 'being held elsewhere'.

When that day came, a Crime Branch officer entered his cell: 'Are you ready?' Ajmal was eager.

The prisoner was driven past the Gateway of India and the Taj, arriving at the JJ Hospital, in Byculla, where the victims of Chabad House had also been taken. 'Are they all badly injured?' Ajmal asked uncertainly, as the door was unlocked and opened. 'You can see for yourself,' the officer said, leading him into a white-walled room.

Nine stainless steel trays lay before him. The brothers who had fought inside the Taj were the hardest to look at. Ali's and Shoaib's faces had been crushed into hideous grins. Umer, the diminutive Taj leader, was burnt beyond recognition, and all that was left of Abdul Rehman 'Bada' was a mangled clump of burnt body parts and singed red material.

Ajmal turned furiously to his police guard, his world imploding: 'Take me away.' He was driven back to his solitary cell, where his interrogator was waiting for him. 'So, Ajmal,' he said, smiling. 'Did you see the glow on their faces and smell the fragrance of roses rising from their bodies?'

Bitterly, Ajmal wept.

Afterword

Terrorism is often described as asymmetrical, and Mumbai provides a chilling illustration of what that means: ten resentful and misguided young men who were able to hold the world's fourth-largest city to ransom, killing 166 and injuring more than 300 over three nights of horror.

Images from the ravaged city travelled the world. There were countless tragic stories. At Chhatrapati Shivaji Terminus, where Ajmal Kasab and his accomplice gunned down fifty-eight commuters, wounding another 104, a thirteen-year-old boy was saved from the firing and taken to a hospital where doctors calculated when to tell him that his parents, an uncle and three cousins had perished. Outside Chabad House, Sandra Samuel, a nanny, clutched the two-year-old Moshe Holtzberg as his parents, Rabbi Gavriel and his pregnant wife, Rivka, were murdered, alongside four other hostages. After the bodies of thirty-two staff and guests were recovered from the Trident–Oberoi hotels, a Turkish Muslim couple, Seyfi and Meltem Muezzinoglu, held captive for eight hours, recalled how they burst into mourning after watching the gunmen execute a group of female hostages. 'We stepped forward, opened our hands and said our prayers out loud,' Seyfi said. 'And you know what happened? One of the gunmen was staring at us with big eyes. He didn't believe it and started looking at the floor. He was ashamed. We spoke our prayers in Arabic, and we spoke them loud, hand in hand in front of those bodies.' There were many more harrowing and life-affirming snapshots from the Leopold Café, from Cama Hospital, the Metro cinema and Rang Bhavan Lane. Also from the city's port area, where one taxi bomb detonated, and at Vile Parle, where another exploded, all of these acts of inhumanity haunting police chiefs all over the world, who pondered how their forces would have coped.

They studied Mumbai's days of reckoning, and picked up on Lashkar's unnerving innovations. Handlers in Pakistan had guided their gunmen in real time using a cheap Internet telephony network, while disguising their location. Equipped with satellite TV and Google Earth, these invisible controllers had simply sat back in Karachi, zooming in and out of the stricken city with the flick of a mouse or remote control. Everyone in Mumbai who called or texted in an interview with a rolling news channel gave these men insights into the strategy of the Indian security forces, alerting them also to fresh targets. Hours of chilling, eavesdropped telephone conversations revealed the cold calculations of the masterminds who pushed their men into a slaughter, before ensuring that they were consumed by it. These extraordinary tapes also exposed the child-like nature of the gunmen, teetering between mania, self-doubt, sadism and exhaustion.

All of the above are compelling reasons for us to write about 26/11, as the attacks became known in India, and we began researching *The Siege* soon after the assaults were over. However, a common reaction among the authorities in Mumbai when we first sought them out was fatigue and suspicion. Rakesh Maria, the city's most famous cop, who was promoted in 2010 to chief of the Anti-Terrorist Squad, replacing his murdered colleague, Hemant Karkare, insisted that those three days in November 2008 simply represented a failure of imagination on the part of the police and intelligence agencies. 'Everything's been said that needs to be,' Maria initially claimed, after we had waited hours to see him in his first-floor office at the ATS headquarters, in Nagpada.

But once we had begun trawling through the evidence the opposite seemed true. While the 9/11 commission of inquiry in the United States enlisted a ten-man bi-partisan board of politicians to probe every facet of the attacks, and the 7/7 inquests in London spent six months recording every detail and witness statement, 26/11 received only a cursory grilling from the Pradhan Commission, a two-man panel formed in Mumbai on 30 December 2008 to explore the 'war-like' attacks on the city.

Having been precluded from cross-examining the intelligence services, politicians or the National Security Guard, it produced a sixty-four-page inquiry report, which was widely lambasted for lacking depth. Pradhan exonerated Mumbai's police force, although it did accuse Police Commissioner Hasan Gafoor of failing to be more visible. Even these weak words were rejected by the state legislature. Gafoor, who responded by blaming other senior officers for the mistakes of 26/11, died of a heart attack in Breach Candy Hospital in 2012, by which time the majority of the Pradhan Commission's recommendations to better detect future attacks (and thwart them) had still not been implemented.

The National Security Guard was also wary of speaking out, eventually confirming in writing to us that it did not want to participate in the book as 'an organization', fearful of India's draconian secrecy laws. Subsequently, many individual officers, some still in service, were so horrified by the fiasco of the NSG's mobilization, which had made them one day late for India's worst ever terrorist attack, that they agreed to tell their stories. The spooks were twitchy and the state-appointed prosecutors self-serving, but they too spoke to us, on condition of anonymity. But none of these responses was as daunting as the Taj's. Caught, tremulously, between needing to create an image for itself once more as the 'House of Magic', and remembering the sacrifice of staff and guests, the hotel as an institution was unresponsive at first, something especially worrying for us as it stood at the dead centre of the book we wanted to write.

Of all the targets hit that night, the Taj was the most iconic, and for that reason it was the first to be chosen by Lashkar. For us the Taj's story, and those of its assailants, staff, guests and liberators, was also a porthole into Chabad House, the CST massacre, and the Trident–Oberoi, giving insight into what was lost and also what was endured and overcome by everyone from the police to *chawl* dwellers, from the gunmen assailing the city to the NSG's gunslingers who eventually neutralized them.

We began slowly, building the confidence of nervous institutions,

reaching out to hundreds of individual Taj staff, guests, police officers and members of the Special Forces, to eyewitnesses and
participants of every kind in Mumbai and Pakistan, in Europe,
the United States, South-East Asia and the Gulf States, using
their memories to construct a time-line. Once we had a location
and a ticking clock, we came back to several dozen crucial inter-
viewees, many of whom have never talked before, and most of
whom have undergone a remarkable change as a result of their
experiences.

We first met Bhisham Mansukhani at the height of the rush hour
in 2010, grabbing a table at the crowded Pizza by the Bay, on Mumbai's Marine Drive, not far from his Breach Candy home. He
revealed that no sooner had he got out of the Taj alive than he began
working out how to quit India too. Bhisham's narrow escape left
him feeling contempt for the authorities that he and many others
accused of prolonging their ordeal, and disillusioned with the
political impasse of cross-border relations with Pakistan. While we
sipped fresh lime sodas, Bhisham took us through his memories
from the Crystal Room into Chambers, talking non-stop for hours,
disdainful of the Friday night crowd that seemed to have forgotten
about the assaults which brought the city to a standstill at shortly
after 9.40 p.m. on 26 November 2008.

Savitri Choudhury, who spent much time with the food critic
Sabina Sehgal Saikia during her last days, was still freelancing in
Mumbai, this time for the Australian Nine Network, when we
emailed each other arranging to meet. Sitting in her high-rise apartment, with its bird's-eye view over many key locations, from the
Bombay Hospital to the jail where Ajmal Kasab was then still incar-
cerated, she recalled Sabina's last hours, dipping into their shared
past too, stories that encapsulated their friendship. Savitri had
arranged for her friend to be embalmed by Danny Michael Pinto
later that day. 'Dead Centre of Town', the sign still says outside
Pinto's, marking his funeral parlour as the city's necropolis, where
Rajiv Gandhi and Mother Teresa were prepared for burial. Savitri

had smiled at that board, knowing that Sabina would have loved it. She bid her a final farewell at the airport, with her husband Vikram at her side, both of them watching as the casket disappeared into the hold of a waiting passenger jet.

Politicians, dress designers, journalists, TV stars and artists attended Sabina's funeral in New Delhi – as she would have wished. Nikhil Segel, her brother, told us: 'As a family we joked that if Sabina had to go, it had to be like this, in a blaze of glory. She would have hated every moment of a slow and uncelebrated death.' Her widower, Shantanu, was more circumspect with us. He still lives in New Delhi with their sixteen-year-old son Aniruddha and their daughter Arundhati, aged nineteen.

Mike Pollack, who took us on his journey from the Tower lobby to the Harbour Bar, and via the Wasabi restaurant to Chambers, told us how he had embraced the opportunity to change, a decision consolidated by finding a photo of himself cowering from bullets outside the Taj splashed on front pages. Staring at the photo, he saw a man who believed he was about to die. When he and Anjali returned to New York, he dissolved the hedge fund he had co-founded in 2001 and they set up the SCA Charitable Foundation to promote 'venture philanthropy' and provide financial backing to social entrepreneurs, primarily in India. Mike also became an adjunct professor of philosophy and business studies at New York University Stern School of Business and he manages his family's investment firm, Pollack Holdings.

When we contacted Will Pike it was initially through his Central London lawyer, who was marshalling a lawsuit against the Taj. At first, Will was reluctant to tell his story. The aftermath of his fall from the third floor felt as though it would never end, he said. After more than a dozen operations and six months at Stanmore Spinal Cord Injury Centre, in North London, Will was told in February 2009 that he would never walk again. He and Kelly Doyle split up in 2011 and he has still not developed a Super 8 video film of them on the beach together in Goa before the attacks, the only surviving record of their ill-fated holiday. After five years of battling the British government, he finally won compensation as a victim of terrorism in January 2013 but his battle to come to terms with life as a paraplegic continues.

Line Kristin Woldbeck, the Leopold Café survivor, escaped physical injury, but has never shaken off the trauma of those days. She and her boyfriend, Arne Strømme, stayed in Mumbai for a month after the attacks, an act she described as an effort 'to heal with the city'. During this time, doctors reattached Arne's severed fingers and sutured his slashed face. Afterwards, Line established a survivors' network and she remains in touch with many she came into contact with on that night, including her 'angel', Amit Peshave, although not the family of Meetu Asrani, her Facebook friend, who bled to death in the café. Line still travels widely, most recently to Cambodia and the Andaman Islands, and describes 26/11 as her 'rebirth'.

Finding the retired banker K. R. Ramamoorthy was difficult. A quiet man, he had been fearful about talking to anyone about his ordeal, and continued to work in far-flung places as an adviser for the World Bank. When we sat down face to face at his home in leafy Bangalore, Ram, surrounded by his family, revealed how he had also narrowly escaped the 1993 bombings in Mumbai before searching for the right words to encapsulate the terror he encountered fifteen years later during 26/11. Ram has returned to Mumbai many times, although he has never shaken off his feelings of disappointment at being brushed aside by the authorities after he was rescued, even though he had spent more time with the four gunmen inside the Taj than anyone else. He persevered, finally giving a statement in the trial of Ajmal Kasab. When we last emailed each other, he was working in Uganda.

Amit and Varsha Thadani, whose wedding reception in the Crystal Room was pivotal to the Taj's schedule on Wednesday, 26 November, went back to building their lives together as soon as they could. Sitting in their Pedder Road apartment, a new baby lying beside them, they described how they decided to leave on a honeymoon to Australia, two days after being rescued, desperate to put the experience behind them, even though some friends thought they should have stayed in the mourning city. But Amit is not one for false sentiment and only he and Varsha knew what they had been through.

Jharna Narang, the sister of Amit's school friend Gunjan Narang, who died along with his parents in the hotel's cellars, still lives in Mumbai too and defied the odds from the moment she was pulled, near dead, out of the Taj. Doctors were staggered that she survived the slaughter, and then were confounded by her recovery. After spending months in hospital, treated with forty-eight bottles of blood, her bowel and kidneys having failed, with both legs paralysed at one stage, Jharna eventually learned to walk again. She put her remarkable survival and recovery down to her Buddhist beliefs, which enabled her to reach beyond the terror.

Bob Nicholls and Captain Ravi Dharnidharka stayed in touch after their escape from Souk. On the first anniversary of the Mumbai attacks, Bob – who stills runs Nicholls Steyn & Associates – and his team were guests of honour at a dinner hosted in the restaurant. His Indian operation is thriving: he still works closely with the Taj's security chief, Sunil Kudiyadi, taking part in the Champions League Twenty20 that was eventually launched in September 2009. Ravi, who returned home to San Diego, became an executive at a Californian aerospace company, but still serves in the 4th Tank Battalion, US Marine Corps Reserve, and remains in contact with his Mumbai family. After his life-threatening experience in the Taj, he married his girlfriend and brought her for dinner in Souk on the second anniversary of the attacks. They now have a young child.

Ratan Kapoor and Nick Edmiston went their own ways after Mumbai, the former moving into India's nascent Formula 1 project and the latter opening new offices in Mexico City, São Paolo and Moscow. They helped Dion Liveras repatriate his father's body to London, where Andreas's daughter told Nick that they felt that his 'circle of life' had been completed. The Liveras family held a lavish funeral at a Greek Cypriot church in North London and in 2010 the *Alysia* was renamed *Moonlight II* and Edmiston sold it on behalf of the family for £60m. After recovering from his own injuries, Andreas's cruise director, Remesh Cheruvoth, returned to work for the Liveras family, running a super-yacht that Dion had named after his father. When we last caught up, he had arrived in London, where he was managing the assets of a Saudi tycoon.

For Vishwas Patil the Mumbai attacks have still not been adequately explained or investigated and they represent anything but a failure of imagination. Despite his personal feelings, Patil became a hero in Maharashtra, a role model for provincial boys from ordinary families who previously viewed the police service as elitist, his public lectures about 26/11 winning millions of hits on YouTube. He was promoted to Additional Commissioner of Police West Region, moving to Bandra, Mumbai's glamorous seaside suburb loved by Bollywood's stars, where we met him in a seafront office with floor-to-ceiling windows. His batch-mate Rajvardhan Sinha was also feted, becoming the new Additional Commissioner Police (economic offences wing) in Mumbai, working from the Crime Branch offices, near Crawford Market.

The Black Cats created a forensic account of every minute wasted and submitted it to the Home Ministry. It is an astonishing document that still makes soldiers angry and details how a combined task force was unofficially mobilized at 10.05 p.m., on Wednesday, 26 November 2008, just twenty-two minutes after the first shots were fired in Leopold's. By 10.30 p.m., the Black Cats were ready to deploy to the technical area of the nearby Palam airstrip, but it would take another seventy minutes for the Cabinet Secretary, the highest civil servant in the land, to contact the NSG Chief, Jyoti Dutt, warning of a mobilization without giving the go-ahead or revealing transport arrangements.

At 00.12 the Joint Secretary Police (Internal Security), called the NSG, also warning mobilization was likely, without giving the green light, but promising to get a plane from the Chief of the Air Staff. Three minutes later, Brigadier Govind Singh Sisodia (DIG

Ops) moved the task force to Palam airstrip. At 00.34 the most senior civil servant in the ministry, Madhukar Gupta, the Home Secretary, called with news that Maharashtra's Chief Minister had finally called for the NSG. They had a 'go' three hours after the first shots had been fired in the Colaba Causeway, the review concluded.

However, when Dutt called the Air Chief asking for their plane, he was informed the transporter was 156 miles away in Chandigarh, leaving him to call the Research and Analysis Wing (RAW), India's insular foreign intelligence service, for help. RAW agreed to lend an Ilyushin 76, parked at Palam airstrip. But it could only carry 120 troops and their kit, meaning the Black Cats would have to make three trips to Mumbai to scramble a force large enough to counter the raids. The crew were also missing, RAW revealed, and the transporter had not been fuelled. Finding them and filling the Ilyushin would delay the mission further.

Dutt was so anxious that he called the Home Secretary at 00.54, only to find that he was stranded in Pakistan, on government business, and could not get a flight until the morning. 'Don't let them take you hostage,' the NSG chief joked bitterly.

Finally, at 01.45, when chief Dutt tried to leave for the airstrip he was requested to pick up the Home Minister from his residence, despite advising the minister's household that this meant a significant deviation from his route. When they arrived at Palam, they found the Black Cats humping their heavy kit by hand into the Ilyushin as no lifting gear was available. The plane took off around 02.30, with a flight time of almost three hours to a city where the slaughter in the Chhatrapati Shivaji Terminus had started and finished, multiple bombs had exploded, and sieges had set in at Chabad House, the Trident–Oberoi and the Taj.

Around 05.30, Thursday, 27 November, the NSG finally touched down in Mumbai, one hour after the gunmen inside the Taj had begun hunting guests down in the hotel's darkened cellars having shot up the Kitchen Brigade. However, the report concluded, the promised convoy to transport them downtown did not show. Although a flurry of white Ambassadors and armed outriders turned out for the Home Minister, there was no convoy to transport the NSG. It would take several more hours to unpack the plane, by hand, commandeer local buses and ferry the Black Cats to the city.

The NSG report also repeated earlier warnings that had been submitted to the ministry as far back as 2006. Then Dutt had written to explain that its mobilization strategy was 'critically flawed'. From Delhi it took more than two and a half flying hours to reach most other cities. The NSG proposed creating four regional hubs, but the proposals went unanswered. So did a second report advising the ministry that the Black Cats were 'limping along' because of corruption and lethargy in procurement. Presently the men were 'woefully ill-equipped'. Applications for lightweight boots, Kevlar helmets and modern body armour, as well as hands-free communications sets, were in limbo. They were short of high-powered thermal-imaging units; their lightweight ladders dated from 1985; and they had no useable night vision devices, with one ministry official conceding that the NSG was 'as good as blind' and 'could only work effectively in daylight'.

When the Black Cats flew into Mumbai it was a triumph of men over machinery, chief Dutt reflected to us. The only thing the NSG could be glad about, touching down in the city, was that eight months earlier when they had been deputed to secure a meeting in Delhi, chief Dutt had insisted that thirty Black Cats don their civvies to mingle in a five-star hotel, the first time any of them had been inside a luxurious establishment.

While the public sector floundered, the private sector marched ahead. On 21 December 2008, three weeks after the siege ended, and after surveyors reported that the hotel had not suffered any significant structural damage, the Tata Group took out newspaper advertisements to announce the hotel would soon be back in business: 'Welcome Home Again . . . Mumbai will rediscover its nesting place and will play host to the world.'

Brigadier Sisodia retired from the NSG and was recruited as Head of Physical Security by the Tata Group. As we walked around the Taj with him, every nook was a foxhole, and every landing a victory relived, all told of in visceral re-enactments. At the Taj, the Chambers, the Tower and most of the restaurants reopened before Christmas that year. The restored Crystal Room, Sea Lounge and other public areas of the Palace wing reopened the following March. Some rooms were renamed, Sabina's Sunrise Suite becoming the Bella Vista Suite. The hotel staged a grand relaunch in August 2010, after spending £24m getting itself straight, having become, in the words of the US President, Barack Obama, who visited that November, 'a symbol of the strength and resilience of the Indian people'.

Backstage, Hemant Oberoi, the hotel's Grand Executive Chef, was reinstalled in his cabin on the first floor and the Kitchen Prayer was put back on the wall of the chefs' staffroom, along with the group photograph by Ian Pereira that shows the senior chefs in their whites, wielding the tools of their trade. With the help of Nitin Minocha, the Golden Dragon chef, whose arm was eventually saved, Oberoi's Kitchen Brigade returned to work, stepping into the blood-logged kitchens to hold a multi-faith puja or cleansing ritual, then organized new uniforms, crockery and menus for all the restaurants. Chef Oberoi also had a marble slab engraved with the names of those who were killed. Chef Raghu came back from the dead, too, and returned to the Taj after making his stand against the gunmen assailing Chambers.

Others looked further afield, including Shamiana's manager, Amit Peshave. Immediately after the attacks, despite having lost so many friends, including Hemant Talim of the Golden Dragon, who succumbed to his injuries four days after the attacks, he returned to the Taj. However, he quit and married in 2009, to try his hand working in Europe, although he hopes to return to Mumbai in the near future. We spent three long evenings with him in London, reliving 26/11 and all that he had witnessed. Amit told us how the six-year-old boy he tried to rescue from the Harbour Bar toilets was eventually reunited with his parents and how he is still in touch with the British man whose life he saved but who wanted to remain anonymous.

Florence Martis also distanced herself from the hotel. Awaking from a deep sleep several days after being rescued by the Black Cats, she finally learned that the body of her father had been located in the Sion Hospital mortuary, where he had been identifiable only by the ring he wore. More than 2,000 people turned out for his funeral, which was widely reported in newspapers and on TV. 'He got the death he wanted, but not in the way he imagined,' Florence said, showing us local newspaper cuttings that had been laminated. A year after the tragedy, she returned briefly to the Taj kitchens to stand in the meat store where her father had been shot. 'It was so cold,' she told us, 'I could not last there even one minute.' Florence now works at the Thane headquarters for the Tata group's Ginger hotels. Her mother took a job at the Taj Public Services Welfare Trust – working to help other victims of the attacks.

Karambir Kang is also still with the Taj group, but no longer in India. One year after 26/11, he married Priya Nagrani, an old college friend, in a low-key ceremony in Pune, and moved to the United States, where he became director of Taj Hotels in the Americas and General Manager of the Taj Boston. He remains in touch with Nikhil, Sabina's brother, both of them having shared many thoughts on loss and grieving.

We discovered many of the most important pieces of the story over the border, in the villages of the Pakistani Punjab, where Lashkar continues to thrive. After months of gruelling exploration, we located many relatives of the team of ten gunmen and found that all had been told the same story by Lashkar in the weeks after 26/11, one that had been later rammed home by the ISI – which warned them of the severe consequences of talking. Their sons/brothers/ nephews had been martyred in Kashmir, they were told. Some had been killed in battle. Others had drowned in rivers or were frozen to death crossing mountain passes. None had been killed in Mumbai. 'That's a fiction created by India and America,' one father told us, unswervingly, even when confronted with photos of his son's body lying in a Mumbai morgue.

In the Punjab, Sindh and Islamabad, we shadowed Pakistan's internal inquiry into the Mumbai assaults, which was a hamstrung affair. The Federal Investigative Authority, the Islamic Republic's would-be FBI, staffed by diligent investigators, had never previously been allowed to probe Lashkar. But following the global outcry generated by 26/11, the FIA was given the go-ahead, although in a limited way, tracing the Mumbai cash and procurements operation, probing the careers of three of the gunmen and several of their controllers, as well as the outfit's quartermaster. One of those at the heart of the investigation, the FIA lawyer and prosecutor Chaudhry Zulfiqar Ali, who provided much insight and many legal documents, told us that the Mumbai inquiry was an albatross. He was gunned down on his way to work in Islamabad in May 2013, and the case remains unsolved. Along the way Pakistan blamed India for failing to present clear and admissible evidence, a gripe that was true in several important instances, although FIA investigators privately wondered at the complexity and reach of Operation Bombay, which many of them believed could not have been carried out without official knowledge and sanction.

There were yet more double-games afoot, according to the FIA. Investigators believed that Washington, too, chose to ignore the building evidence against Lashkar, wary of unsettling the Pakistan military whose support was needed to aid the US fight against the Afghan Taliban and Al-Qaeda. David Headley was also tolerated by his sponsors in the US intelligence community, these same investigators believe, so long as he remained a potential source that might eventually lead them to the most prized goal in those days: Osama bin Laden.

These views have powerful backers among the French and British security sources, who told us about the dossier given to the Americans in 2007, warning of a new global terror axis with Lashkar at its centre.

Sajid Mir had come up on the radar of Western intelligence services as far back as 2003, when he began to recruit Caucasian and African converts, 'clean skins', to mobilize for future operations that were in breach of Lashkar's covenant with Pakistan's military to focus solely on Indian-administered Kashmir.

In compelling detail, the European dossier explained how one of these operations involved a French convert recruited by Lashkar whose arrest in October 2003 exposed a well-advanced plot by the outfit to strike against a nuclear installation in Australia. This plot was one of Lashkar's first attempts at an international spectacular. The French detainee's interrogation led Western intelligence agencies to identify dozens more recruits like him in Europe and the US, jihadi 'sleepers' who were waiting to be activated to mount attacks that included 'multiple raids on luxury hotels in London, and a strike on English synagogues'.

The report noted that Mir referred to his UK lynchpin as 'Dukan', an Urdu word for 'store'. But as British detectives prepared to raid Dukan's home, he fled. 'Lashkar looks as if it will break apart or metamorphose into an Al Qaeda-style outfit that is trying its best to strike at US and British interests at home and abroad, with India particularly vulnerable,' the White House was warned. Less than a year later, almost all of what had been predicted in the dossier came to the fore in Mumbai.

One month after 26/11, David Headley's father, Syed Saleem Gilani, died in Lahore. Headley was out of the country but Pakistan's Prime Minister visited the Gilani family home to offer his condolences. Headley mentioned this in an email to his Al-Qaeda-supporting friend Pasha, who attended Gilani's funeral. Dismissing subsequent reports that the Pakistani government and Headley were in league, Headley's half-brother Danyal issued a statement, saying the PM had visited out of courtesy 'because I was his PRO and also because my father was a renowned broadcaster'.

In December 2008, there was a flurry of email correspondence between David Headley and Major Iqbal concerning the fallout in Pakistan from 26/11. Headley was worried that Sajid Mir and Pasha had both gone to ground, and he had learned that M2 (Faiza) and Chand Bhai were being questioned by the Pakistani authorities.

After receiving a message that *chacha* Zaki was likely to buckle if arrested and rumours that Pasha had also been 'picked up by [ISI] counter guys in Pindi' he ceased most of his digital communications. Soon, however, he was distracted by a new plot, the so-called Mickey Mouse Project, a plan to attack the Danish newspaper *Jyllands-Posten*, which had published cartoons said to lampoon the Prophet Mohammed. Once again Headley was dispatched to conduct surveillance directed by Pasha and Major Iqbal, who both reappeared unscathed by Mumbai.

Headley was finally arrested at O'Hare International Airport, Chicago, in October 2009, en route to Pakistan. Although the US State Department would claim Headley was snared as the result of electronic surveillance connected to the controversial Prism programme, he was arrested after a British intelligence tip-off. Earlier that year he had travelled to the UK to meet one of Sajid Mir's jihadi sleepers, who lived in Derby. In January 2013 Headley was convicted for his role in the Mumbai attacks. But after making another deal with the authorities, he was only sentenced to thirty-five years in prison and was protected from extradition to India.

Tahawwur Rana, his co-accused and former cadet college friend, was found not guilty of the Mumbai attacks. David Headley's second wife, Shazia, and his four children still live in Chicago, while Faiza Outalha, his third wife, returned to Morocco. Washington has never formally admitted Headley's role as a double agent, despite the over-whelming evidence, but family members told us they believed this to be true.

Indian investigators filed an 11,000-page charge sheet against Ajmal Kasab, who was found guilty of waging war and sentenced to death by the Supreme Court of India in August 2012. His plea for clemency was rejected by the Indian president on 5 November 2012 and, after he had made a formal request that his mother be informed, he was hanged at Yerwada Jail in Pune, at 7.30 a.m. on 21 November 2012, and his body buried inside the prison grounds.

After the attacks, his family had received a hand-delivered letter, written by Ajmal before he had set out. 'Venerable parents! Today, Inshallah, I leave for Occupied Kashmir in order to fulfil my duty. The groans and cries of the Muslim brothers and sisters cry out to me . . . Life and death are in Allah's hands, but no death is comparable to death that occurs on the battlefield.'

The remains of his nine co-attackers remained in the JJ Hospital morgue until January 2010, when they were buried at a secret location. None of the ten bodies were claimed. As Kasab feared, none of them were going home.

Both Headley and Kasab (as well as the captured Indian *mujahid* Abu Hamza) claimed that Sajid Mir *was* Brother Wasi, one of the handlers in the Karachi control room, overheard by the ATS. In 2011, Mir, who had used the pseudonym 'Wasi' in some of his email correspondence with Headley, was indicted in absentia by a US district attorney for conspiracy to murder in Mumbai, where six US citizens were killed. He remains at large.

Lashkar's *amir*, Zaki-ur-Rehman Lakhvi, was arrested by the FIA in February 2009, along with Abu Al-Qama, one of the Karachi handlers, and Zarrar Shah, Lashkar's media organizer and resident computer expert. Zaki is awaiting trial in Adiala Prison in Rawalpindi, where he is living well, allowed the use of a mobile phone and full conjugal rights with his wife, who recently gave birth. After 26/11, the ISI's chief, Lieutenant General Shuja Pasha, visited him in jail, but vehemently denied any state involvement in the Mumbai attacks. Interestingly, the pseudonym Wasi was the nom de guerre chosen by *chacha* Zaki's son, Mohammed Qasim, who died in battle in Kashmir in 2007. Abu Hamza, the Indian *fidayeen* trainer who taught the attackers Hindi, was extradited from Saudi Arabia to India in 2012, where he is awaiting trial.

The handler Abu Qahafa, 'the Bull', has never been identified. Nor has Major Iqbal, David Headley's ISI contact, who recruited 'the Mice', his information gatherers in Mumbai, and who boasted of an Indian double agent called 'Honey Bee'. None of these sources have ever been found or identified.

In April 2012 the US government announced a $10m bounty on the head of Hafiz Saeed, the co-founder of Lashkar and *amir* of Jamaat-ud-Dawa, its parent organization, for his role in the Mumbai attacks. But Saeed remains a free man. When we met him in the outfit's sprawling campus at Muridke, protected by legions of armed guards and checkpoints, Saeed was dismissive of the claims made against him, playing up to an audience of several thousand religious students graduating from the outfit's college. 'I am the West's bogeyman,' he said scoffing, 'worth millions of dollars to someone. But I am not in hiding. I am here only, sitting with you.' He combed through his beard, and then gestured with two open arms to his students, who cheered: 'God is Great.' Then Saeed stood, pointing to the heavens. 'They have not come for me, from up there,' he said, referencing the drone strikes that have killed so many in Al-Qaeda and the Taliban, 'or from there.' He pointed to the dusty lanes outside, evoking the extraordinary renditions that saw terror suspects detained and transported to CIA black sites. 'And that is because America needs me to distract their people away from the collapse of their own country.' Cheers rang out, as Saeed nodded in appreciation, shuffling out to the awaiting convoy of pick-ups, with their armed outriders, many of whom sported the same tidy, institutionalized look: Aviator shades, ironed khaki strides, army short back and sides and assault rifles. The recent assassination of the FIA investigator and prosecutor Chaudhry Zulfiqar Ali will ensure that the truth about Mumbai and Hafiz Saeed's involvement in it will remain suppressed just that little while longer.

RIP

In total, 166 people were killed and over 300 injured during the terrorist attacks of November 2008. Thirty-three died at the Taj:

Vijay Banja – chef, killed in kitchens

Willem-Jan Berbers – Belgian–Dutch guest, shot while he was
   checking in

Senator Ralph Burkei – German politician and TV producer, died
   from his injuries after falling from a window

Gautan Gosain – chef, killed in kitchens

Chaitlall Gunness – guest, shot in room 551

Rajan Kamble – Taj engineer, shot in Chambers evacuation

Kaizad Kamdin – chef, killed in kitchens

Neeti Singh Kang – wife of Karambir, died in room on sixth floor

Samar Veer Kang – aged five, son of Karambir

Uday Singh Kang – aged twelve, son of Karambir

Hematlata Kasipillai – Malaysian woman, her body was found
   in room 637

Feroz Khan – killed while visiting an MP in the hotel

Ravindra Jagan Kuwar – security officer, shot in hotel

Andreas Liveras – British entrepreneur, killed in Chambers

Douglas Markell – Australian businessman, shot trying to escape
   third floor

Faustine Martis – head waiter in the Sea Lounge, killed in kitchens

Zaheen Mateen – chef, killed in kitchens

Michael Stuart Moss – Canadian GP, killed by pool

Gunjan Narang – friend of Amit Thadani, shot in cellars

Nilam Narang – mother of Gunjan, killed in cellars

Vishnu Narang – father of Gunjan, shot in cellars

Sadanand Patil – trainee manager, shot in head in lobby

Rupinder Randhava – teacher, killed in Chambers evacuation

Boris Rego – chef, killed in cellars

Elizabeth Russell – nurse from Canada, shot by pool

Sabina Sehgal Saikia – writer, died in Sunrise Suite

Rajiv Sarasvati – guest, killed in room on fourth floor above Will Pike and Kelly Doyle

Rehmatullah Shaukatali – head waiter in Shamiana, shot in restaurant

Maqsood Shiekh – killed while visiting an MP in the hotel

Rahul Shinde – reserve constable in SRPF, killed during exit from CCTV room

Hemant Talim – chef, shot in kitchens

Sandeep Unnikrishnan – Major from NSG killed in Palm Lounge

Thomas Varghese – head waiter, killed in kitchens

Lucy the sniffer dog – shot by the Palace lobby

A Note on Sources

There were many challenges in getting to grips with the siege of the Taj hotel. Crises breed confusion. People under fire or captive in a burning building can have wildly differing memories of the same events, making it difficult for us to build a reliable timeline with which to reconstruct events as they happened. Mindful of this, we interviewed hundreds of people for this book across four continents, and in ten countries: guests, Taj staffers, Special Forces, police, soldiers, eye-witnesses, journalists covering the attacks, foreign investigators, diplomats, and foreign and Indian intelligence agents (serving and retired), as well as many members of the Indian emergency services, including firefighters, ambulance drivers and hospital orderlies, along with surgeons and nurses.

Once we had amassed a dossier of views, we identified key scenes and then tried to build a consensus for each of them, matching the transcribed statements to hard data. Mobile phones were useful. Often a text message sent by a guest, a hotel manager or a policeman would lock down the disputed time of a particular scene. We recovered hundreds of text messages, and dated and timed photographs taken on phones, some of which we reference in the text, but the majority were deployed in the invisible service of anchoring events in the right time and place.

We obtained audio files and transcripts from the wiretaps placed on the gunmen's phones from Indian, US and British security sources, the most complete to be assembled, which includes material never published before. They were translated and cross-checked as multiple languages were spoken, using idioms that were sometimes hard to pin down. We compared wiretap transcripts of the gunmen talking inside the hotel with the memories of captive Taj staffers and guests who were in the room with them as they took advice from their controllers in Karachi, which enabled us to home in on the timing and accuracy of an event.

CCTV footage was also matched to events recounted in interviews. However, some of the hotel footage continues to throw up questions for us regarding the identities of two of the Taj attackers. Although the police remain insistent that Abu Ali was the attacker in yellow and therefore part of the front lobby team and that Abu Umer was the attacker dressed all in black and part of the Leopold team, we believe that the CCTV footage proves the reverse to be the case. In transcripts of the terrorists' intercepted conversations with their handlers in Pakistan, Ali claims repeatedly that he has an injured leg and cannot perform his duty properly – police say he was hit by a ricocheting bullet when the gunmen attacked and killed the Taj's sniffer dog team in the Palace lobby. On the CCTV film the only terrorist with any visible leg injury is the terrorist in black, who is limping, with one shoe off and a piece of cloth tied around his foot. If these two identities have been switched then all the trial court documents are inaccurate. We found numerous other inconsistencies regarding which gunmen were in which location, and photographs of the bodies of Abu Umer and Abu Rehman 'Bada' have never been made available.

We accessed thousands of unpublished court documents from the trial of Ajmal Kasab, including his multiple interrogations. Many of these accounts were conflicting, but we incorporated them into our timeline, the affidavits amplifying the statements given to us. Similarly, police contacts allowed us to read many thousands of pages from Crime Branch evidence books, amassed during the criminal inquiry into 26/11, including all of the witness statements and forensic evidence reports. We also accessed the confidential annexes submitted to the Pradhan Commission, as well as appraisals by foreign intelligence services that lent technological assistance to India during the assault and forensic services afterwards. We studied the FBI analysis provided to investigators in Mumbai and the more complex intelligence dossier shared with domestic and foreign intelligence in New Delhi.

Inevitably, some of these reconstructed events will jar with individual memories that placed a person somewhere else, at a different time, as might some of the dialogue, although we have tried to show every re-created scene to as many parties as possible to ensure accuracy. A few quotations have been compared to or directly extracted from interviews survivors gave at the time to cable news channels and newspapers, so as to capture the authenticity of that moment – the thoughts they had back then, rather than with the benefit of hindsight.

During the research for this book we viewed thousands of photographic stills of the attacks, using newspaper libraries in India and the UK, and hundreds of hours of TV footage from most of the Indian and international cable news channels. Among the most dramatic accounts was *Terror in Mumbai*, the award-winning film made by the British director Dan Reed that was broadcast around the world. We also translated Sachin Waze's written account of the attacks, *Jinkun Harleli Ladhai (A Battle Won and Then Lost)* from its original Marathi. As Waze is a retired police officer and encounter specialist and he interviewed a great number of police officers who were still serving, his work provides an interesting perspective from within the force, albeit different from ours in many instances. The book *26/11 Mumbai Attacked*, edited by Harinder Baweja, published in 2009, is an early take on the attacks, but contains some solid forensic reporting, especially by Ashish Khetan, investigations editor for *Tehelka* magazine, who examined the intelligence trail that foretold of the attacks and the security briefings ignored by the Taj and other Mumbai institutions. For a broader view on the historic problems facing the Mumbai police force it is also worth reading, as we did, *The Untouchables*, Srinivasan Jain's overview first published in *Open* magazine.

The sections that relate to Pakistan, Lashkar-e-Toiba and the country's security apparatus are the culmination of eighteen years' work as foreign correspondents, writers and filmmakers in the Islamic Republic, in which we have amassed a large number of contacts working in counter-terrorism and de-radicalization, and students of sectarianism in its multiple guises. For *The Siege* we spent many months in Pakistan, working with civil servants, retired intelligence officials, diplomats, serving and retired soldiers, and civilian investigators, as well as Pakistani academics and journalists. A group of researchers continued on our behalf when we left. On several occasions, they were asked to leave a village or town by men claiming to be intelligence agents. The ISI remains extremely sensitive about the issue and is keen for it not to be probed too deeply.

We reached out to dozens of serving and former Lashkar cadres, including most of the leadership of the various factions (welfare, religious, military), visiting some of their training and education centres in Muzaffarabad and Muridke. This took many months to broker, some of it done via the offices of retired intelligence officials. We also interviewed key members of and office holders within other Sunni sectarian groups that have closely observed Lashkar and know this world, including Sipah-e-Sahaba, renamed Ahle Sunnat Wal Jamaat in 2002, and Lashkar-e-Jhangvi. Both organizations have been outlawed as terrorist outfits in Pakistan and the US, making these meetings drawn out and sensitive but extremely useful when they eventually came off. All of these interviews provided the clearest thoughts on the context for Operation Bombay, the growing suspicions about David Headley within Lashkar – that eventually concluded he was 'a useful US spy' – and the aftermath.

Numerous insights were given by the FIA, whose inquiry did what it could, within the remit set. FIA agents, serving and retired, from all over the country, many of whom have a long history of analysing terror, provided invaluable commentary on Lashkar's recruiting strategy and procurement operation. A foreign intelligence service showed us the evidence pack assembled by the FIA and we had access to its complete prosecution dossier for thirteen named offenders, most of them intermediaries in the final operation. We also read the interrogation reports for those on trial.

On Lashkar, we learned much picking through the three volumes of *Ham Ma'en Lashkar-e-Taiba Ki* (*We, the Mothers of Lashkar-e-Taiba*), which runs to more than 1,000 pages, and was written by Umme-Hammad, the head of Lashkar's women's section, allegedly the mother of two Lashkar cadres who died in combat. It contains fascinating insights into the formation of the outfit and its philosophy, by charting the lives and deaths of 184 'martyrs'. An exceptional review of this work, by C. M. Naim, was published by *Outlook* magazine on 15 December 2008. In April 2013, the Combating Terror Center, at West Point, published *The Fighters of Lashkar-e-Taiba: Recruitment, Training, Deployment and Death*. It analysed the paths of 900 fighters, taking material from Lashkar's Urdu publications, with the aim of spotlighting the outfit's methodology given the 'broader international consciousness' about it after 26/11. It is statistically interesting but quite distant from the essence of Lashkar. Finally, Steven Tankel's *Storming the World Stage: The Story of Lashkar-e-Taiba*, is a good attempt at charting the rise of Lashkar and the 26/11 attacks, which contains some interesting translations of Lashkar's own material.

We learned much from parallel inquiries into Lashkar run in the UK, France, Germany, Australia and the US, all of which were especially helpful in describing the role of Sajid Mir, Lashkar's deputy head of foreign operations, and David Headley, painting a compelling picture of the latter as a DEA provocateur and a US intelligence source/informer. These accounts by credible agencies and veteran observers, with clearances to access classified material, all come down on the side of Headley being tolerated by elements within the US intelligence community, as he promised, tantalizingly, to lead investigators ever closer to arresting Osama bin Laden. The US intelligence community itself is less eager to describe Headley as anything other than a terrorist, with the CIA and FBI declining to comment on the record. Headley's American relatives gave us their own opinions. David Headley's own account of events comes primarily from his FBI and Indian intelligence interrogations.

Jean-Louis Bruguière, the former Vice-President of the Tribunal de Grande Instance, in Paris, one of France's leading investigative magistrates who dealt with counter-terrorism, provided a clear view of the operation to track Sajid Mir and what that revealed about Lashkar's attempts to transform itself into a global brand similar to Al-Qaeda. In turn, the best published work done on Headley to date is by Sebastian Rotella, for *ProPublica* and PBS, who described forensically, and even-handedly, Headley's rise and fall. Rotella has written a useful e-book too, *Pakistan and the Mumbai Attacks: The Untold Story*, while Bruce Riedel's *Deadly Embrace: Pakistan, America, and the Future of Global Jihad* is essential reading for anyone who wishes to understand the relationship between the Pakistan deep state and jihad.

Some in the Mumbai police force helped considerably, allowing us access to some of the Control Room logs, evidence books and analyses, which we married with what was secured using right-to-information legislation by Vinita Kamte, the widow of the slain police officer Ashok Kamte. Vinita and her family have struggled to pin down an accurate picture of the killings in Rang Bhavan Lane, and have worked doggedly to draw out detail from officers who it seems have done what they can to fog events. These logs give a compelling snapshot of the chaos that overwhelmed the force. The full interrogation video and transcript prepared at Nair Hospital, where Kasab was first questioned after being captured, were also invaluable.

The stories from within the Taj were painstakingly drawn from Taj staffers and their families, as well as guests and diners. Without them, and especially the Taj chefs and managers, we would never have understood the sacrifices they made in the hours before any rescue took shape. Without doubt, the unarmed Taj security team, the Black Suits, as well as the hotel's chefs and managers, saved hundreds of lives.

Acknowledgements

An enormous and heartfelt thank you to everyone at the Taj Mahal
Palace Hotel in Mumbai who took a risk in collaborating with us. In
some cases they did this physically, walking us through Mumbai and
the hotel. Others spent hours reliving the events from afar. Thanks
especially to Amit Peshave, Mallika Jagad, Grand Executive Chef
Hemant Oberoi and Sous-Chef Nitin Minocha, who patiently
explained the internal workings of the vast Taj machine so that we
could understand the minutiae of its processes. We hope we have
created some kind of consensus and also a testament to the staff
who survived and those who succumbed. Thanks also to Florence
Martis and family for opening up the life of the remarkable Faustine
Martis.

Thanks to Nikhila Palat, Director of PR at the Taj, for being
patient, even when the hotel's goals differed from ours. Also to
Deepa Misra Harris, Senior Vice-President of sales and marketing.
Thanks to Padmini Mirchandani, publisher at Pictor, for *The Taj on
Apollo Bunder*, which brilliantly depicted the history of the hotel,
including a chapter on the attacks. We also need to thank Charles
Allen, who wrote it, along with Sharada Dwivedi, Mumbai's *prima*
historian. There are many others inside the hotel who have asked
not to be named. Thanks to all of you for talking to us.

Dozens of soldiers and police officers who spoke to us also do
not want to be named, and we are very grateful to them.

Thanks to Rakesh Maria for giving us his time. Particular thanks
must go to Vishwas Nangre Patil and Rajvardhan Sinha for giving
us detailed accounts of the police's best attempts at detecting the
attacks and then containing them. Deven Bharti was key to our
understanding of the ending of the siege and the electronic monitoring of Lashkar's handlers. Deepak Dhole and several others from

the stations that surrounded the Taj were patient with us, while officials in state and national domestic intelligence took risks in expanding on the trail of warnings, explaining, frankly, the electronic monitoring operation during the days of terror. One Intelligence Bureau stalwart has moved into a different area of public service, while the other continues to serve. Two more are retired and took considerable risks in coming forward. Thank you, Brigadier Govind Singh Sisodia and family, for walking us through many aspects of the National Security Guard (NSG) operation. Thanks also to J. K. Dutt, whose overview of the NSG mobilization and modernization was critical.

Thank you to the counter-terrorism practitioners and experts in Britain (Scotland Yard and the Foreign Office), in France, and especially the US, where we broke much new ground thanks to the enthusiasm of retired operatives who worked for the Joint Terrorism Task Force, the FBI and CIA. Also a huge thank you to those members of David Headley's family who took a chance to open up to us about their 'sociopath' relative, with his split personality; a heavy weight for any family to bear. Thanks to Jean-Louis Bruguière for his insight and detailed account of the Sajid Mir operations in France and beyond. Thanks too to Marc Sageman, Senior Fellow of the Foreign Policy Research Institute who was the CIA's foremost Al-Qaeda expert. He was brought in as an expert witness during the trial of Tahawwur Rana, and shared with us his knowledge in so many areas.

Thank you to Sachin Waze (and family) for a 1 a.m. dinner in Thane and much banter afterwards over email.

Special thanks go to Vinita Kamte, the widow of Additional Commissioner East Ashok Kamte, and family, who have risked much to try and understand the circumstances surrounding the Rang Bhavan Lane shootings. Vinita Kamte's book, *To the Last Bullet*, written with journalist Vinita Deshmukh, is a bold epitaph for her 'braveheart'. They have recently forced a government probe into the alleged tampering with police call log records for 26/11.

Thanks to Suketu Mehta and Jeet Thayil for writing *Maximum*

City and *Narcopolis*, two of the best contemporary works on Mumbai. Thanks to Sheela Bhatt, managing editor at Rediff, who has continually given advice, contacts, friendship and provided great 'Guj' food. Also to Hussain Zaidi, the crime reporter, who knows Thayil's Brown Crows better than anyone. Zaidi was a great counsellor and a good man to chow down with at midnight in Bandra. Thank you also to his family for the idli and samba, and for his book *Headley and I*, which gives a colourful and insightful account of the bizarre relationship that blossomed between David Headley and Rahul Bhatt, the Bollywood actor and bodybuilder. Ashish Khetan did not help us, but has wrestled long and hard with differences between the public and private versions of 26/11. Thank you, Meenal Baghel, editor-in-chief of the *Mumbai Mirror*, who is also an accomplished writer. Her powerful *Death in Mumbai*, an account of a shocking Bollywood murder, was the first of its kind of crime writing in the city. Thank you to the photographer Ian Pereira for taking such a great portrait of the chefs at the Taj and to Harinder Baweja for editing *26/11 Mumbai Attacked*, which, as an early take on those days, was remarkably shipshape.

All the Taj guests who dared go back with us into their memories require a vote of thanks. Thank you, K. R. Ramamoorthy and family, for the company, stories and reflections. Thank you, Remesh Cheruvoth, for recalling his former boss Andreas Liveras so vividly. Nick and Woody Edmiston brought the days and night aboard the Alysia to life for us, as did Ratan Kapoor in Delhi, and Will Christie and Tomaso Polli in London. Thanks to Will and Nigel Pike for putting up with our constant questions and intrusive demands. Thank you especially to Nikhil Segel and to Savitri Choudhury (and family) for introducing us to Sabina Sehgal Saikia and her world. Thank you also, Ambreen Khan, for sharing your innermost thoughts, and Sunil Sethi for setting us on the right path.

Amit and Varsha Thadani. This was your wedding. Thanks for reliving it for us, which we know was arduous, given how busy your lives are. Sir Gulam Noon was endlessly patient with us, as we probed and picked apart his account of being trapped in the Taj.

Presently working in Singapore, Dr Mangeshikar talked us through the Chambers and more, as did Bhisham Mansukhani, a great writer and observer of life, who has a remarkable recall of the hours trapped in Chambers and the final evacuation. Thanks to Rory Steyn and Bob Nicholls for the networking and the tales of Souk. One day we hope all to be in Mumbai at the same time. Ravi Dharnidharka, with a pilot's eye for remote detail, got us from Souk down to the Gateway.

Thanks to the resourceful Mike Pollack. And special thanks to Line Kristin Woldbeck for getting us from Leopold's to the Bombay Hospital. It took some courage to go back, and put us in touch with her circle of survivors.

In Pakistan, many who helped us have asked for anonymity. Those that can be named for their long-term support and advice include Syed Kaleem Imam, the former Inspector General of Police in Islamabad, Samina Pervez, the Director General of External Publicity at the Ministry of Information, and Wajid Shamsul Hasan, the Pakistan High Commissioner in London. We look forward to sharing a cigar in North London. Syed Zulfikar Gardezi, Deputy High Commissioner in London, dealt with our demands helpfully, as did Muneer Ahmad, press attaché, and our good friend, Shabbir Anwer, the Minister Press, who will hopefully be enjoying a well-deserved retirement by the time this book is published. Naghma Butt, the High Commissioner's social secretary, has got us into many meetings, and was always a pleasure to call.

We must thank Sabookh Syed from Geo News and Tamur Khan Yusufzai, who worked with us in Swat and elsewhere. Smart and insightful, he is emerging as a formidable guide to Khyber Pakhtunkhwa. Thanks also to his father, Rahimullah Yusufzai, one of the country's most modest but knowledgeable and well-connected journalists. Over many years Rahimullah has given us advice, lent expertise, made calls on our behalf, and tested hypotheses, challenging laziness and crass assumptions. We await his definitive book on Pakistan.

Our hearts sank when Tariq Parvez retired as chief of Pakistan's

National Counter-Terrorism Authority. With a long view from the Punjab force, where he was head of CID, to the Federal Investigation Agency in Islamabad, which as Director General he revamped, Parvez went some way in creating Pakistan's first real counter-terrorism force. He continues to work hard connecting people and ideas. So does the formidable Additional Inspector General of Police Syed Asif Akhtar, who travelled from Pakistan to Interpol and now, in retirement, to Karachi. Special thanks to Khalid Qureshi, head of the Special Investigations Group (SIG) at the FIA, and to his Waziri deputy, Sohail Tajik, who is now a Senior Superintendent in the Punjabi heartland city of Bahawalpur.

Thank you, Dr Feriha Peracha, for introducing us to your work on deradicalizing young men and boys in Swat and elsewhere. Thanks to her assistant Sadia Khan. Condolences to the family of the diligent and enthusiastic Dr Mohammed Farooq Kahn, a pragmatic and optimistic man who believed his work in educating young extremists about the true messages of Islam could make a difference. A devout and hard-working academic, he spoke with us at length in Swat in July 2010, but by October he was dead, killed by Pakistan Taliban gunmen.

Sarah Tareen, executive producer and CEO of Concordia Productions in Lahore, thanks for your help, as always, and congratulations on getting your first feature, *Tamanna*, to the big screen, with award-winning music by Rahat Fateh Ali Khan. Thanks to Major Muhammed Ali Diyal at the Pakistani Army's Inter-Services Public Relations (ISPR), who dealt with our burgeoning requests politely and efficiently, getting us up and down the country.

In Mumbai, thank you to Pranati Mehra, a skilful journalist, who made the running on some of Mumbai's biggest stories, in its darkest days of serial bombings and communal riots, and who helped us marshal research and contributors. Thanks also to Shree Thaker Bhojanalay, in Dadisheth Agyari Lane, off Kalbadevi Road, for keeping us refuelled in between driving, meeting and talking. Thank you to the accident-prone fixer Nandan Kini, who tirelessly wrangled locations and people with humour, precision and calmness. In

Acknowledgements

London, thanks to the team at True Vision Television, who continually support and promote our projects.

A huge thanks goes to our agent, David Godwin, for his invaluable support and to his colleagues at David Godwin Associates: Anna Watkins and Kirsty Mclachlan. Thanks to our army of editors at Penguin for marshalling and honing down the manuscript across three continents and through its multiple forms: Joel Rickett in London, Chiki Sarkar in New Delhi and Emily Baker in New York. Thanks also to our copy-editor, Mark Handsley, for his painstaking rereading of the manuscript. Thanks finally to friends and family in London, who put us up and fed us during our constant comings and goings between Europe and South Asia: Katy and Kevin Whelan, Lesley Thomas, Ninder and Ajay Khandelwal, and Karen and Jeremy Levy.

Index

Index

Index

He just wanted a decent book to read ...

Not too much to ask, is it? It was in 1935 when Allen Lane, Managing
Director of Bodley Head Publishers, stood on a platform at Exeter railway
station looking for something good to read on his journey back to London.
His choice was limited to popular magazines and poor-quality paperbacks –
the same choice faced every day by the vast majority of readers, few of
whom could afford hardbacks. Lane's disappointment and subsequent anger
at the range of books generally available led him to found a company – and
change the world.

*'We believed in the existence in this country of a vast reading public for intelligent
books at a low price, and staked everything on it'*
Sir Allen Lane, 1902–1970, founder of Penguin Books

The quality paperback had arrived – and not just in bookshops. Lane was
adamant that his Penguins should appear in chain stores and tobacconists,
and should cost no more than a packet of cigarettes.

Reading habits (and cigarette prices) have changed since 1935, but
Penguin still believes in publishing the best books for everybody to
enjoy. We still believe that good design costs no more than bad design,
and we still believe that quality books published passionately and responsibly
make the world a better place.

So wherever you see the little bird – whether it's on a piece of
prize-winning literary fiction or a celebrity autobiography, political tour
de force or historical masterpiece, a serial-killer thriller, reference book,
world classic or a piece of pure escapism – you can bet that it represents
the very best that the genre has to offer.

Whatever you like to read – trust Penguin.